ROME

CONDENSED

Antonios' at the Pantheon

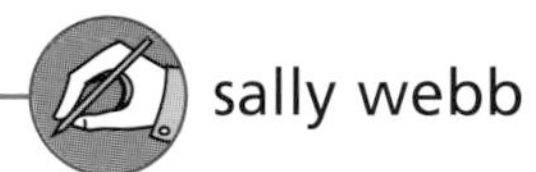

sally webb

LONELY PLANET PUBLICATIONS
Melbourne • Oakland • London • Paris

contents

Rome Condensed
1st edition – June 2001

Published by
Lonely Planet Publications Pty Ltd
ABN 36 005 607 983
90 Maribyrnong St, Footscray, Vic 3011, Australia

Lonely Planet Offices
Australia Locked Bag 1, Footscray, Vic 3011
USA 150 Linden St, Oakland, CA 94607
UK 10a Spring Place, London NW5 3BH
France 1 rue du Dahomey, 75011 Paris

Photographs
Many images in this guide are available for licensing from Lonely Planet Images (email: lpi@lonelyplanet.com.au). Images also used with permission of Ministero per i Beni e le Attività Culturali. Thanks to Bridgeman Art Library, London, for the following: p. 19 *Saint Sebastian* (oil on panel) by Pietro Perugino (c.1445-1523) and *Sacred and Profane Love,* c.1515 (oil on canvas) by Titian (Tiziano Vecellio) (c.1488-1576) from Galleria Borghese, Rome, Italy; p. 22 *A Gaul Committing Suicide,* Pergamon School, 3rd century BC (marble) (b/w photo) Palazzo Altemps, Rome, Italy; p. 23 *Sleeping Hermaphrodite* (marble) (b/w photo) Palazzo Massimo alle Terme, Rome, Italy; p. 28 Interior View of the Main Altar of San Clemente, Rome, photo credit: Bridgeman Art Library.

Front cover photographs
Top: Ponte Sant'Angelo (Jon Davison)
Bottom: Staircase, Vatican Museums (Greg Elms)

ISBN 1 86450 360 2

Printed by Colorcraft Ltd, Hong Kong

how to use this book

KEY TO SYMBOLS

- ✉ address
- ☎ telephone number
- e email/web site address
- nearest bus (or electric bus) route
- M nearest metro station
- nearest tram route
- auto route, parking details
- ⓘ tourist information
- opening hours
- $ cost, entry charge in Lire (L)/euro(€)
- ♿ wheelchair access
- child-friendly
- ✕ on-site or nearby eatery
- V good vegetarian selection

COLOUR-CODING

Each chapter has a different colour code which is reflected on the maps for quick reference (eg all Highlights are bright yellow on the maps).

MAPS & GRID REFERENCES

The fold-out maps on the front and back covers are numbered from 1 to 6. All sights and venues in the text have map references which indicate where to find them; eg (2, C3) means Map 2, grid reference C3. All sights and significant venues are marked on the maps. For items not marked, the street is marked. While official neighbourhood names are labelled on the maps, the author has used their commonly known names in the text.

PRICES

Price gradings (eg L5000/3000, €2.58/1.55) usually indicate adult/concession entry charges to a venue in both lire and euro prices. As euro prices are direct conversions of the lire prices current at the time of writing, there may be some price variations after the adoption of the euro as the sole currency. For more information, see Money and the Lire-Euro Conversion table on page 112.

WARNING & REQUEST

Things change – prices go up, schedules change, good places go bad and bad places improve or go bankrupt. So, if you find things better or worse, recently opened or long since closed, please tell us and help make the next edition even more accurate. Everyone who writes to us will find their name and possibly excerpts from their correspondence in one of our publications (let us know if you *don't* want your letter published or your name acknowledged). They will also receive the latest issue of *Planet Talk*, our quarterly printed newsletter, or *Comet*, our monthly email newsletter. Subscriptions to both newsletters are free. The very best contributions will be rewarded with a free guidebook.

Send all correspondence to the Lonely Planet office closest to you (p. 123).

Lonely Planet books provide independent advice. Lonely Planet does not accept advertising in guidebooks, nor payment in exchange for listing or endorsing any place or business. Lonely Planet writers do not accept discounts or payments in exchange for positive coverage of any sort.

facts about rome

Rome is a beautiful, beguiling, chaotic, fascinating, frustrating and romantic city where a phenomenal concentration of history, legend and monuments coexists with an equally phenomenal concentration of people busily going about everyday life. It is easy to pick the tourists because they are the only ones to turn their heads as the bus passes the Colosseum.

The Eternal City has always inspired wonder and awe in its visitors. Its ruined, but still imposing, monuments represent a point of reference for a city which, through the imperial, medieval, Renaissance and Baroque periods, has undergone many transformations and which has produced an archaeological archive of Western culture. The historical sites are merely the tip of the iceberg. Tourists wandering around the city with their eyes raised to admire the architecture should know that about 4m under their feet exists another city, with traces of numerous other settlements deeper still.

When in Rome do as the Romans do. This is a city for the senses, where the minutiae of daily life possess a charm unimaginable in other capitals. Get your cultural fill but make sure to leave time for more hedonistic concerns: eat till you can eat no more, get drunk on wine, architecture and sunshine. There's still plenty of *dolce vita* left in Rome.

Dan Herrick

Throughout the ages, visitors have found that Rome can be a hard habit to break.

HISTORY

Foundation of Rome

The agreed date of the foundation of Rome, when Romulus became its first king, is 21 April 753 BC. The kingdom lasted until about 507 BC when a revolt against the tyrannical Etruscan king, Tarquin the Proud, established the Republic.

Romulus & Remus

When the twin sons of a Latin princess, Rhea Silvia, and the war god Mars were abandoned on the banks of the Tiber river, they were raised by a she-wolf. According to legend, Romulus killed his brother during a battle over who should govern and then established the city of Rome on the Palatine. Later Romulus disappeared, either taken up by the gods or, more gruesomely, secretly murdered by senators.

Republic to Empire

The city prospered under a more democratic form of government, the civic structure benefited and roads and aqueducts were constructed. Surrounding tribes became allies of the city and its influence extended to Sicily and northern Africa. With its victory in the Punic wars over rival Carthage, Rome became the dominant Mediterranean power. Struggles among the patrician ruling classes resulted in a series of omnipotent dictators, among them Gaius Julius Caesar, who was murdered by conspirators. There ensued 17 years of civil war, until 27BC when Octavian (using the title of Augustus) became Rome's first emperor.

Augustus oversaw a new era of political stability and artistic achievement, boasting that 'he found Rome in brick, and left it in marble'. By AD100, the city had more than 1.5 million inhabitants, and taxes from the Empire's vast domains brought wealth and prosperity. Hadrian's era marked the peak of the Roman Empire, when stability was enjoyed on the borders and in internal politics. Diocletian halved the Empire, governing the east and allocating the west to Maximian.

Constantine became the first Christian emperor in 312. When he moved his power base to Byzantium in 330, Rome's period as Caput Mundi (capital of the world) was over.

Hailed Caesars

Some notable emperors included:

27BC - AD14	Augustus
14 - 37	Tiberius
54 - 68	Nero
69 - 79	Vespasian
79 - 81	Titus
81 - 96	Domitian
98 - 117	Trajan
117 - 138	Hadrian
161 - 180	Marcus Aurelius
193 - 211	Septimius Severus
211 - 217	Caracalla
285 - 305	Diocletian/Maximian
312 - 337	Constantine the Great

Christian Rome & the Middle Ages

Christianity had been spreading slowly through the Empire since the apostles Peter and Paul had joined a small group of Christians in Rome; they were persecuted but the religion flourished.

In the 5th century Goths and Vandals invaded the city, but Gregory I's papacy (590-604) rescued Rome from demise. Four of the city's great basilicas were built during this time and missionaries were dispatched throughout Europe to encourage pilgrimages to Rome. In 774, Rome's place as centre of the Christian world was cemented when Pope Leo III crowned Charlemagne as Holy Roman Emperor. Clement V moved the papal court to Avignon in 1309, leaving Rome in the hands of aristocratic ruling families. The Papal State was restored to Rome in 1379.

The Renaissance

The popes of the 15th and early 16th centuries saw that the best way to ensure political power was to rebuild the city. The leading artists and architects of the Florentine Renaissance were summoned to Rome to work on the Sistine Chapel and St Peter's among other projects. Power struggles in Europe still affected the papacy and in 1527 Pope Clement VII was forced to take refuge in Castel Sant'Angelo when the troops of Charles V sacked Rome.

Martin Moos

Castel Sant'Angelo's guardian angels kept Pope Clement VII safe.

Counter-Reformation & the Baroque

The broad-minded curiosity of the Renaissance gave way to a period of intolerance. The Roman Church's determination to regain papal supremacy over the Protestant churches set the stage for the persecution of intellectuals and free thinkers such as Giordano Bruno and Galileo Galilei. The Chiesa del Gesú was the prototype of Rome's great Counter-Reformation churches, built to accommodate huge congregations. In the 17th century, under the popes and grand families of Rome, the theatrical exuberance of the Baroque found masterful interpreters in Bernini and Borromini.

Napoleonic Occupation

Over the centuries the popes had acquired a group of provinces in central Italy that was known as the Papal States, with Rome as their capital. They were a strategic prize for Napoleon in his bid for power. In 1805 Napoleon crowned himself king of Italy and later named his infant son king of Rome; three years later he demanded the pope's abdication, and annexed Rome.

Unification

After Napoleon's defeat, patriots Giuseppe Mazzini and Giuseppe Garibaldi led the movement to unify Italy. Rome was briefly declared a republic in 1848, but Garibaldi's forces were driven out by papist French troops. In 1861 the Kingdom of Italy was declared under King Vittorio Emanuele II, but the French-supported pope was still sovereign of Rome. Troops stormed the city in 1870 and Rome became capital of Italy.

Fascism & WWII

Discontent and social unrest after WWI favoured the rise of Benito Mussolini, and his Fascist Party, which won the national elections in 1924 following a campaign marked by violence and intimidation. By the end of 1925 Mussolini's regime had expelled opposition parties from parliament and gained control of the press and trade unions. In 1929, Mussolini and Pope Pius XI signed the Lateran Pact, whereby Catholicism was declared the sole religion of Italy and the Vatican recognised as an independent state.

Declared an open city, Rome was largely spared from destruction during WWII, although many Jews were deported and killed in the Nazi death camps. In a 1946 referendum the Italian people abolished the monarchy.

Modern Times

In 1960, Rome hosted the Olympic Games. Student revolt and then terrorism marked the 1960s and '70s. The 1980s saw significant economic growth in Italy (and ostentatious spending in Rome) under socialist prime minister Bettino Craxi, but neither he nor many other politicians escaped the 'Tangentopoli' corruption investigations of the 1990s. Preparations for the Jubilee Year of 2000 marked the final decade of the millennium.

Holy Years

Pope Boniface VIII instituted the first Christian Jubilee or Holy Year in 1300, when pilgrims visited the major religious sites in Rome. In return, they were granted indulgences (effectively annulling time in purgatory due for sins committed).

Jubilee Years are usually held every 25 years. The last one (in 2000) gave authorities the impetus to clean up and modernise the city for the new millennium. Many of Rome's historic buildings emerged from behind scaffolding like butterflies from a cocoon, with their facades cleaned of centuries of dirt and grime. At just over 2750 years old, Rome's never looked better.

Martin Moos

ORIENTATION

Rome is a vast city, but the *centro storico* (historic centre) is relatively small, defined by the twisting Tiber river to the west, the sprawling Villa Borghese park to the north, the Roman Forum and Palatine Hill to the south and the central train station, Stazione Termini, to the east. The Vatican City and the charming Trastevere are on the west bank of the Tiber.

In ancient times, the city was enclosed by defensive walls, the Mura Serviane, only traces of which remain. From AD271 Emperor Aurelian built a second defensive wall, most of which is still standing.

The Seven Hills of Rome

Rome's best known geographical features are its seven hills: Palatine, Capitoline, Aventine, Celian, Esquiline, Viminal and Quirinal. Two other hills, the Gianicolo, above Trastevere, and the Pincio, above Piazza del Popolo, were not part of the ancient city.

Most major sights are located within the historic centre, which makes sightseeing relatively simple and walking the best way to get around town. Some major churches and parks, and the catacombs lie outside the walls.

ENVIRONMENT

The city of Rome covers an expanse of roughly 150,000 hectares, of which 37% is built-up urban area, 15% is parkland and 48% is under agricultural use. Traffic and air pollution are Rome's greatest environmental problems. Efforts to reduce traffic have increased dramatically in recent years, and special permits are needed to drive in the centre. There are strict regulations governing levels of gas emissions from motor vehicles and *motorini* (scooters) – although not everyone adheres to them. Many of the city's monuments, the Colosseum included, remain at risk from pollution.

Martin Moos

St Peter's dome casts a long shadow.

Recent public works have concentrated on improving roads, public transport and other infrastructure to relieve pressure on the environment. New tram lines are being built and old ones extended, and several small electric buses buzz around the centre. Subway lines have been extended and improved, and public spaces that were formerly parks for cars are being reclaimed as piazzas for people.

Recycling is widespread, although it is a well-known fact that Mafia interests control waste management in Italy, and not all rubbish destined for recycling actually gets recycled.

GOVERNMENT & POLITICS

Rome's municipal government is headed by a *sindaco* (mayor) elected by the public, who appoints a *giunta*, a body of councillors called *assessori* who hold ministerial positions as heads of municipal departments of the *comune* (council). The assessori are appointed from the *consiglio comunale*, a body of elected officials, much like a parliament.

Rome is also the seat of national government and capital of the *regione* of Lazio. A parliamentary republic, Italy is headed by a president, who appoints the prime minister. The parliament consists of two houses – a Senate and a Chamber of Deputies – both with equal legislative power.

Rome's former mayor Francesco Rutelli, who brought a dash of Paul Newman glamour to the job, is now active in national politics (at the time of writing he was facing off against Silvio Berlusconi in the prime ministerial race). He oversaw significant improvements to the city's neglected services and facilities, ushering in a pre-2000 renewal with a speed that took many Romans' breath away. A plus for visitors is that dozens of world-class museums and archaeological sites have been revamped and reopened.

ECONOMY

The local economy is based on tourism, banking, fashion, insurance, printing and publishing. The comune itself is one of the biggest employers and a good proportion of Romans working in the private sector are self-employed.

The mainstays of the city's budget are the annual 'garbage tax' paid by residents (a form of municipal tax) and its share of taxes paid to the national government. In comparison with other cities, Rome receives a fairly low share of the tax pool – L290,000 annually per capita – while Milan receives L449,000 and Naples L1,015,000.

Recent infrastructure spending has soared, including more than L2000 billion on a much-improved rail network. After a slow start Rome has taken a great leap forward in digital communications and L1,800 billion has been invested laying fibre optic cables to modernise the city's telecommunication network.

Did you Know?

- **Population** 2.6/3.8/5.2 million Rome City/Greater Rome/Lazio % by age: 17.1/65.5/17.4% under 20/20-64/over 65yrs
- **Inflation rate** 1.7%
- **Italian GDP per capita** US$21,400
- **Unemployment** 12.5% (but around 22% for 14-29yr olds)

Friends, Romans, countrymen...

SOCIETY & CULTURE

The ageing Roman population echoes the demographic trend throughout Italy, which is the only country in the world where the old outnumber the young. Italy has had a negative birth rate for the past seven years; its current birth rate is the lowest in the world and the lowest in its history. Despite deaths outnumbering births, latest available figures (1997) show that Lazio's population is growing thanks to the arrival of around 30,000 immigrants.

Estimates of the number of foreigners in Rome vary, although it is thought that one fifth of the total number of immigrants in Italy live in Rome. The official number is around 211,000 (or around 8% of the city's population). However, there are also around 33,000 illegal immigrants living in the city. Of the foreigners in Rome, around 21% are in the city for religious reasons.

Romans have an ambiguous relationship with immigrants. Many would say that immigrants and natives live together harmoniously (and indeed the 1990s saw an increasing number of mixed marriages) but on the other hand, incidences of intolerance and xenophobia demonstrate that racism is alive and well here.

Sally Webb

Luckily there are some activities that appeal to both young and old.

Some 85% of Italians profess to be Catholic; the remainder are split between a growing number of Muslims (around 700,000), and other communities such as Protestants, Jehovah's Witnesses and Jews. A fitting symbol for demographic shift in the heart of Christendom was the inauguration in 1995 of Rome's first mosque.

Do's and Don'ts

In churches you are expected to dress modestly. This means no shorts (for men or women) or short skirts, and shoulders should be covered. Dress regulations are stringently enforced at St Peter's Basilica. Churches are places of worship. If you really must visit one during a service, try to be as inconspicuous as possible.

Smoking

Smoking practises in Rome, like in many other European cities, tend to be a little confronting for those more used to restriction on where and when people can light up. There are very few places where it's not OK to smoke.

ARTS

While Rome is one of the world's great art treasure troves, it's difficult to argue that the contemporary arts scene rates highly. There are active exhibition programs in public spaces (such as the Palazzo delle Esposizioni, p. 37) and private galleries. Check *Wanted in Rome* and *Roma C'e* for current shows.

Other key areas in recent Roman artistic life are film (p. 98) and fashion, where local artisan tradition has translated into beautiful wares for sale. Milan may be Italy's undisputed high-fashion capital, but all top clothing, accessory and homeware designers have boutiques here (pp. 61-71). And, of course, food has been elevated into a joyful Roman art form (pp. 76-89).

Architecture

The Romans learned their building skills from the Etruscans. From the 1st century BC, they made a quick-curing concrete for arches and domes (such as the Pantheon); marble was used from the 2nd century BC. As Rome's power grew, new buildings were needed to reflect the city's status; artistic concerns took second place to impressive engineering, evident in structures such as the Terme di Diocleziano (AD298).

The first Christian churches in Rome were based on the basilica form – oblong with three naves. From the 11th to 13th centuries churches featured the rounded arches of the Romanesque style, influenced by ancient Rome.

Classical orders and proportion provide the key to Renaissance architecture; Donato Bramante (1441-1514) being the chief exponent. During the Counter-Reformation art and architecture were entirely at the service of the Church, and the Jesuits created grand churches to attract and overawe worshippers.

Neil Setchfield

Symmetry is the order of the day at EUR.

Two great architects of 17th century Rome were Francesco Borromini (1599-1667) and Gian Lorenzo Bernini (1598-1680). Under Urban VIII's patronage, Bernini transformed the face of the city; his churches, palaces, piazzas and fountains remain landmarks.

The Baroque love of grand gesture continued in the 18th century with the Trevi Fountain and the Spanish Steps. Mussolini and the fascists made their architectural mark with monumental building schemes such as the Foro Italico sports centre and Esposizione Universale di Roma (EUR; p. 45).

Painting & Mosaic

From the 1st century BC Romans used fresco and mosaic, both legacies from the Greeks and Etruscans, to decorate buildings. Stunning mosaic decorations were used in Christian churches from the 4th to the 9th century. In the Middle Ages the Cosmati revolutionised mosaic art by reusing fragments of coloured glass and marble from ruins to create patterned pavements, ornaments and pulpits. One of the greatest artists of the period, and a precursor of the Renaissance, was Pietro Cavallini (c 1250-1330).

From 1481-83 Botticelli, Perugino, Ghirlandaio, Pinturicchio and Signorelli were employed by Sixtus IV to decorate the Sistine Chapel walls; Michelangelo frescoed the ceiling (1508-12), while Raphael worked on designs for the Stanze di Raffaello nearby. Michelangelo confirmed his painterly genius with the *Last Judgement* (1535-41).

The arrival in Rome of Caravaggio (1573-1610) heralded a move away from the confines of the High Renaissance towards a new and controversial naturalism. More successful in their day were the academic painters Guido Reni (1575-1642) and Domenichino (1581-1641). The fashion for ceiling frescoes continued well into the 17th century, when Pietro da Cortona (1596-1669) was one of the most sought-after decorators of Baroque Rome.

By the 18th century Rome's artistic attention turned to the antique; grand tourists sought Giovanni Battista Piranesi's etchings of ancient ruins. The late 19th century saw the emergence of Italian post-Impressionism with the *Macchiaioli,* who produced a version of pointillism. The futurists of the early 20th century – Boccioni, Balla and others – were inspired by urbanism, industry and the idea of progress. Important post-WWII artists include Burri and Manzoni and the Transavanguardia whose exponents include Francesco Clemente and Mimmo Paladino.

Sculpture

During the Republic and the Empire, sculpture was at the service of the state and provides a compelling record of the city's history. The first 'Roman' sculptures were actually made by Greek artists or were copies of imported classical Greek works. Michelangelo was the outstanding Renaissance sculptor (see p. 42). In Rome, Baroque sculpture meant one thing: Bernini. The sculptor could do things with marble that no one before or since has managed, making cold hard stone appear to be soft flesh and a solid static figure seem to be dynamic. The neoclassicism of the late 18th and early 19th centuries – best represented by Antonio Canova (1757-1822) – was a reaction to the excesses of the Baroque and a response to the renewed interest in the classical world.

Martin Moos

Bernini's Fontana dei Quattro Fiumi, Piazza Navona

highlights

It doesn't matter how much time you've got to spend in Rome, it won't be enough. The popular saying *'Roma non basta una vita'* (Rome, a lifetime isn't enough) pretty much sums it up. It is a city on so many levels that most Romans have yet to see it all. And it is constantly changing, as new excavations unearth yet more ancient treasures.

Most of the major attractions are in the historic centre and quite close to each other, so depending on your level of museum fatigue you could see a few sights the same day. However, few people would be able to handle more culture after a visit to the Vatican or Capitoline museums.

The major sights like the Colosseum and St Peter's get hopelessly overrun at any time of the year. At the Vatican Museums, avoid the worst of the crowds and tour groups by being first in line in the morning or waiting until the early afternoon. You can always get away from the crowds at the Palatine and you'll often have galleries to yourself at Villa Giulia, Palazzo Massimo or Palazzo Altemps.

Culture vultures in Rome for several days who really want to *do* the sights should consider buying a five-day ticket (L30,000, €15.49) which gives admission to the Colosseum, Palatine, and the four Museo Nazionale Romano sights – Palazzo Massimo alle Terme, Terme di Diocleziano, Palazzo Altemps and Crypta Balbi.

Stopping Over?

One Day Visit the Vatican Museums and Sistine Chapel and St Peter's Basilica in the morning. Relax over lunch around Piazza Navona, then head to the Roman Forum and Colosseum. Make a night of it in the streets, piazzas, restaurants and bars of Trastevere.

Two Days Check out the market at Campo de' Fiori. Visit the Pantheon and the Capitoline Museums. Do some serious retail therapy around Via Condotti then take an evening *passeggiata* (walk) from Piazza di Spagna to the Trevi Fountain.

Three Days Get a sense of Rome's multi-layered history at the San Clemente Basilica. Wander through Villa Borghese park and visit the magnificent Museo Borghese. Enjoy the ancient delights of Palazzo Massimo or the excavated wonders of the Domus Aurea. Have a slap up meal at one of the city's best eateries.

Rome Lowlights

Some things make Rome 'eternal' in all the wrong ways:

- Traffic, pollution, Roman drivers
- Crowds at the Sistine Chapel
- Restaurant-to-restaurant vendors of roses and cigarette lighters
- Roman shop assistants

COLOSSEUM (4, J14)

More than any other monument, the Colosseum is *the* symbol of the Eternal City. Its construction was started by Vespasian in AD72 in the grounds of Nero's private Domus Aurea. Originally known as the Flavian Amphitheatre, after the family name of Vespasian, it was inaugurated by his son Titus in AD80. The massive structure could seat more than 50,000, and bloody gladiator fights and wild beast shows were held there. Inaugural games lasted for 100 days and nights, during which some 5000 animals were slaughtered. Trajan once held games which lasted for 117 days, during which 9000 gladiators fought to the death.

With the fall of the Empire, the Colosseum was abandoned and became overgrown with exotic plants; seeds had inadvertently been transported with the wild beasts that appeared in the arena (including crocodiles, bears, tigers, elephants and hippos). In the Middle Ages the Colosseum became a fortress, occupied by two of the city's warrior families: the Frangipani and the Annibaldi.

Damaged several times by earthquake, it was later used as a quarry for travertine and marble for Palazzo Venezia and other buildings. Despite this, it remains an evocative spot to explore while imaging yourself in the latest Hollywood sword-and-sandals epic, giving Russell Crowe a run for his money.

Russell Mountford

INFORMATION

- ✉ Piazza del Colosseo
- ☎ 06 399 67 700
- 🚌 numerous ATAC services (see map); J4, J5
- Ⓜ Colosseo
- 🕐 varies; usually from 9am to: 6pm Mar-Apr, 7pm May-Aug, 6.30pm Sept-Oct, 4.30pm Nov-Feb
- $ L10,000/5000, €5.16/2.58; museum pass valid
- ⓘ guided tours (in Italian) hourly, L6000/€3.10
- ♿ limited
- ✕ Pasqualino

Martin Moos

Go, Gladiator, Go!

Gladiatorial games were a popular but gruesome form of entertainment. The combatants were usually prisoners of war or slaves; some were armed with swords and shields while others fought only with a net and a trident. Bouts were not necessarily to the death; a defeated gladiator could appeal to the crowd and the presiding magistrate who could signal that he had fought well and deserved to be spared. Thumbs down, however, meant death, which the defeated man was expected to face with quiet dignity. Successful gladiators became popular heroes, with some running their own training schools.

CAPITOLINE HILL & MUSEUMS (2, A9)

The Capitoline Hill *(Campidoglio)*, now the seat of the city's municipal authorities, was the centre of government of ancient Rome, and is the geographical centre of the modern city. It is especially beautiful at night, when it is usually deserted.

The piazza was designed by Michelangelo in 1538. It is bordered by three buildings (also by Michelangelo): the **Palazzo Nuovo** and the **Palazzo dei Conservatori**, both of which the **Capitoline Museums**, and the **Palazzo Senatorio** at the rear.

The bronze equestrian **statue of Marcus Aurelius** (below) in the centre of the piazza is a copy made from a mould created through computer-generated photographs. The 2nd century original was badly damaged by pollution and pigeon poo and was removed in 1981. It has been restored and is now housed behind glass inside the Palazzo Nuovo.

For the greatest visual impact, approach the Capitoline from Piazza d'Aracoeli and ascend the **cordonata**, a stepped ramp also designed by Michelangelo. It is guarded at the bottom by two ancient Egyptian granite lions and at the top by two mammoth statues of Castor and Pollux, which were excavated from the nearby ghetto area in the 16th century.

At the foot of the Capitoline Hill, next to the staircase leading up to the church of **Santa Maria in Aracoeli** (pp. 43-4), are the ruins of a Roman

INFORMATION

- ✉ Piazza del Campidoglio
- ☎ 06 399 67 800
- 🚌 numerous ATAC services (see map); J4, J5, J7
- Ⓜ Colosseo
- 🕘 Tues-Sun 10am-9pm
- $ museums L12,000/ €6.19
- ♿ excellent (access via road to right of cordonata)
- ✕ museum cafe, Vezio's Bar

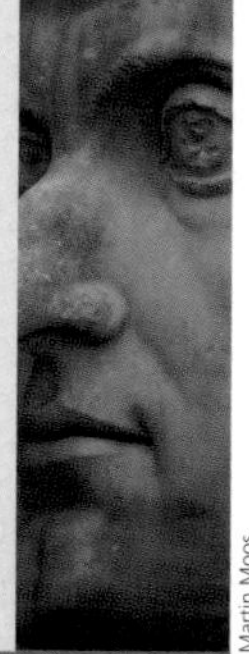

Martin Moos

Martin Moos

Top: Constantine the Great
Above: Diana of Ephesus

A Case of Mistaken Identity

The equestrian statue of Marcus Aurelius (who ruled AD161-180) is one of only a handful of ancient bronzes not to have been melted down. It survived because it was incorrectly identified as Constantine, the first Christian emperor. Traces of the gold paint that covered the original statue are still visible on the emperor's face and coat and on the horse's head and back.

Jenny Jones

Jon Davison

Rear view of Palazzo Nuovo's masterwork Dying Gaul

insula (apartment block). Buildings of this type were used to house the urban poor, who lived in cramped and squalid conditions.

The Capitoline Museums (Musei Capitolini) are the world's oldest public collection, started in 1471 with Pope Sixtus IV's donation of bronze sculptures to the city. The Palazzo Nuovo houses many important works, including statues of Roman emperors and other famous personages. Busts of philosophers, poets and politicians, among them Sophocles, Homer, Epicurus and Cicero line the Sala dei Filosofi. The impressive *Galata Morente* (Dying Gaul) is a Roman copy of a 3rd century BC Greek original, and the red marble *Satiro Ridente* (a satyr holding a bunch of grapes) is the *Marble Faun* of Nathaniel Hawthorne's novel.

A tunnel links Palazzo Nuovo to Palazzo dei Conservatori opposite and gives access to the **Tabularium** beneath Palazzo Senatorio, where important inscriptions of the republic and empire were kept.

The inner courtyard of the Palazzo dei Conservatori contains the head, a hand and a foot of a colossal acrolith of **Constantine** originally in the Basilica di Massenzio in the Roman Forum. A highlight here is the famous **She-wolf** (Lupa Capitolina), an Etruscan bronze statue from the 6th century BC. Suckling figures of Romulus and Remus were added by Antonio Pollaiolo around 1509. Also of interest in this wing is the 1st century BC **Spinario**, a delicate bronze statue of a boy removing a thorn from his foot.

If the sculpture hasn't worn you out, head up to the **Pinacoteca** to see magnificent paintings by Giovanni Bellini, Caravaggio, Guido Reni, Federico Zucchari, Salvator Rosa, Domenichino, Pietro da Cortona, van Dyck and Rubens.

DON'T MISS • *Capitoline Venus* • Caravaggio's *San Giovanni Battista* • view of the Forum from the Tabularium • Guercino's *Santa Petronilla* altarpiece

DOMUS AUREA (5, J1)

Nero didn't do things by halves. His massive Domus Aurea (Golden House), built after the fire of AD64, extended over the Palatine, Oppian and Celian hills. The gold paint that covered the facade gave the Domus Aurea its name and the banqueting halls, nymphaeum (a room or outdoor area with fountains, statues and gardens), baths and terraces were decorated with frescoes and mosaics, a few of which remain. Its extensive grounds had vineyards, game and an artificial lake.

Nero didn't have long to enjoy his palace. After his death in 68, his successors were quick to remove all trace of his excesses, razing much of the Domus Aurea to the ground. Vespasian drained the lake and built the Colosseum in its place, Domitian built his palace on the Palatine, and Trajan constructed a baths complex (Terme di Traiano) on top of the Oppian hill ruins – this is this area that has been excavated.

Many of the original loggias and halls were walled when Trajan's baths were built and significantly, the light which filtered through the Domus Aurea's pavilions was completely lost. It is quite confusing trying to identify the parts of the original complex and the later baths.

The baths and underlying ruins were abandoned by the 6th century. During the Renaissance, artists (including Ghirlandaio, Perugino and Raphael) lowered themselves into the ruins in order to study the frescoes. Some left their own graffiti – not quite 'Pinturicchio woz 'ere', but not far off – and all copied motifs from the Domus Aurea frescoes in their work in the Vatican and other parts of Rome.

INFORMATION

- ✉ Viale della Domus Aurea
- ☎ 06 399 67 700
- 🚌 85, 87, 117, 175, 186, 810, J4, J5
- Ⓜ Colosseo
- 🕘 Wed-Mon 9am-8pm
- $ L10,000/€6.20
- ⓘ booking required
- ♿ good

Sally Webb

Sally Webb

Top: The Laocoön, *removed from the Domus Aurea site, is now in the Vatican's Museo Pio-Clementino (p. 32)*
Above: Galata Morente

Nutty Nero's Nick-Nacks

Nero was a great pillager, and had hundreds of Greek bronzes and marble copies of Greek statues placed in his palaces. Among them were the *Galata Morente* and *Galata Suicida* (now in the Capitoline Museums and Palazzo Altemps; see pages 17 & 22 respectively) which were displayed in the octagonal room of the Domus Aurea. The *Laocoön*, now in the Vatican Museums, is also thought to have once been in the Domus Aurea.

GALLERIA BORGHESE (3, D6)

The 'queen of all private collections' was formed by Cardinal Scipione Borghese, the most passionate and knowledgeable connoisseur of his day. The collection and the mansion were acquired by the Italian state in 1902; a lengthy restoration took place in the 1990s.

The ground floor contains some important classical statuary, intricate Roman floor mosaics and Antonio Canova's daring sculpture of Paolina Bonaparte Borghese as a reclining *Venere Vincitrice,* her diaphanous drapery leaving little to the imagination. But Bernini's spectacular carvings – flamboyant depictions of pagan myths – are the stars. His precocious talent is evident in works such as *Rape of Proserpine,* where Pluto's hand presses into Proserpine's solid marble thigh, and in the swirling *Apollo and Daphne,* which depicts the exact moment when the nymph is transformed into a laurel tree, her fingers becoming leaves, her toes turning into tree roots, while Apollo watches helplessly.

INFORMATION

- ✉ Piazzale Scipione Borghese
- ☎ 06 328 10
- 🚌 52, 53, 88, 95, 116, 490, 495, 910
- 🕐 Tues-Sun 9am-7pm
- $ L14,000/8000, €7.23/4.13
- ⓘ book in advance; timed admissions
- e www.galleriaborghese.it
- ♿ good
- ✕ museum cafe

Bridgeman Art Library

Bridgeman Art Library

Top: Perugino's Saint Sebastian
Above: Titian's Amor Sacroe Amor Profano

There are six Caravaggios including early works such as *Bacco Malato* (Ailing Bacchus) and the luscious *Ragazzo con Canestro di Frutta* (Boy with a Basket of Fruit), both with magnificent representations of still life. The wonderfully naturalistic *Madonna dei Palafrenieri* (Madonna with the Serpent) is one of Caravaggio's masterpieces; its uninhibited realism led to its rejection by its ecclesiastical commissioners, so Scipione snapped it up.

The paintings on the 1st floor are testimony to Scipione's connoisseur's eye, and include masterworks by Giovanni Bellini, Giorgione, Veronese, Botticelli, Guercino, Domenichino and Rubens among others. Highlights are Raphael's *Deposizione di Cristo* (Deposition) of 1507 and Titian's early masterpiece *Amor Sacroe Amor Profano* (Sacred and Profane Love). After you've had a an art-attack, go for a wander in the gorgeous grounds (see p. 50).

DON'T MISS

• *Sleeping Hermaphrodite* • Pietro Bernini's bas-relief of horse & rider • Bernini's *Davide* • Correggio's erotic *Danae* • Fra Bartolomeo's *Adoration of Christ Child* • Perugino's *Madonna with Child*

MUSEO NAZIONALE ETRUSCO DI VILLA GIULIA (3, D4)

Vignola, Vasari and Michelangelo all had a hand in the design of Villa Giulia, Pope Julius III's summer residence (1550-55), complete with its frescoed loggias and much imitated sunken nymphaeum. It is home to the national collection of Etruscan treasures, many found in tombs at necropoli throughout Lazio.

INFORMATION

- ✉ Piazzale di Villa Giulia 9
- ☎ 06 320 19 51
- 🚌 88, 95, 628
- Ⓜ Flaminio
- 🚊 2, 3, 19
- ⏲ Tues-Sun 8.30am-7.30pm
- $ L8000/4000, €4.13/2.07
- ⓘ free guided tours, Sun 11.15am; summer concerts (p. 95)
- ♿ good
- ✖ museum cafe

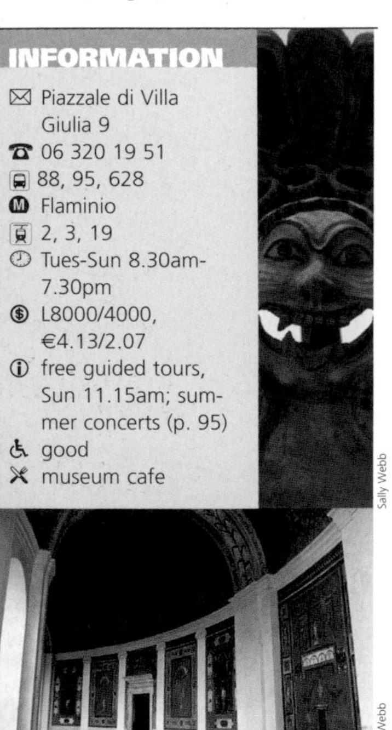

Sally Webb

Sally Webb

A meeting of artful ages: Etruscan statuary (top) and Renaissance loggia (above)

There are thousands of exhibits including domestic objects, cooking utensils, terracotta vases and amphoras, distinctive black bucchero tableware, bronze mirrors engraved with mythological scenes and the remains of a horse-drawn chariot. An Etruscan tomb has been reconstructed complete with burial objects and armchairs sculpted into the rock.

Of particular note is the polychrome terracotta statue of Apollo and other pieces found at Veio, dating from the late 6th century or early 5th century BC. Another highlight is the **Sarcofago degli Sposi** made for a husband and wife, from a tomb at Cerveteri. This finely sculpted sarcophagus demonstrates the heights of creativity and skill that Etruscan artists reached. It has been restored several times, most recently in 1998 when a cleaner in the museum knocked one of the wife's arms off.

Among the most fascinating exhibits are the personal items, such as safety pins and hairclips, and the small bronze figurines. The display of Etruscan (and later) jewellery and gemstones is dazzling. Take a close look at the stunning jewellery (in a room of its own) and you'll see that design hasn't progressed all that much since.

Etruscan Enigmas

Most of what is known about Etruscan culture, which reached its peak in the 7th and 6th centuries BC, has been gleaned from the archaeological evidence of their tombs and religious sanctuaries. Their belief in life after death gave rise to the practice of burying the deceased with everything that he or she might need in the next life: food and drink, clothes, ornaments and jewellery. You can't help but ask: if these are their burial objects, what was their civilisation like?

PALATINE (4, J13)

The Palatine (Palatino) is the mythical founding place of Rome, and the remains of Iron Age huts have been discovered there. During the Republican era it was the most desirable spot for wealthy Romans to build their homes and later became the realm of the emperors – inspiring the word 'palace'. It remained an important centre in Roman life until the Middle Ages.

A vast complex built for Emperor Domitian served as the main imperial palace for 300 years. The **Domus Augustana** (the emperor's private residence) was built on two levels, in characteristically Roman style with rooms leading off a *peristilio* (peristyle, or garden courtyard) and an elaborate colonnaded facade overlooking Circus Maximus (Circo Massimo). The **Domus Flavia** (the official imperial palace) nearby comprised several large halls and a *triclinio* (banqueting hall) paved in coloured marble. Domitian was terrified of being assassinated and had the building's peristyle lined with shiny marble slabs so that he could see who was approaching.

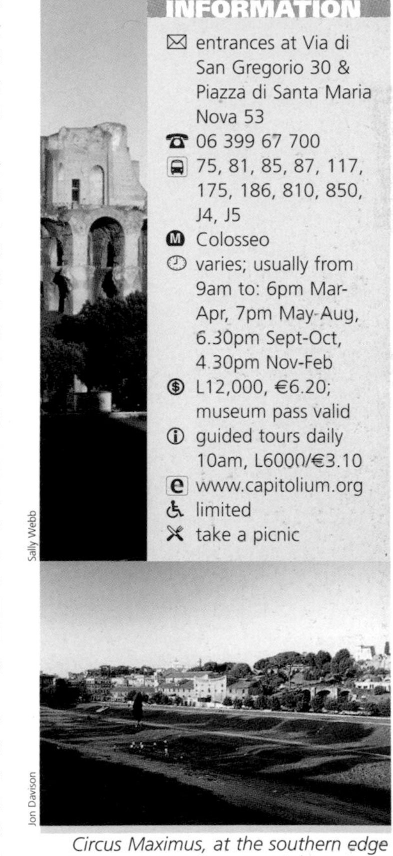

Sally Webb

Jon Davison

Circus Maximus, at the southern edge of the Palatine

INFORMATION

- ✉ entrances at Via di San Gregorio 30 & Piazza di Santa Maria Nova 53
- ☎ 06 399 67 700
- 🚌 75, 81, 85, 87, 117, 175, 186, 810, 850, J4, J5
- Ⓜ Colosseo
- 🕘 varies; usually from 9am to: 6pm Mar-Apr, 7pm May-Aug, 6.30pm Sept-Oct, 4.30pm Nov-Feb
- $ L12,000, €6.20; museum pass valid
- ⓘ guided tours daily 10am, L6000/€3.10
- e www.capitolium.org
- ♿ limited
- ✗ take a picnic

The Domus Flavia was constructed over earlier edifices. One of these (not always open) is the **Casa dei Grifi** which has a stucco relief of two griffins in one of the rooms. Dating from the late 2nd or 1st century BC, it is the oldest building on the Palatine and was excavated in the 18th century.

Among the best preserved buildings on the Palatine is the so-called **Casa di Livia** (west of the Domus Flavia) whose walls are decorated with frescoes – of mythological scenes, landscapes, and fruits and flowers – which are still *in situ*.

DON'T MISS

• the stadium • Palatine artefacts and artworks in Museo Palatino • *Criptoportico,* Nero's 128m tunnel • Orti Farnesini gardens

PALAZZO ALTEMPS (4, E8)

The prestigious Ludovisi collection forms the main body of the exhibits in this branch of the Museo Nazionale Romano, housed in a Renaissance and Baroque palazzo designed by Antonio da Sangallo the Elder, Baldassarre Peruzzi and Martino Longhi for generations of the noble Altemps family.

INFORMATION

- ✉ Piazza Sant' Apollinare 46
- ☎ 06 683 35 66
- 🚌 70, 81, 87, 116, 186, 492
- 🕘 Tues-Sun 9am-7.30pm
- $ L10,000/5000, €5.16/2.58; museum pass valid
- ⓘ guided tours Sat & Sun hourly (in English on request)
- ♿ good
- ✕ Il Primoli or Orso 80 (p. 82)

Bridgeman Art Library

Cardinal Ludovico Ludovisi, a nephew of Pope Gregory XV, was a ravenous collector of the ancient sculpture which was regularly unearthed in the building boom of Counter-Reformation Rome. He employed leading sculptors – including Bernini and Alessandro Algardi – to repair and 'enhance' the works, replacing missing limbs or sticking a new head on a headless torso.

Baroque frescoes provide a decorative backdrop for the sculpture. Landscapes and hunting scenes are seen through trompe l'oeil windows in the Sala delle Prospettive Dipinte and a fresco by Melozzo da Forlì (in the Sala della Piattaia, once the main reception room of the palazzo) displays a cupboard full of wedding gifts.

The *Trono Ludovisi,* discovered in the late 19th century, is one of the prize exhibits. Most scholars believe the carved marble throne came from a Greek colony in Italy and dates from the 5th or 6th century BC.

Ministero per i Beni e le Attività Culturali

Top: Galata suicida *Above:* Trono Ludovisi

In the Sala del Camino, intricate carvings graphically depict a Roman battle scene on a giant marble sarcophagus. The expression and movement extracted from a huge lump of stone is astonishing. Equally impressive is the sculpture *Galata suicida* (Gaul Committing Suicide). Blood spurts out of his flesh as the Gaul knifes himself to death.

DON'T MISS • sarcophagi relief of ritual foot bathing, south loggia • Bernini's touch-ups (see *Ares Ludovisi*) • head of Juno (c 600BC) • north loggia frescoes

PALAZZO MASSIMO ALLE TERME (5, E2)

Rome's best museum of sculpture, statuary and painting from the late Republican to late Imperial era cannot be missed. The commissioned portraits of emperors, statesmen and their families (in the ground-floor galleries) are idealised representations of the ruling classes. Realism had little to do with these busts and statues; self-glorification was the order of the day.

Sala VII contains a superb 5th century BC Greek sculpture of a young woman extracting an arrow from her back. It was found in the Horti Sallustiani (now the Via Veneto area), which once belonged to Julius Caesar. The badly damaged **Apollo del Tevere** in Sala VI shows what a lengthy bath in polluted water can do to marble; this piece was excavated from the Tiber's banks in the late 19th century. In the same room are two marble discus throwers copied from one of the most famous of all Greek bronzes.

Bridgeman Art Library

INFORMATION

- ✉ Largo di Villa Peretti 1
- ☎ 06 489 03 500
- 🚌 numerous ATAC services (see map)
- Ⓜ Termini, Repubblica
- ⏲ Tues-Sun 9am-7.45pm
- $ L12,000/6000, €6.20/3.10; museum pass valid
- ♿ good
- ✕ Monti area (p. 83)

The highlights of this seat of the Museo Nazionale Romano are the sensational Roman paintings and mosaics, including frescoes (datable to 20-10BC) from the excavated Villa Livia, which belonged to the wife of Augustus. These stunning frescoes depict an illusionary garden with cypresses, pines, oleander, myrtle and laurel, and fruit trees abundant with ripe pomegranates and quinces.

Fresco fragments from a Roman villa in the Trastevere area (excavated in the 19th century) are among the most important examples of Roman painting that survive, clearly illustrating the style and taste of the period. Dating from around 20BC, they include landscapes, narrative friezes with an almost Egyptian appearance, and illusionary architectural elements such as columns, cornices and vases.

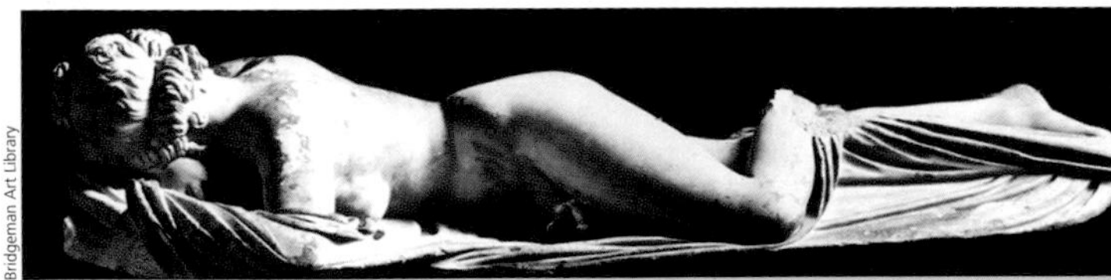

Bridgeman Art Library

Top: Roman fresco of a seated woman Above: Hermaphroditus Asleep

DON'T MISS

• statue of Minerva • portrait head of Livia • terracotta artefacts from the Palatine's Domus Tiberiana • wall mosaics from Nero's villa at Anzio • ancient and medieval coin collection

PANTHEON (6, C5)

The Pantheon, or 'temple to all the gods', is the best-preserved ancient Roman building. Originally built by Marcus Agrippa, top general and son-in-law of Augustus, in 27BC, it was rebuilt by Hadrian around AD120.

INFORMATION

- ✉ Piazza della Rotonda
- ☎ 06 683 00 230
- 🚌 46, 62, 64, 70, 81, 87, 186, 116, 492, 628
- 🕒 Mon-Sat 8.30am-7.30pm, Sun 9am-6pm
- $ free
- ♿ good
- ✕ L'Angoletto, Osteria dell'Ingegno (p.80)

Martin Moos

Christopher Groenhout

Looking through the eye of the gods

Its dramatic, imposing interior is the kind of place that inspires people to become architects. The height and diameter of the interior both measure 43.3m and the extraordinary dome – the largest masonry vault ever built – is considered the most important achievement of ancient Roman architecture. Light is provided by the oculus, a 9m opening in the dome; small holes in the marble floor beneath it allow any rain that enters to drain away.

The weight of the dome is supported by brick arches embedded in the structure of the walls which are evident from the exterior. Rivets and holes in the brickwork indicate where the original marble veneer panels have been removed. The 16 massive Corinthian columns of the portico are each a single block of stone.

After being abandoned under the first Christian emperors, the Pantheon was converted into a church in 609 and dedicated to the Madonna and all martyrs. Over the centuries it has been consistently plundered and damaged. In 667 the gilded roof tiles were removed by the Byzantine emperor Constans II. Pope Urban VIII had the bronze ceiling of the portico melted down to make the *baldacchino* (canopy) for St Peter's and cannons for Castel Sant'Angelo.

The Italian kings Victor Emmanuel II and Umberto I and the artist Raphael are buried here.

In the Writer's Words

Stendhal was impressed. In this *Promenades dans Rome* he wrote that he had never met anyone who could remain impassive at the sight of the Pantheon's interior, where its great dome vault creates a sense of the sublime. But he also had other senses to satisfy. The great thing about the Pantheon, he wrote, is that you can visit it so quickly.

PIAZZA DI SPAGNA (4, C11)

The piazza, famous Spanish Steps (Scalinata della Trinità dei Monti) and church above are a masterpiece of urban planning and have long provided a gathering place for foreigners. Built with a legacy from the French in 1725, but named after the Spanish Embassy to the Holy See (which is still located in the piazza), the steps lead to the French church, **Trinità dei Monti**. In the 18th century the most beautiful women and men of Italy gathered here, waiting to be chosen as an artist's model. Today models (and the rest of us) swan from boutique to boutique in a fashion frenzy (see pp. 62-6).

Martin Moos

INFORMATION

- ✉ Piazza di Spagna
- 🚌 116, 117, 119
- Ⓜ Spagna
- ♿ good; lift to the top from the metro
- ✕ Al 34, Otello alla Concordia (p. 81)

In April each year the steps are decorated with pink azaleas. Viale della Trinità dei Monti at the top of the steps leads to the **Pincio** (see p. 49). Halfway along the road on the right is the **Villa Medici**, home of the French Academy, which has hosted and funded the Roman sojourns of talented French artists, writers and musicians since 1666.

In the piazza is the fountain of a sinking boat, called the **Barcaccia**, by Pietro Bernini, father of the famous Gian Lorenzo. To the right as you face the steps is the house where John Keats died in 1821, now a museum (Keats-Shelley House; see p. 36). Further to the right, in Piazza Mignanelli, is the **Colonna dell 'Immacolata**, crowned with a statue of the Virgin Mary. Rome's firefighters have traditionally placed a wreath on her arm on 8 December; in his more nimble years, Pope John Paul II climbed up the firefighter's ladder to do the same.

Jon Davison

Superlative sit and stare stairs

Literary Rome

Writers have been flocking to Rome for centuries since the days when Ovid, Virgil and Horace worked for Emperor Augustus. The 18th century saw an unprecedented influx of foreign writers inspired by Rome's classical past, including Edward Gibbon, who wrote *The Decline and Fall of the Roman Empire,* and Goethe.

The English Romantics – Keats, Shelley, Mary Shelley and Byron – came *en masse* and formed a virtual colony in the Piazza di Spagna area together with the many grand tourists. Other writers who came, saw and were inspired include Robert and Elizabeth Barrett Browning, Charles Dickens, Augustus Hare and Henry James. A list of Rome-inspired tomes can be found on page 74.

PIAZZA NAVONA (6, B3)

Lined with Baroque palaces, this vast and beautiful piazza – a popular gathering place for Romans and tourists alike – was laid out on the ruins of a stadium built by Domitian in AD86. Originally called the Circus Agonalis, it became known in the Middle Ages as the Campus Agonis, which in time became 'n'agona' and eventually 'navona'. The arena was used for festivals and sporting events, including jousts, until the late 15th century, when it was paved over and transformed into a marketplace and public square.

The central **Fontana dei Quattro Fiumi** by Bernini was completed in 1651. It depicts four rivers – the Nile, Ganges, Danube and Rio Plata. The obelisk above once stood in the Circo di Massenzio on the Via Appia Antica.

The **Fontana del Moro** at the southern end of piazza was designed by Giacomo della Porta in 1576; Bernini added the central figure of the Moor. The 19th century **Fontana del Nettuno** at the other end has a figure of Neptune fighting a sea monster, surrounded by sea nymphs.

Facing the Fontana dei Quattro Fiumi is the **Chiesa di Sant' Agnese in Agone**, designed by Bernini's bitter rival, Borromini. The largest building in the piazza is the elegant **Palazzo Pamphilj** built between 1644 and 1650 by Girolamo Rainaldi and Borromini for Giovanni Battista Pamphilj when he became Pope Innocent X. It was later occupied by his domineering sister-in-law, Olimpia Maidalchini, who, like other members of the pope's family, received enormous riches and favours during his pontificate. It is now the Brazilian Embassy.

INFORMATION

- ✉ Piazza Navona
- 🚌 81, 87, 116, 186, 492, 628
- ⓘ Christmas market and funfair early Dec-6 Jan
- ♿ good
- ✕ Ditirambo, Tre Scalini, Paladini (p. 78 & 88-9)

Alan Benson

Bernini vs Borromini: A Brilliant Blue

The enormous rivalry that existed between Bernini and Borromini has, over time, fuelled the idea that one statue in Bernini's Fontana dei Quattro Fiumi is shielding his eyes from Borromini's church. The truth is that Bernini completed the fountain two years before his contemporary started work on the facade of Sant'Agnese in Agone.

Guy Moberly

ROMAN FORUM (4, H13)

Built over 900 years, the Roman Forum (Foro Romano) was the commercial, political and religious centre of ancient Rome from the Republican era until the 4th century AD. Its importance declined along with the Empire. During medieval times the area was used to graze cattle and extensively plundered for its precious marble. During the Renaissance, with the renewed appreciation of all things classical, the Forum provided inspiration for artists and architects. The area was systematically excavated in the 18th and 19th centuries, and you can see archaeological teams at work in ongoing digs.

The **Via Sacra** crosses the forum from north-west to east. At its western end is the 100m-long **Basilica Aemilia**, built in 179BC. Its two storey portico was once lined with shops. Beyond it is the **Curia**, once the Roman Senate's meeting place, which was rebuilt several times and converted into a church in the Middle Ages. The triumphal **Arco di Settimio Severo** was erected in AD203 in honour of the emperor Septimius Severus and his sons, Caracalla and Geta. To its south are eight granite columns from the **Tempio di Saturno**, inaugurated in 497BC, once the city's treasury.

Back on the Via Sacra is the **Casa delle Vestali**, home of the Vestal virgins who tended the sacred flame in the adjoining temple. **Arco di Tito** at the eastern end was built in AD81 in honour of the victories of Titus against the Jews.

Russell Mountford

INFORMATION

- ✉ entrances at Largo Romolo e Remo 5-6, Piazza Santa Maria Nova 53 & Via di Monte Tarpeo
- ☎ 06 399 67 700
- 🚌 numerous ATAC services (see map); J4 & J5
- Ⓜ Colosseo
- 🕘 varies; usually from 9am to: 6pm Mar-Apr, 7pm May-Aug, 6.30pm Sept-Oct, 4.30pm Nov-Feb
- $ free
- ⓘ kiosk at Via dei Fori Imperiali has maps
- e www.capitolium.org
- ♿ limited
- ✕ Osteria Gli Angeletti (p. 83)

Recycling, Roman Style

Ironically, the physical destruction of ancient Rome can't be blamed on invading barbarians or natural disasters, but on Romans themselves. Over the years, in the name of progress, the Romans dismantled the ancient city brick by brick in order to build other palaces, churches and monuments.

DON'T MISS

• Basilica di Costantino (or Basilica di Massenzio) • the Rostra • the ever-upright Colonna di Foca • Umbilicus Urbis, centre of ancient Rome

SAN CLEMENTE BASILICA (5, K1)

This church defines better than any other the multi-level history of Rome. The 12th century church was built over a 4th century church which was, in turn, built over a 1st century Roman house containing a late 2nd century AD temple to the god Mithras (an eastern deity especially popular with soldiers). It is believed that Republican era foundations lie beneath the house.

INFORMATION

- ✉ Via di San Giovanni in Laterano
- ☎ 06 704 51 018
- 🚌 85, 87, 117, 186, 850
- Ⓜ Colosseo
- 🕘 9am-12.30pm, 3-6pm (from 10am Sun)
- $ free; crypt L4000/ €2.07
- ♿ limited (access to medieval church only)
- ✕ Pasqualino (p. 83)

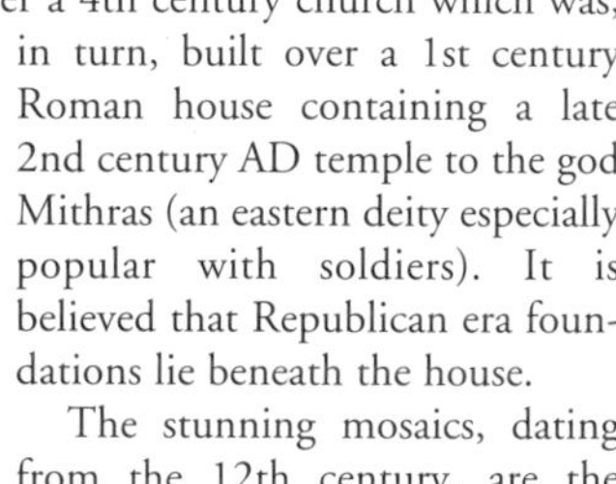
Bridgeman Art Library

The stunning mosaics, dating from the 12th century, are the highlight of the medieval church. The gold background is typical of the later Byzantine mosaic style, although the designs were probably based on and built with mosaics from the earlier church. On the triumphal arch are Christ and the symbols of the four Evangelists. In the apse is the **Triumph of the Cross,** with 12 doves symbolising the apostles, and the Madonna and saints encircled by a vine growing from the foot of the cross.

Bridgeman Art Library

San Clemente's glorious triumphal arch

Not much remains of the 4th century church, which was virtually destroyed by Norman invaders in 1084, although some 11th century Romanesque frescoes illustrating the life of St Clement can be seen at the eastern end. The *piscina,* a deep pit discovered by archaeologists in 1967, was probably used as a font or fountain.

Descending another level, you arrive at the 1st century Roman house. At the eastern end is a catacomb with 16 wall tombs dating from the 5th or 6th century. The **Temple of Mithras,** containing an altar with a sculpted relief of Mithras slaying the bull, is situated directly under the apse of the 4th century church.

DON'T MISS

- Masolino da Panicale's frescoes in Cappella di Santa Caterina
- 6th century marble choir
- Cosmati Paschal candlestick

SAN GIOVANNI IN LATERANO (3, H7)

Founded by Constantine in the 4th century, San Giovanni was the first Christian basilica constructed in Rome. It is Rome's cathedral and the pope's seat as Bishop of Rome. It has been destroyed by fire twice and rebuilt several times. In 1425 Martin V had the floor inlaid with stone and mosaic looted from other derelict Roman churches.

Borromini transformed the interior in the mid-17th century. The **bronze doors** of the eastern facade were moved here from the Curia in the Roman Forum. Alessandro Galilei's **portico** (1736) is surmounted by colossal statues representing Christ with Saints John the Baptist and John the Evangelist and the 12 apostles. The Gothic **baldacchino** over the papal altar contains relics including the heads of Saints Peter and Paul. The apse was rebuilt in the 19th century; its mosaics are copies of the originals.

Fortunately the beautiful 13th century **cloister** escaped the fires. Built by the Vassalletto family in Cosmati style, the cloister has columns and an architrave which were once completely covered with inlaid marble mosaics. The outer walls are lined with sarcophagi and sculpture, including an inscription of a Papal Bull of Sixtus IV.

The domed **baptistry**, near Domenico Fontana's northern facade, was also built by Constantine, but has been remodelled several times. Sixtus III gave it its present octagonal shape which became the model for many baptistries throughout the Christian world. The adjoining **Palazzo Laterano** (see Scala Santa, p. 47), now housing diocesan offices, was the papal residence until the popes moved to Avignon.

INFORMATION

- ✉ Piazza San Giovanni in Laterano 4
- ☎ 06 698 86 452
- Bus: 16, 85, 87, 117, 186, 218, 650, 850
- M: San Giovanni
- Tram: 3, 8
- ⌚ Basilica 7am-6pm, to 7pm summer; cloister 9am-5pm, to 6pm summer; baptistry Mon-Thurs 9am-1pm, 4-6pm, Fri & Sat 9am-1pm
- $ free, cloister L4000/ €2.07
- ♿ good

Martin Moos

Sally Webb

Divine mosaic and Cosmati work star here.

DON'T MISS

• Borromini's sculptural frames and oval windows • baptistry's exquisite mosaics, especially in the Capella di San Venanzio

ST PETER'S BASILICA (4, D2)

In 315, Constantine ordered construction of a basilica on the site of St Peter's tomb, and this first church was consecrated in 326. In the mid-15th century, Pope Nicholas V put architects, including Alberti, to work on its reconstruction. Serious work began in 1506 when Bramante designed a new basilica on a Greek cross plan.

INFORMATION

- ✉ Piazza San Pietro
- ☎ multilingual infoline 06 698 81 662; St Peter's Tomb booking 06 698 85 318, fax 06 698 85 518
- 🚌 46, 62, 64
- Ⓜ Ottaviano
- 🕘 basilica 7am-6pm, to 7pm Apr-Sept
- $ free; dome L6000/ €3.10
- e www.vatican.va
- ♿ good
- ✕ Da Cesare, Osteria dell'Angelo (p. 86)

Martin Moos

It took more than 150 years to complete, involving the contributions of Bramante, Raphael, Antonio da Sangallo, Michelangelo, Giacomo della Porta and Carlo Maderno. It is generally held that San Pietro owes most to Michelangelo, who took over the project in 1547 at the age of 72 and was responsible for the dome. Maderno designed the facade and portico and was also instructed to lengthen the nave towards the piazza, creating a Latin cross.

The cavernous interior, decorated by Bernini and Giacomo della Porta, holds up to 60,000 people. It contains treasures including Michelangelo's superb *Pietà*. Bernini's Baroque **baldacchino** stands 29m high in the centre of the church. The bronze used to make this extraordinary work of art was taken from the roof of the Pantheon. The high altar, at which only the pope can serve, stands over the site of St Peter's grave.

Michelangelo's **dome**, a majestic architectural masterpiece, soars 119m above the high altar. Its balconies are decorated with reliefs depicting the so-called Reliquaire Maggiori (major relics). Entry to the dome (see p. 51) is to the right as you climb the stairs to the atrium of the basilica. Those without a head for heights might want to book in advance for a tour of the excavations of the original church, an early Christian cemetery and the tomb of St Peter under the basilica.

Eric L Wheater

Christendom's wealth on glorious display

• bronze plates in the floor showing the sizes of the world's largest churches • Sacre Grotte Vaticane • bronze statue of St Peter, whose right foot has been worn down by the kisses and touch of pilgrims

TRASTEVERE (2, D3)

Separated from the historic centre by the river, Trastevere is the most charming part of town. The many bars and restaurants tucked into its labyrinthine laneways make it the most popular area of the city to eat out or just hang out. Its traditionally proletarian nature is changing as crumbling old palazzi become gentrified and wealthy foreigners move in.

Tamsin Wilson

INFORMATION

- 🚌 23, 44, 75, 280, H
- 🚊 8
- ♿ limited
- ✕ see pp. 84-5

The heart of Trastevere is the lovely **Piazza Santa Maria in Trastevere**. It's a true Roman square – by day peopled by mothers with strollers, chatting locals and guidebook-toting tourists, by night with artisans selling their craftwork, young Romans looking for a good time, and the odd homeless person looking for a bed. Stop to admire the Roman fountain, restored by Carlo Fontana in 1692.

The **Basilica di Santa Maria in Trastevere** has a stunning 12th century mosaic on its Romanesque facade, but those inside are even better. If your insides are calling, stop for a hot chocolate or gelato at Bar San Calisto.

From the piazza, Vicolo del Piede leads to the pretty **Via della Scala**; residents of the streets east of here (Via del Leopardo, Via del Mattonato and Vicolo Bologna) have the most photographed washing in the world.

The **Basilica di Santa Cecilia in Trastevere** was built in the 9th century on the spot where St Cecilia was martyred in 230. She sang her way through several botched attempts to finish her off and became the patron saint of music. The impressive apse mosaic was executed in 870 and features Christ with Cecilia and other saints.

Martin Moos

DON'T MISS

- Piazza San Cosimato market • food shops on Via Natale del Grande
- Pietro Cavallini's *Last Judgement* in the nun's choir at Santa Cecilia

VATICAN MUSEUMS & SISTINE CHAPEL (4, C2)

You'll need several hours and *lots* of energy to do justice to the immense papal collections – and that's before you even get to the Sistine Chapel. Early Christian antiquities? Head for the **Museo Pio-Cristiano**. Pagan Greek and Roman statuary? Try the **Museo Gregoriano Profano**. And for paintings, make a bee-line for the **Pinacoteca**, which houses a magnificent collection including paintings by Giotto, Filippo Lippi, Federico Barocci, Guido Reni, Guercino, Nicolas Poussin, van Dyck and Pietro da Cortona.

INFORMATION

- ✉ Viale del Vaticano
- ☎ 06 698 84 341, 06 698 84 947, fax 06 698 85 863
- 🚌 34, 46, 49, 62, 64, 98, 492, 982
- Ⓜ Ottaviano, Cipro-Musei Vatican
- ⏲ Mon-Fri 8.45am-4.45pm (last admission 3.30pm), Sat 8.45-1.45pm (last admission 12.45pm), Sun closed except last Sun of month 9am-1pm
- $ L18,000/€9.30, L12,000/€6.20; free on last Sun of month
- ⓘ CD audioguides
- e www.vatican.va/museums
- ♿ excellent (information folder available)
- ✕ museum cafe

Sally Webb

Two mummies are among the fascinating Egyptian pieces in the **Museo Gregoriano Egizio**. Burial objects from Etruscan tombs including a 7th century BC bronze funeral carriage, the *Mars of Todi* bronze and some spectacular gold jewellery are showcased in the **Museo Gregoriano Etrusco**.

Masterpieces of classical sculpture such as the **Apollo Belvedere**, a Roman copy in marble of a 4th century BC Greek bronze (boasting a seriously good six-pack), and the **Laocoön** and other artefacts taken from the Domus Aurea(see p. 18) are in the **Museo Pio-Clementino**.

The tapestries opposite the windows in the **Galleria degli Arazzi** were designed by students of Raphael and woven in the Brussels workshop of Pieter van Aeist. The fascinating **Galleria delle Carte Geografiche** (at left) is frescoed with topographical maps of Italian regions, painted between 1580 and 1583.

The **Stanze di Raffaello**, Pope Julius II's private apartments, are named after Raphael's paintings therein, such as his masterpiece, *Expulsion of Heliodorus from the Temple,* and his best known work, *School of Athens,* featuring philosophers and scholars. The lone figure in the foreground is a portrait of Michelangelo (who was painting the Sistine Chapel at the time); Raphael also included a self-portrait (second figure from right).

The **Sistine Chapel** (Cappella Sistina), completed in 1484 for Pope Sixtus IV, is used for the conclave which elects the popes. It is best known for two of the most awe-inspiring acts of individual creativity in the history of the visual arts: Michelangelo's **frescoes** on the barrel-vaulted ceiling (1508-12), and his **Giudizio Universale** (Last Judgement) on the end wall

Worth a little pain in the neck.

(completed in 1541). Restorations over the past two decades have brought back to life Michelangelo's rich, vibrant colours.

It took the great artist four years to paint the ceiling, working on scaffolding lodged under the windows. The frescoes down the middle represent nine scenes from the book of Genesis, including the Division of Day from Night, the Creation of Adam, the Expulsion of Adam and Eve from the Garden of Eden, and the Flood. These main images are framed by the **Ignudi**, athletic male nudes; next to them, on the lower curved part of the vault, are large figures of Hebrew **Prophets** and androgynous pagan **Sibyls**. In the lunettes over the windows are the ancestors of Christ.

More than 20 years later Michelangelo was commissioned to paint the *Last Judgement*. The dramatic, swirling mass of predominantly naked bodies caused a scandal when it was unveiled, and Pope Pius IV had Daniele da Volterra (one of Michelangelo's students) do a cover-up job with fig leaves and loin cloths in appropriate places.

The chapel's walls were painted by top Renaissance artists including Botticelli, Domenico Ghirlandaio, Pinturicchio and Luca Signorelli. Try to drag your attention away from Michelangelo's frescoes to appreciate these late 15th century works, depicting events in the lives of Moses and Christ; thanks to a recent restoration, they are as stunning as the ceiling. Botticelli's **Tentazione di Cristo** and the **Purificazione del lebbroso** (second fresco on the right) is particularly beautiful, with its typical Botticelli maiden in a diaphanous dress. The first frescoes in each cycle, the Finding of Moses and the Birth of Christ by Perugino, were destroyed to make way for the Last Judgement – a great controversy at the time.

Russell Mountford

Papal Audiences

On Wednesday the pope meets his flock. To be present at an audience, write in advance to the Prefettura della Casa Pontificia, 00120 Città del Vaticano, requesting the date you'd like to attend. If you're already in Rome, call into the Prefettura (open Mon-Fri 9am-1pm) through the bronze doors under the colonnade to the right of St Peter's.

DON'T MISS

- Raphael's *Trasfigurazione* & Leonardo's unfinished *San Gerolamo*, Pinacoteca
- Fra Angelico frescoes, Pope Nicholas V's private chapel

sights & activities

Sightseeing in Rome is exhilarating and exhausting. That it wasn't built in a day is quickly evident when you start exploring Republic-era temples, imperial residences, early Christian basilicas, medieval churches, Renaissance palazzi and Baroque fountains.

The vast majority of things to see and do are in the *centro storico* (historic centre), and walking between them is a sightseeing exercise in itself. Medieval, Renaissance and Baroque Rome is on display between Piazza del Popolo, Piazza Venezia and Piazza Navona. Look up at building facades and bell towers, look down at cobblestone streets, church crypts and ruins of Roman edifices several metres below current street level. Look at the people, the shops, the restaurants, the bars and cafes – in short, watch the theatre of life that makes Rome, well, Rome.

Ruins of the ancient city can be seen around the Capitoline and Palatine hills. In the Esquiline and Quirinal areas you'll find small churches, some dating from the early Christian era, with magnificent mosaics. Across the Tiber, the marvels of the Vatican attract tourists and pilgrims alike, while Trastevere appeals to more epicurial senses.

Be flexible with your sightseeing, as unpredictability is a fact of life in Rome. It's not unusual to find churches, museums or archaeological sites on your well planned itinerary closed when you get there, due to ongoing excavations or lack of staff. Relax, have a cappuccino or a gelato, and head for the next ancient wonder or Baroque architectural delight on your list.

Off the Beaten Track

With the evidence of 2000 years of civilisation around you, and thousands of tourists to deal with at any time of year, getting off the beaten track in Rome is easier said than done.

However, crowds at thin out at smaller museums such as **Casa di Goethe**, **Centrale Montemartini**, and the **Museo Barracco** (see pp. 35-6). Keats and Shelley find **Cimitero Acattolico per gli Stranieri** (p. 45) a restful place. And when it all gets too much, a snooze under a parasol pine in **Villa Doria Pamphilj** can be the perfect pick-me-up (p. 50).

Neil Setchfield

Pietro da Cortona's amazing ceiling fresco, Palazzo Barberini

MUSEUMS

Museums rarely charge for under 18s or over 65s, and student and youth discounts are common. Prices here indicate full or full/concession admission.

Ara Pacis Augustae (4, C9) The marble reliefs of this 13BC altar commemorating Augustus' victories mark the point at which Roman sculpture became a distinct entity. Closed at the time of writing, a Richard Meier designed museum complex should open in 2002.
✉ Piazza Augusto Imperatore ☎ 06 688 06 848 🚌 81, 117, 119, 628, 913, J9 🕐 closed at time of writing; call for information $ free ♿ good

Casa di Goethe (4, B10) The apartment where Johann Wolfgang von Goethe stayed between 1786 and 1788 is now a museum, with drawings and etchings by the great author as well as documents relating to his Italian sojourn.
✉ Via del Corso 18 ☎ 06 326 50 412 e www.casadigoethe.it 🚌 117, 119 Ⓜ Flaminio 🕐 Wed-Mon 10am-6pm $ L5000/€2.58

Centrale Montemartini (3, K4) Ancient sculpture (hidden for decades in Capitoline Museum storage vaults) is on display against industrial machinery in a former power plant. The unusual juxtaposition – originally a stop-gap measure to house the collection during major Capitoline renovations – has been so successful that it's now a permanent fixture.
✉ Via Ostiense 106 ☎ 06 574 80 30 🚌 23, 702 Ⓜ Piramide 🕐 Tues-Fri 10am-6pm, Sat & Sun 10am-7pm $ L12,000/6000, €6.20/3.10 ♿ limited

Lauren Sunstein

Centrale Montemartini

Crypta Balbi (2, A7) Based around the ruins of medieval and Renaissance structures built atop a grand Roman portico and theatre (from 13BC), this new museum (part of the Museo Nazionale Romano) is testament to Rome's multi-layered history.
✉ Via delle Botteghe Oscure 31 ☎ 06 481 55 76 🚌 46, 62, 63, 64, 70, 87, 492, H, J5 🚋 8 🕐 Tues-Sun 9am-7.45pm $ L10,000/5000, €5.16/2.58; museum pass valid ♿ good

Crypt of Santa Maria della Concezione (4, C13) See p. 50.

Galleria Colonna (4, F12) Palazzo Colonna's Baroque galleries house one of the city's most important private art collections. Vibrant ceiling paintings fight for attention with religious works by Salvator Rosa, Guido Reni and Guercino, but it's the delightful *Mangi fagiuoli* (Bean Eater) attributed to Annibale Caracci that you'll remember best.
✉ Via della Pilotta 17 ☎ 06 679 43 62 e web.tin.it/galleriacolonna/ 🚌 40, 64, 70, 170, H 🕐 Sat 9am-1pm; closed Aug $ L10,000/8000, €5.16/4.13

Galleria Doria Pamphilj (6, D8) Dazzling even by Roman standards, the Doria Pamphilj collection was started by Pamphilj Pope Innocent X. Elaborate picture galleries – and the stunning private apartments – are crammed from floor to ceiling with paintings, although Velasquez's portrait of Innocent X dazzles in its own chamber.
✉ Piazza del Collegio Romano 2 ☎ 06 679 73 23 e www.doriapamphilj.it 🚌 46, 62, 63, 64, 70, 81, 87, 117, 119, 160, 175, 186, 492, 628 🕐 Fri-Wed 10am-5pm $ L14,000/11,000, €7.23/5.68; private apartments L6000, €3.10 ♿ g

Galleria Nazionale d'Arte Moderna (3, D4) The *belle époque* palace built for the 1911 Rome International Exhibition shows 19th and 20th century painting and sculpture.

There's Carrà, De Chirico, Lucio Fontana and Guttuso, the futurists (Boccioni, Balla), and the *Transavanguardia* (Clemente, Cucchi, Paladino) here. Degas, Cézanne, Kandinsky, Mondriaan, Henry Moore and Cy Twombly are international collection standouts.
✉ Viale delle Belle Arti 131 ☎ 06 32 29 81 e www.gnam.arti.beniculturali.it 🚊 2, 3, 19 🕘 Tues-Sun 8.30am-7.30pm $ L12,000/6000, €6.20/3.10 ♿ excellent

Best of Bernini

- Colonnade (Piazza di San Pietro; 4, D3)
- *Elefantino* (p. 44)
- Fontana dei Quattro Fiumi (Piazza Navona; p. 26)
- Fontana del Tritone (Piazza Barberini, below)
- *Rape of Proserpine* and *Apollo & Daphne* (Galleria Borghese; p. 19)
- Sant'Andrea al Quirinale (p. 43)

Sally Webb

Piscean pecs

Galleria Spada (2, A4) Rome's prettiest *palazzo* houses the Spada family art collection (acquired by the state in 1926) with works by Titian, Andrea del Sarto, Guido Reni, Guercino and Titian. The highlight is Borromini's clever trompe l'oeil perspective in the courtyard – which is only a quarter of the length it appears to be.
✉ Piazza Capodiferro 13 ☎ 06 686 11 58 e www.galleriaborghese.it/spada/en/einfo.htm 🚌 23, 116, 280 🕘 Tues-Sat 8.30am-7.30pm, Sun 8.30am-6.30pm $ L10,000/5000, €5.16/2.58

Keats-Shelley House (4, C11) Memorabilia and a vast library of work relating to Keats, Shelley, Mary Shelley, Byron and other Romantic poets occupy the apartment next to the Spanish Steps where John Keats died in 1821 after his brief sojourn in Rome.
✉ Piazza di Spagna 26 ☎ 06 678 42 35 e www.keats-shelley-house.org Ⓜ Spagna 🕘 Mon-Fri 9am-1pm, 2.30-5.30pm $ L5000/€2.58

Museo delle Anime dei Defunti (4, D8) See p. 50.

Museo Barracco (6, E3) One of Rome's most charming museums, the Barracco boasts exquisite Greek, Roman, Assyrian and Egyptian sculpture and artefacts. Beneath the museum are remains of what is said to be a Roman fish shop, complete with counter and a water trough.
✉ Corso Vittorio Emanuele II 166 ☎ 06 688 06 848 🚌 46, 62, 64, 116 🕘 Tues-Sun 9am-7pm $ L5000/3000, €2.58/1.55

Museo Canonica (3, D5) Sculptor and musician Pietro Canonica lived in this delightful villa in Villa Borghese park from 1927 until his death in 1959. Wander through the sculpture collection (mostly Canonica's own work), private apartment and studio.
✉ Viale Pietro Canonica 2 ☎ 06 884 22 79 🚌 88, 95, 116, 490, 495 🕘 Tues-Sat 9am-7pm, Sun 9am-1.30pm $ L5000/3000, €2.58/1.55

Museo della Civiltà Romana (1, C6) See p. 51.

Museo della Comunità Ebraica & Synagogue (2, C7) Roman Jewish history is chronicled in this small but interesting museum, part of the city's main synagogue. The 19th century building is under armed guard after a bomb exploded here in 1983, killing a small child.
✉ Lungotevere dei Cenci ☎ 06 684 00 661 🚌 23, 63, 280, 780 🕘 9.30am to: 4.30pm Mon-Thurs, 1.30pm Fri, noon Sun $ L8000/€4.13 (includes synagogue tour)

Museo delle Mura (3, J6) See p. 51.

Museo Nazionale del Palazzo di Venezia (6, E9) This often overlooked museum has a superb collection of Byzantine and early Renaissance paintings, and decorative arts from the

medieval period to the 18th century: jewellery, tapestries, silver, ivories, ceramics, hundreds of 15-17th century bronze figurines, 18th and 19th century pastels, carved wooden wedding chests as well as a collection of arms and armour.
✉ Via del Plebiscito 118 ☎ 06 679 88 65 🚌 46, 62, 63, 64, 70, 81, 87, 186, 492, 628, 810 ⏲ Tues-Sat 9am-2pm, Sun 9am-1pm $ L8000/4000, €4.13/2.06 ♿ good (call ahead)

Museo Nazionale delle Paste Alimentari (4, E12) See p. 51.

Palazzo Barberini (4, D14) Carlo Maderno, Bernini and Borromini all worked on the rural villa for Barberini pope Urban VIII, which houses the National Art Collection (Galleria Nazionale d'Arte Antica). Highlight works are by Guido Reni, Bronzino and Guercino, an ethereal *Annunziazione* by Filippo Lippi, and Caravaggio's *Judith with the Head of Holfernes,* a gruesome masterpiece of theatrical lighting. In the *Gran Salone* Pietro da Cortona's ceiling fresco is dazzling.
✉ Via Barberini 18 ☎ 06 481 45 91 e www.galleriaborghese.it/barberini/en/ Ⓜ Barberini ⏲ Tues-Sat 9am-7pm, Sun 9am-8pm $ L12,000/€6.20 ♿ good

Palazzo Corsini (2, B1) The poorer half of the National Art Collection (see Palazzo Barberini, above) still boasts some masterpieces: van Dyck's superb *Madonna della Paglia* and Murillo's *Madonna and Child;* Guido Reni's richly coloured *St Jerome* and melancholy *Salome;* Giovanni Lanfranco's lovely *St Peter Healing St Agatha;* and Guercino's haunting *Ecce Homo*. Trompe l'oeil frescoes decorating the galleries are alone worth the visit.
✉ Via della Lungara 10 ☎ 06 688 02 323 e www.galleriaborghese.it/corsini/en/ 🚌 23, 280 ⏲ Tues-Fri 9am-7pm, Sat 9am-2pm, Sun 9am-1pm $ L8000/4000, €4.13/2.06

Lunedi Chuiso

The city takes a while to emerge from its weekend hangover, and if it's Monday, you might find yourself stumped at every turn. Most shops are open only in the afternoon and many eateries take the day off. On top of that, virtually all the city's museums are closed on Monday, except for Casa di Goethe, Galleria Doria Pamphilj, Keats-Shelley House, Museo della Comunità Ebraica, Villa Farnesina and the Vatican Museums. Some archaeological sites – Foro Romano, the Palatino and the Colosseum – also remain open.

Palazzo delle Esposizioni (4, F14) Rome's purpose-built exhibition centre dates from 1882. It's had a chequered history, having housed the Communist Party, been a mess for allied soldiers, a polling station and a public loo. Today it's a vibrant multimedia centre, with a changing program of art exhibitions, performances and cinema.
✉ Via Nazionale 194 ☎ 06 474 59 03 🚌 64, 70, 170, J2 ⏲ Wed-Mon 9am-9pm $ L15,000/8000, €7.75/4.13 ♿ good

Terme di Diocleziano (5, D2) Ancient epigraphs and artefacts from Italian protohistory are the focus of this Museo Nazionale Romano gallery, though its elegant Renaissance cloister is lined with classical sarcophagi, capitals and (mostly headless) statues. The halls of the 4th century Diocletian's Baths host temporary exhibits. This vast complex of libraries, concert halls and gardens was the largest in ancient Rome and held 3000 people.
✉ Viale Enrico de Nicola 78 ☎ 06 481 55 76 Ⓜ Repubblica, Termini ⏲ Tues-Sun 9am-7pm $ L8000/4000, €4.13/2.06; museum pass valid ♿ good

Villa Farnesina (2, B1) Baldassarre Peruzzi's delightful villa (1508-11) is decorated with frescoes: Raphael's superb *Galatea* and works by his pupils; and Peruzzi's illusionary perspective of a colonnade and panorama of Rome.
✉ Via della Lungara 230 ☎ 06 688 01 767 e www.lincei.it/english.version/farnesina.html 🚌 23, 280 ⏲ Mon-Sat 9am-1pm $ L6000/€3.10

ANCIENT MONUMENTS & SITES

Arch of Costantine
(4, J14) Built in AD312 to honour Constantine's victory at Ponte Milvio, this triumphal arch is an assemblage of earlier pieces. The round hunting scenes are from Hadrian's reign (AD117-138), while four reliefs depicting Trajan's battle against the Dacians are possibly by the sculptor who carved Colonna di Traiano.
✉ Via di San Gregorio 🚌 75, 85, 87, 117, 175, 186, 810, 850, J4, J5 Ⓜ Colosseo ♿ good

Dan Herrick

Catnap at Area Sacra di Largo Argentina.

Area Sacra di Largo Argentina (6, F5)
The four Republic-era temples, discovered during construction work in the 1920s, get lost among the heavy traffic skirting the archaeological area. The ruins are home to hundreds of stray cats cared for by the volunteers at the cat sanctuary at the south end.
✉ Largo di Torre Argentina 🚌 46, 62, 63, 64, 70, 87, 186, 780, 810, H 🚋 8 🕘 closed to public

Castel Sant'Angelo
(4, D6) Hadrian's mausoleum was converted into a papal fortress in the 6th century AD. Linked to the Vatican in 1277 by a wall and passageway, it was used by popes to escape in times of threat. During the sack of Rome in the 16th century by Emperor Charles V, hundreds of people lived in the fortress for months.
✉ Lungotevere Castello ☎ 06 681 91 11 🚌 23, 64, 87, 280 🕘 Tues-Sun 9am-8pm $ L10,000/5000, €5.16/2.58

Catacombe di San Callisto (3, M7)
Over 60 martyrs and early popes are buried in these catacombs, covering an area of 15ha. In the 20km of tunnels explored so far, archaeologists have found the sepulchres of some 500,000 people, as well as Greek and Latin inscriptions and frescoes.
✉ Via Appia Antica 110 ☎ 06 51 30 15 80 ⓔ www.catacombe.roma.it 🚌 218, 660, J3; ATAC shuttle bus to/from Colosseum (Sun only) 🕘 Thurs-Tues 8.30am-noon, 2.30-5.30pm (to 5pm Oct-Mar) $ L8000/€4.13

Catacombe di San Sebastiano (3, M8)
These catacombs were a safe haven for the remains of SS Peter and Paul during the reign of Vespasian. The 1st level is now almost completely destroyed, but frescoes, stucco-work, epigraphs and three perfectly preserved mausoleums can be seen on the 2nd level. The basilica dates from the 4th century and preserves one of the arrows used to kill St Sebastian.
✉ Via Appia Antica 136 ☎ 06 788 70 35 ⓔ 🚌 see Catacombe di San Callisto 🕘 Mon-Sat 8.30am-noon, 2.30-5.30pm (to 5pm Oct-Mar); closed mid-Nov-mid-Dec $ church free; guided tour L8000/€4.13 ♿ limited

Circo di Massenzio
(1, C6) Archaeologists believe this stadium, built by Maxentius around AD309, was never finished. It is well preserved, and chariot starting stalls can still be made out. In front is a tomb built for Maxentius' son Romulus and next to it are ruins of an imperial residence.
✉ Via Appia Antica 153 ☎ 06 780 13 24 🚌 see Catacombe di San Callisto 🕘 Tues-Sun 9am-7pm (to 5pm Oct-Mar) $ L5000/3000, €2.58/1.55

Jon Davison

Impenetrable Tiber-side Castel Sant'Angelo

Colonna Antonina
(6, A8) You'll get a pain in the neck – literally – gazing at the intricate reliefs on this 30m column, erected in AD180 to commemorate Marcus Aurelius' victories over barbarian tribes of the Danube. A statue of Marcus Aurelius crowning the column was replaced by a bronze figure of St Paul in 1589.
✉ **Piazza Colonna** 🚌 **62, 63, 81, 85, 95, 117, 119, 492**

Intricate Colonna Antonina

Colonna di Traiano
(4, G12) Erected to celebrate victories over the Dacians, Trajan's column is decorated with superb reliefs depicting battles between the Roman and Dacian armies. A golden statue of Trajan once topped the column, but it was lost during the Middle Ages and replaced with St Peter.
✉ **Via dei Fori Imperiali** 🚌 **84, 85, 87, 175, 186, 810, 850**

Roman Underworld

The catacombs are underground corridors and passageways built as communal burial grounds. The best known are the Christian catacombs along the Via Appia Antica although there are Jewish and pagan ones as well. Scholars are divided as to whether the catacombs were also clandestine meeting places of early Christians in Rome, although they were often used to hide important relics from the Christians' persecutors.

Fori Imperiali (4, H13)
The imperial forums – Foro di Traiano (see below), Foro d'Augusto, Foro di Cesare, Foro di Nerva and Foro di Vespasiano – were built between 42BC and AD112. In 1933 Mussolini's grand thoroughfare from Piazza Venezia to the Colosseum was built over them, and their hidden treasures are only now being excavated and evaluated.
✉ 🚌 **see Colonna di Traino** 🕘 **closed to public**

Foro di Traiano
(4, G12) The last and most splendid of the imperial forums was built between AD107 and 113. Its vast complex comprised a massive basilica, Greek and Latin libraries, the Colonna di Traiano and the Mercato di Traiano.
✉ 🚌 **see Colonna di Traino** 🕘 **closed to public**

Forum Boarium (2, E8)
The Forum Boarium (cattle market) was an important commercial centre with its own port. The two 2nd century BC temples – the round Tempio di Ercole Vincitore and the Tempio di Portunus – were consecrated as churches in the Middle Ages. Cattle dealers used to shelter from sun and rain under the Arco di Jano, which dates from the 4th century AD.
✉ **Piazza della Bocca della Verità** 🚌 **81, 160, 170, 628, 715, 716**

Mausoleo di Augusto
(4, C9) This litter-covered mound of earth, once one of the most imposing monuments in ancient Rome, was built in 28BC, as a mausoleum for Augustus and his descendants. Nerva was the last to be interred there, in AD98, and it's since been used as a fortress, vineyard and travertine quarry.
✉ **Piazza Augusto**

Jon Davison
Augustus is surely turning over over the state of his grave.

Imperatore ☎ 06 671 03 819 🚌 81, 117, 119, 628, 913, J9 🕘 Sat-Sun 10am-1pm (by prior booking only) $ L10,000/€5.16

Mercati di Traiano
(4, G12) Built in the early 2nd century and comprising six floors of shops and offices, Trajan's markets were the precursor to the modern shopping mall. Wine, oil, vegetables, flowers, imported silks and spices were sold here.
✉ Via IV Novembre
☎ 06 679 00 48
🚌 64, 70, 117, 170
🕘 Tues-Sun 9am-7pm
$ L12,000/€6.20

Martin Moos

World's first mall, Mercati di Traiano

Portico d'Ottavia
(2, B7) Only the fragmented pediment and a few columns remain from the enormous square colonnade, enclosing temples and libraries, built by Augustus in 23BC. A fish market was established here in the Middle Ages, and excavations have uncovered remains of a fishmonger's stand.
✉ Via del Portico d'Ottavia 🚌 23, 63, 280, 780, H, J4, J5 🚋 8

Sites: from Ancient to Web

The Comune of Rome's Web site offers further information and the occasional virtual tour through the cultural wonders on offer in the city. Although the homepage is in Italian only, many of the individual site pages are translated into English. Visit the following:

- www.comune.roma.it/cultura/italiano/monumenti/monumenti/antichi/index.htm
- www.comune.roma.it/cultura/italiano/musei_spazi_espositivi/musei/index.htm

Piramide di Ciao Cestio (3, J4)
This white marble tomb set in the Aurelian wall is an incongruous – but unmissable – landmark. Its occupant, Caius Cestius, a wealthy Roman magistrate, died in 12BC.
✉ Piazzale Ostiense 🚌 23, 75, 175, 280, 716 🚋 3, 8

Teatro di Marcello
(2, C8) Only 12 of the original 41 arches, made of large travertine blocks, remain from the theatre, built around 13BC by Augustus and dedicated to his nephew. In the 16th century, Baldassarre Peruzzi built a palace on top of the ruins for the Orsini family.
✉ Via del Teatro di Marcello 🚌 23, 63, 280, 780, H, J4, J5 🚋 8

Tempio di Adriano
(6, B7) The remains of the temple dedicated to Hadrian – 11 marble Corinthian columns – are incorporated into a 17th century building, most recently used as the Roman stock exchange.
✉ Piazza di Pietra 🚌 62, 63, 81, 85, 95, 117, 119, 160, 175, 492, 628, 850

Terme di Caracalla
(3, J5) The Baths of Caracalla are the best preserved of the imperial bath complexes in Rome. Covering 10 hectares, they could hold 1600 people and in addition to the caldarium, tepidarium and frigidarium there were shops, gardens, libraries and gym facilities. Excavations of the baths in the 16th and 17th centuries unearthed important sculptures which found their way into the Farnese family collection.
✉ Viale delle Terme di Caracalla 52 ☎ 06 575 86 26 🚌 628 🕘 Tues-Sat 9am-6pm (to 4pm Tues-Sat), Sun & Mon 9am-1pm
$ L8000/€4.13

Tomba di Cecilia Metella (3, M8)
Money talked in Roman times, and Cecilia Metella's fabulously wealthy in-laws made sure she was buried in style. This grand tomb was used as a fortress by the Caetani family in the early 14th century. Not far past it is a section of the original Via Appia.
✉ Via Appia Antica
☎ 06 780 24 65
🚌 218, 660, ATAC shuttle bus to/from Colosseum (Sun only)
🕘 Tues-Sat 9am-6pm (to 4pm Nov-Mar), Sun & Mon 9am-1pm
$ L4000/€2.06

CHURCHES

Not surprisingly for the centre of the Christian world, Rome has its fair share of churches – over 400 in the historic centre alone – many of which are repositories for some of the city's great artworks. A definite bonus is that unless otherwise indicated here, they are free to visit.

Chiesa del Gesù (6, F7)
Rome's first Jesuit church represents the epitome of Counter-Reformation architecture and highlights the Jesuits' aim to attract worshippers with splendour and breathtaking artworks. In Baciccia's vault fresco, the foreshortened figures appear to tumble onto the coffered ceiling. He also created the cupola frescoes and the stucco decoration. St Ignatius' opulent marble and bronze tomb with lapis lazuli-encrusted columns is in the north transept.
✉ **Piazza del Gesù**
☎ **06 69 70 01** 🚌 **46, 62, 64, 70, 81, 87, 186, 492, 628** 🕘 **6am-12.30pm, 4-7.15pm**
♿ **limited**

Domine Quo Vadis? (3, K7) There's nothing special about the present-day church, but it *was* built at the spot where St Peter, as he was escaping the Neronian persecution, allegedly had a vision of Christ. Peter asked 'Domine, quo vadis?' ('Lord, where are you going?'). When Jesus replied that he was going to Rome to be crucified again, Peter took the hint and returned to the city, where he was martyred.
✉ **Via Appia Antica**
🚌 **218, 660, ATAC shuttle bus to/from Colosseum (Sun only)**
🕘 **7.30am-noon, 4.30-7pm**
♿ **good**

A Truly Artistic Temperament

Trouble with the law was a fact of life for Michelangelo Merisi da Caravaggio (1573-1610) who arrived in Rome around 1590. He fled the city in 1606 after killing his opponent in a ball game, spent four years on the run and died in Tuscany aged 36.

Caravaggio's paintings were as controversial as his behaviour. His innovative and dramatic use of lighting influenced generations of artists. His use of peasants and prostitutes as models gave the Madonnas and saints of his paintings a realism that was not always well received. Often church commissions had to be redone as the subjects were deemed to be too lifelike: saints would *not* have had such dirty feet!

You can do a Caravaggio crawl through the following: Capitoline Museums (pp. 16-7), Galleria Borghese (p. 19), Galleria Doria Pamphilj (p. 35), Palazzo Barberini (p. 37), San Luigi dei Francesi (at right), Santa Maria del Popolo (p. 43), Sant'Agostino (p. 42) and the Vatican Museums (pp. 32-3).

San Carlo alle Quattro Fontane
(4, E14) Completed in 1641, the Chiesa di San Carlo is one of Borromini's masterpieces. The curves of the facade, the play of convex/concave surfaces inside and the dome lit by hidden windows are a clever solution to the tiny site. Borromini also designed the small cloister.
✉ **Via del Quirinale 23**
☎ **06 488 32 61**
🚌 **64, 70, 170, H**
🕘 **9.30am-12.30pm**
♿ **limited**

San Lorenzo Fuori le Mura (3, E8)
Constantine's 4th century church built over the martyred St Laurence's burial place was joined with another early Christian church nearby; medieval additions and WWII bombing raids give us the basilica we see today, highlights of which are the Cosmati floor, 13th century frescoed portico, and the Catacombe di Santa Ciriaca where St Laurence was buried.
✉ **Piazzale del Verano 3**
☎ **06 49 15 11**
🚌 **71, 448, 492** 🚊 **3, 19** 🕘 **7.30am-noon, 4-6.30pm** ♿ **limited**

San Luigi dei Francesi
(6, B4) Caravaggio's canvases of St Matthew's life are the top draws of the French national church, although the tombs of eminent French citizens (including a monument to

Claude Lorrain), are also noteworthy. Giacomo della Porta designed the facade.
✉ **Piazza San Luigi dei Francesi** 🚌 **70, 81, 87, 116, 186, 492, 628** 🕘 **8am-12.30pm, 3.30-7pm , Thurs 8am-12.30pm** ♿ **limited**

San Paolo Fuori le Mura (1, C6)
The basilica built by Constantine on the site of St Paul's burial was destroyed by fire in 1823. The 5th century mosaics on the triumphal arch, a Romanesque paschal candlestick, and the marble tabernacle (c1285) by Arnolfo di Cambio survived. The reconstruction recreates some sense of the huge scale of the original. The cloisters survived the fire and are a masterpiece of Cosmati work, with elaborate mosaic-encrusted columns.
✉ **Via Ostiense 186** ☎ **06 541 03 41** 🚌 **23, 170** Ⓜ **San Paolo** 🕘 **7.30am-6.30pm** ♿ **good**

San Pietro in Vincoli (4, H15) Pilgrims flock to this church to see the chains of St Peter, but art lovers come in droves to see Michelangelo's unfinished tomb of Pope Julius II, with his powerful *Moses* flanked by statues of *Leah* and *Rachel.* Some 40 figures were planned for the tomb, but few were completed: a couple of figures of slaves ended up in the Accademia in Florence; others in the Louvre.
✉ **Piazza San Pietro in Vincoli 4a** ☎ **06 488 28 65** 🚌 **75, 84, 117** Ⓜ **Cavour** 🕘 **7am-12.30pm, 3.30-7pm** ♿ **limited**

Sant'Agnese Fuori le Mura & Santa Costanza (3, C8)
Sant'Agnese, named after St Agnes who was buried here in 304, has a beautiful 7th century apse mosaic of the saint with popes. The 4th century Santa Costanza, built as a mausoleum for Constantine's daughters Constantia and Helena, has a circular dome and an ambulatory covered with beautiful 4th century mosaics of fruit, flowers, vines and animals.
✉ **Via Nomentana 349** ☎ **06 861 08 40** 🚌 **36, 36b, 60, 62, 136, 137** 🕘 **Mon-Sat 9am-noon, Tues-Sun 4-6pm** $ **basilica free; catacombs L8000/€ 4.13**

Sant'Agostino (6, A4)
This 15th century church contains two great artworks: Raphael's fresco of Isaiah on the 3rd column in the nave, which shows the influence of Michelangelo (both artists were working in the Vatican when Raphael painted it); and Caravaggio's *Madonna dei Pellegrini*, one of his best works.
✉ **Via di Sant'Agostino** 🚌 **70, 81, 87, 116, 186, 492, 628** 🕘 **7.30am-noon, 3.30-7pm**

Michelangelo: When Are You Gonna Finish?

Michelangelo came to work in Rome for Pope Julius II who wanted a grand marble tomb for himself which would surpass any funerary monument ever built. Michelangelo spent eight months in the marble quarries of Carrara in Tuscany selecting and excavating suitable blocks. However, the tomb was never completed (see San Pietro in Vincoli, above), and Julius II lies in an unadorned grave in St Peter's.

For some of the master's completed works visit:

- *Pietà* in St Peter's (p. 30)
- Sistine Chapel ceiling (p. 33)
- *Last Judgement* (p. 33)
- Dome of St Peter's (p. 32 & 51)
- *Moses,* San Pietro in Vincoli (above)
- Capitoline Museums (pp. 16-7)
- Palazzo Farnese (p. 46)

Sant'Andrea al Quirinale (4, E14)
Bernini designed this frothy masterpiece with an elliptical floor plan and a series of chapels opening on to the central area. The interior is decorated with rose-coloured marble, stucco and gilding, and topped off by cherubs flying around the lantern of the dome.
✉ Via del Quirinale 29 ☎ 06 489 03 187 🚌 64, 70, 170, H 🕐 Mon-Fri 9am-noon, 4-7pm, Sat 9am-noon ♿ limited

Sant'Ignazio di Loyola (6, C8) Rivalling the Gesù for opulence and splendour, this sumptuous interior is covered with paintings, stucco, coloured marble and gilt. The ingenious ceiling perspective by Jesuit artist Andrea del Pozzo features an illusionary dome (stand on the yellow dot in the nave for the best vantage point).
✉ Piazza di Sant'Ignazio ☎ 06 679 44 06 🚌 62, 63, 81, 85, 95, 117, 119, 160, 175, 492, 628 🕐 7.30am-12.30pm, 4-7.15pm ♿ limited

Sant'Ivo alla Sapienza (6, D4) A masterpiece of Baroque architecture, this is considered to be one of Borromini's most original creations. The walls alternate between being convex and concave, and the bell tower is crowned by a distinctive twisted spiral.
✉ Corso del Rinascimento 40 ☎ 06 686 49 87 🚌 46, 64, 70, 81, 87, 116, 492, 628 🕐 Sun 9am-noon ♿ good

Santa Croce in Gerusalemme (3, H8)
This pilgrimage church was founded in AD320 by St Helena, Constantine's mother, who brought Christian relics, including a piece of the cross on which Christ was crucified, to Rome from Jerusalem. The bell tower was added in 1144, the facade and oval vestibule in 1744.
✉ Piazza di Santa Croce in Gerusalemme 12 ☎ 06 701 47 69 🚌 81, 186, 810, 850, J5 Ⓜ San Giovanni 🕐 6.30am-12.30pm, 3.30-7.30pm ♿ limited

Christopher Wood

Sant'Ivo alla Sapienza's dizzying heights

Santa Maria degli Angeli (5, D1)
Michelangelo incorporated the main hall and *tepidarium* of Terme di Diocleziano's baths into this church's design, although only the great vaulted ceiling remains from his original plans. The meridian in the transept traces both the polar star and the time of the sun's zenith (visible at noon).
✉ Piazza della Repubblica ☎ 06 488 08 12 Ⓜ Repubblica, Termini 🕐 8am-12.30pm, 4-7pm ♿ good

Santa Maria della Vittoria (4, C15)
Who says you can't get excited by religion? St Teresa is quite obviously having a *seriously* good time here. The small Cornaro chapel resembles a miniature theatre, and Bernini's centrepiece is astonishing. Natural light shines onto the sculpture from a concealed window making the moment of ecstasy, depicted by the gilt rays that are part of the sculpture, even more incandescent.
✉ Via XX Settembre 17 ☎ 06 482 61 90 🚌 62, 175, 492 Ⓜ Repubblica 🕐 6.30am-noon, 4.30-7pm ♿ good

Santa Maria del Popolo (4, A9)
This smorgasbord of art treasures dates from 1099. Bramante designed the apse, and the vault frescoes (c1509) are by Pinturicchio who also painted the lunettes and the *Adoration* in the Della Rovere chapel. Raphael designed the Cappella Chigi, which features a macabre mosaic of a kneeling skeleton, but it was completed by Bernini 100 years after Raphael's death. Don't miss Caravaggio's *Conversion of St Paul* and *Crucifixion of St Peter* in the Cerasi chapel.
✉ Piazza del Popolo ☎ 06 361 08 36 🚌 81, 95, 117, 119, 628 Ⓜ Flaminio 🚊 2, 3 🕐 Mon-Sat 7am-noon, 4-7pm, Sun 8am-2pm, 4.30-7.30pm ♿ limited

Santa Maria in Aracoeli (2, A10)
Legend says the Tiburtine Sybil foretold of the birth of Christ on this site, and there's been a church here

Belli sposi, *SM in Aracoeli*

since the 6th century. The facade of the present Romanesque structure was never completed. The church features frescoes by Pinturicchio (c1480), and it was noted for its olive-wood statue of the baby Jesus – until the statue was stolen in 1994.
✉ **Piazza Santa Maria in Aracoeli ☎ 06 679 81 55 🚌 46, 62, 64, 70, 81, 85, 87, 186, 492, 628, 810 🕐 7am-noon, 4-6.30pm**

Santa Maria sopra Minerva (6, D6)
The resting place of the headless body of St Catherine is one of the few Gothic-style churches in Rome. Superb frescoes by Filippino Lippi (c1489) in the Cappella Carafa depict events in the life of St Thomas Aquinas. Left of the high altar is Michelangelo's statue of *Christ Bearing the Cross* completed around 1520 (although the bronze drapery was added later).
✉ **Piazza della Minerva 42 ☎ 06 679 39 26 🚌 46, 62, 63, 64, 70, 87, 116,186, 810, H 🕐 7am-7pm**

Santa Maria in Cosmedin (2, E9)
Built by Pope Hadrian I in the 8th century, this fine medieval church incorporated an imperial era colonnade and a 7th century Christian building. The distinctive seven storey bell tower and portico were added in the 12th century. Cosmati inlaid marble decorates the floor, high altar and choir.
✉ **Piazza Bocca della Verità 18 ☎ 06 678 14 19 🚌 23, 44, 81, 160, 175, 280, 628, 715 🕐 9am-1pm, 2.30-6pm ♿ good**

Santa Maria Maggiore (5, F2)
There's a harmonious blend of architectural styles in this great basilica: a triple nave from the original 5th century building, a Romanesque bell tower, Cosmati marble floor, a 15th century gilded coffered ceiling, and an altar canopy decorated with bronze cherubs. The 5th century mosaics of biblical scenes are the most important of this period in Rome, and the 13th century *Coronation of the Virgin* is equally as fine.
✉ **Piazza di Santa Maria Maggiore ☎ 06 48 31 95 🚌 16, 71, 75, 84 Ⓜ Cavour, Vitt 🕐 7am-6.30pm ♿ good**

Santa Prassede (5, G2)
Pope Paschal I had mosaic artists brought from Byzantium (later Constantinople) to decorate the church he built in the 9th century. The resulting jewel-coloured mosaics – on the triumphal arch, apse and in the small Cappella di San Zenone – are breathtaking, and not to be missed.
✉ **Via Santa Prassede 9a ☎ 06 488 24 56 🚌 16, 71, 75, 84, 590 Ⓜ Cavour, Vittorio 🕐 7.30am-noon, 4-6.30pm ♿ good**

Pachyderm in the Piazza!

Bernini's *Elefantino* in Piazza della Minerva is one of Rome's most popular monuments. The 6th century BC Egyptian obelisk supported by the elephant was found among the ruins of a temple to Isis in the monastery garden at Santa Maria sopra Minerva (left). The white marble elephant (sculpted in 1667 by Ercole Ferrata to Bernini's design) is a symbol of strength and wisdom.

Santa Pudenziana
(5, F1) The magnificent apse mosaic dating from AD390 is the oldest of its kind in Rome. An enthroned Christ is flanked Saints Peter & Paul and the apostles dressed as Roman senators. A 16th century restoration chopped off two apostles and amputated the legs of the others.
✉ Via Urbana 160 🚌 71, 75, 84 Ⓜ Cavour 🕘 8am-noon, 3-6pm

Santa Sabina (3, H4)
One of Rome's most important and elegant early Christian basilicas, Santa Sabina was founded by Peter of Illyria in AD422. The 5th century door to the left of the portico features 18 carved wooden panels including the oldest crucifixion scene in existence.
✉ Piazza Pietro d'Illiria 1 ☎ 06 574 35 73 🚌 81, 160, 628 🕘 6.30am-12.45pm, 3.30-7pm ♿ good

Santi Cosma e Damiano (4, H13)
Dedicated to SS Cosmas & Damian (doctors with miraculous healing powers), and occupying a hall which formed part of the Foro di Vespasiano, the church boasts a stunning 6th century mosaic of Christ flanked by saints. Don't miss the Neapolitan *presepe* (nativity scene) off the cloister.
✉ Largo Romolo e Remo ☎ 06 699 15 40 🚌 75, 85, 87, 117, 175, 186, 810, 850, J4, J5 Ⓜ Colosseo 🕘 basilica 9am-1pm, 4-7pm; presepe 9.30am-12.30pm, 3-6.30pm $ basilica free; presepe L1000/ €0.52 ♿ good

Santo Stefano Rotondo (3, H6)
This fascinating round building (built 468-83) was one of Rome's earliest Christian churches. The walls are lined with 16th century frescoes (by Pomarancio) depicting the gruesome ways in which saints were martyred: vivid impalings, boilings in oil and beheadings.
✉ Via di Santo Stefano Rotondo 7 ☎ 06 704 93 717 🚌 81, 117, 673 🕘 Mon 1.50-4.20pm, Tues-Sat 9am-1pm & 1.50-4.20pm, 2nd Sun of each summer month 9am-noon ♿ limited

Snowball's Chance in Rome

According to legend, in 352 Pope Liberius had a dream in which he was instructed by the Virgin Mary to build a church in the exact place where he found snow. On the following morning (5 August, which just happened to be in the middle of a blazing summer) snow fell on the Esquiline Hill. Obeying instructions, he built Santa Maria della Neve, which later became Santa Maria Maggiore. Each year there's a service there during which white flower petals are released from the ceiling to commemorate the miracle.

NOTABLE BUILDINGS & MONUMENTS

Chiostro di Bramante
(6, B2) Bramante built this beautiful cloister next to the church of **Santa Maria della Pace** in 1504. The architect employed classical rules of proportion in this two storey arcade, creating a monumental feeling in a relatively small space. It is regarded as one of his finest works in Rome, and now hosts exhibitions.
✉ Via della Pace ☎ 06 688 09 036 🚌 70, 81, 87, 116, 492 🕘 Tues-Sun 10am-1.30pm & 3.30-7pm (during exhibitions only) $ varies ♿ limited

Cimitero Acattolico per gli Stranieri (3, J4)
The Protestant cemetery – final resting place of numerous distinguished foreigners, including John Keats, who died in Rome in 1821, and Percy Bysshe Shelley – is a shady place for a peaceful wander.
✉ Via Caio Cestio 6 ☎ 06 574 19 00 🚌 23, 75, 280, 716 Ⓜ Piramide 🕘 Tues-Sun 9am-6pm $ donation

EUR (1, C6)
You'll find some fine examples of fascist architecture – including the Palazzo della Civiltà del Lavoro, a square building with arched windows known as the 'Square Colosseum' – are the legacy of Mussolini's ideal suburb, EUR (Esposizione Universale di Roma), planned for a 1942 international exhibition

which was never held.
✉ **EUR** 🚌 **160** Ⓜ **EUR Magliana, EUR Palasport, EUR Fermi** ♿ **limited**

Mausoleo delle Fosse Ardeatine (3, M7)
When a brigade of Roman partisans blew up 32 German military police in WWII, the Germans retaliated by taking 335 random prisoners (including 75 Jews) to the Ardeatine Caves and shooting them. This moving mausoleum honours the dead.
✉ **Via Ardeatina 174** ☎ **06 513 67 42** 🚌 **218, ATAC shuttle bus to/from Colosseum (Sun only)** 🕒 **8.15am-5.15pm (Sun to 5.45pm)** ♿ **limited**

Palazzo della Cancelleria (6, E2)
This late 15th century Renaissance palace once housed the Papal Chancellery and is still used by the Vatican. Beneath it are ruins of an early Christian church. It's thought that Bramante designed the double loggia in the magnificent interior courtyard.
✉ **Piazza della Cancelleria 1** ☎ **06 681 36 738** 🚌 **46, 62, 64, J5** 🕒 **open during exhibitions** $ **varies**

Palazzo del Quirinale (4, E13) Built between 1574 and the early 18th century, the Quirinale Palace was the papal summer residence from 1592 until 1870, when it became the royal palace of the kings of Italy. Now it's the official residence of the president of the republic. Domenico Fontana designed the facade, Carlo Maderno designed the chapel and Bernini was responsible for the long wing along Via del Quirinale.
✉ **Piazza del Quirinale** ☎ **06 469 92 568** 🚌 **64, 70, 71, 117, 170, H, J2** 🕒 **Sun 8.30am-12.30pm** $ **L10,000/€5.16** ♿ **good**

Vittoriano bookends one side of the Piazza Venezia.

Palazzo di Montecitorio (4, E10)
Built in 1650 by Bernini for the Ludovisi family, Montecitorio has been the seat of the Chamber of Deputies, Italian parliament's lower house, since 1871. It was expanded by Carlo Fontana in the late 17th century and given a larger facade by Art Nouveau architect Ernesto Basile in 1918.
✉ **Piazza di Montecitorio** ☎ **06 676 01, 06 676 04 565** e **english.camera.it/** 🚌 **62, 63, 81, 85, 95, 117, 119, 492** 🕒 **10am-5pm 1st Sun of the month** $ **free**

Palazzo di Venezia (6, E9) Rome's first great Renaissance palace was built (1455-64) for the Venetian cardinal Pietro Barbo, who later became Pope Paul II. Mussolini used it as his official residence and made some of his famous speeches from the balcony.
✉ ☎ 🚌 🕒 $ ♿ see museum review p. 36

Palazzo Farnese (2, A3)
This magnificent Renaissance building, now the French Embassy, was built for Cardinal Alessandro Farnese (later Pope Paul III) and is famous for its frescoes by Annibale and Agostino Caracci. It was started in 1514 by Antonio da Sangallo, continued by Michelangelo and completed by Giacomo della Porta.
✉ **Piazza Farnese** 🚌 **23, 64, 116, 280, J5** 🕒 **not open to public**

Palazzo Madama (6, B4) Originally the Medici's Rome residence, Palazzo Madama has been the seat of the Senate, the upper house of the Italian parliament, since 1871. The building is named after 'Madama' Margaret of Parma, the illegitimate daughter of Charles V, who lived here (1559-67).
✉ **Corso del Rinascimento** ☎ **06 670 61, 06 670 62 225** e **www.parlamento.it/e_tour/palmad.htm** 🚌 **70, 87, 116, 186, 492, 628** 🕒 **10am-6pm 1st Sat of the month** $ **free**

Scala Santa & Sancta Sanctorum (3, H7)
Some believe that the Scala Santa (Holy Staircase) hails from the Jerusalem palace of Pontius Pilate where Christ himself had trod. It's so holy that you can climb on it only on your knees. It leads to the Sancta Sanctorum, once the pope's private chapel.
✉ **Piazza San Giovanni in Laterano 14**
☎ **06 704 94 619**
🚌 **81, 85, 87, J3, J5**
Ⓜ **San Giovanni**
🕘 **Scala Santa 6.15am-noon, 3.30-6.45pm; Sancta Sanctorum Tues, Thurs & Sat 10.30-11.30am & 3-4pm**
$ **Scala Santa free; Sancta Sanctorum L5000/€2.58**

Tempietto di Bramante (2, E1)
Bramante's circular Tempietto (dated c1502), next to the church of **San Pietro in Montorio**, was built on a site wrongly assumed to be the place of St Peter's crucifixion. Despite its tiny scale, it is a Renaissance masterpiece of classical proportion and elegance, and was used as a model by numerous architects in the 16th century.
✉ **Piazza San Pietro in Montorio** ☎ **06 581 39 40** 🚌 **44, 75, 870**
🕘 **9am-noon, 4-6pm**

Vittoriano (2, A10)
The monument commemorating Vittorio Emanuele II and the united Italy is often dubbed the 'typewriter' or the 'wedding cake'. It's the biggest modern building in Rome's centre, rivalling St Peter's in scale and visibility. It incorporates the Altare della Patria (Altar of the Fatherland), the tomb of the unknown soldier and some lovely Art Nouveau murals and sculpture.
✉ **Piazza Venezia**
☎ **06 699 17 18**
🚌 **44, 46, 60, 62, 63, 64, 85, 87, 175, 186, 492, 628, 810, 850, H, J2, J4, J5** 🕘 **Tues-Sun 10am-1hr before sunset**

PIAZZAS & PUBLIC SPACES

Campo de' Fiori (6, F2)
By day the occupants of this lively piazza are Roman mamas with their market baskets and by night beer-clutching bright young things. Towering over them all is Giordano Bruno, who was burned at the stake for heresy here in 1600.
🚌 **46, 62, 64, 116**
♿ **good**

Campo de' Fiori cops

Circus Maximus (3, H5)
In its heyday Rome's largest stadium was decorated with statues and columns and surrounded by stands for over 200,000 spectators. It was used and continually expanded from the 4th century BC until AD49, but these days it's dogs rather than chariot racers who exercise here.
✉ **Via del Circo Massimo** 🚌 **60, 75, 81, 160, 175, 628, 715, J4**
🚋 **3** Ⓜ **Circo Massimio**
♿ **limited**

Fontana delle Tartarughe (2, A7)
Rome's most delightful fountain (see p. 53) was created by Taddeo Landini in 1585. Legend has it that it was built in a single night for the Duke of Mattei, who owned the surrounding palaces. Landini had just lost all his money, and consequently his fiancée, and wanted to prove himself to her father.
✉ **Piazza Mattei**
🚌 **46, 62, 63, 64, 70, 87, 186, 810**

Martin Moos

No man is an island on Isola Tiberina.

Isola Tiberina (2, D7)
Reputedly the world's smallest inhabited island, the Tiber Island is connected to the Ghetto by Ponte Fabricio, Rome's oldest standing bridge. Since the 3rd century BC, it has been associated with healing, and is still the site of the Ospedale Fatebenefratelli.
23, 63, 280, 780, H

Piazza della Repubblica (5, D1)
Formerly known as Piazza dell'Esedra, the piazza follows the line of the exedra of the adjacent Terme di Diocleziano. The Fontana delle Naiadi by Mario Rutelli features a central bronze of Glaucus wrestling with a fish, surrounded by four water nymphs. When they were unveiled in 1901, the curvaceous, scantily-clad figures caused a furore.
40, 64, 70, 170, 492, H Repubblica limited

Piazza del Popolo (4, A9) This magnificently restored piazza, at the northern gateway to the city, was laid out in 1538 and redesigned in neoclassical style by Giuseppe Valadier in 1823. The central obelisk, which once graced Circus Maximus, was brought by Augustus from Heliopolis. 'Twin' Baroque churches on the southern side are almost – but not quite – identical.
95, 117, 119
Flaminio limited

Piazza di Sant' Ignazio (6, B7)
This small square in front of the church of Sant'Ignazio is one of the frivolous delights of Rome. The theatrical piazza was designed by Filippo Raguzzini in the early 18th century. The picturesque and elegant buildings opposite the church are wasted as a police station.
62, 63, 64, 81, 85, 87, 175, 492 limited

Trevi Fountain (6, A10)
Nicola Salvi completed this high-Baroque fountain in 1762. It's one of Rome's most famous monuments, and where Marcello Mastroianni and Anita Ekberg frolicked in Fellini's *La Dolce Vita.* Neptune's chariot is led by Tritons with seahorses – one wild, one docile – representing the moods of the sea. The word Trevi refers to the three roads (*tre vie*) which converged at the fountain.
Piazza di Trevi
117, 119 limited

Via Giulia (4, F6)
Bramante designed this elegant street for Pope Julius II as a new approach road to St Peter's. It is lined with Renaissance palaces, antique shops and art galleries. Spanning its southern end is Michelangelo's Arco Farnese from which ivy tendrils hang like stalactites. The arch was intended to be part of a bridge across the Tiber connecting Palazzo Farnese with the Villa Farnesina.
Via Giulia 23, 116, 280 limited

Three Coins in the Fountain

The famous custom at the Trevi Fountain is to throw a coin into the water (over your shoulder while facing away) to ensure you return to Rome. Toss a second coin and you'll fall in love with an Italian. Chuck a third coin at your peril – it will have you marrying him or her! On average, L230 million (around €119,000) is recovered from the basin each year. Italian currency goes into city council coffers and the foreign coins are given to the Red Cross. No stats are available on Trevi-induced marriages...

Bethune Carmichael

PARKS & GARDENS

Can't take the heat or handle the noisy traffic? Then head to a green space to chill out and cool down. All parks are free unless otherwise stated here.

Orto Botanico (4, J5) Formerly the private grounds of Palazzo Corsini, the botanical garden has some of the rarest plants in Europe, including an avenue of palms, Mediterranean succulents, a cactii collection and a rock garden of mountain flowers from the Apennines and other ranges in Europe and Africa.
✉ Largo Cristina di Svezia 24 ☎ 06 686 41 93 🚌 23, 280 🕘 Mon-Sat 9am-6.30pm (to 5.30pm Oct-Mar) $ L4000/€2.06 ♿ limited

Pincio (4, A10) The view of St Peter's from the Pincio just *has* to be seen. Giuseppe Valadier designed the shady gardens (which adjoin Villa Borghese) around 1809-14. Roman families, cyclists and skaters continue the tradition of past strollers, including Keats, Severn, Richard Strauss, Mussolini, Ghandi and King Farouk.
✉ access from Piazza del Popolo, Viale Trinità dei Monti or Villa Borghese 🚌 95, 117, 490, 495, 590, 628, 926 🕘 open 24hrs ♿ good (from Viale Trinità dei Monti)

Roseto Comunale (3, H5) Stop and smell the roses in the city rose garden with its backdrop of Circus Maximus and the Palatine. An international rose competition is held annually in May.
✉ Via di Valle Murcia ☎ 06 574 68 10 🚌 81, 160, 628 🕘 8am-7pm ♿ good (from Clivo dei Publicii)

Jenny Jones

Playground of popes

Vatican Gardens (4, D1) Fortifications, grottoes and fountains dating from the 9th century to the present day are features of the Giardini Vaticani. The 30 full-time gardeners tend a flower-filled French parterre, a formal Italian garden and a naturalistic English wood. There is even a kitchen garden which provides produce for the pontifical household, although tours don't get close enough to check out the papal tomatoes.
✉ Città del Vaticano ☎ 06 69 88 44 66 e www.vatican.va 🚌 49, 62, 64, 81, 492, 991 Ⓜ Ottaviano, Cipro-Musei Vaticani 🕘 Mon, Tues & Thurs-Sat on pre-booked tours only $ L17,000/€8.78 ♿ good

Villa Ada (3, B6) Rolling lawns, huge shady trees, lakes and ponds are features of Villa Ada, which is a popular park year round and in summer hosts music and cinema festivals. The villa itself, once the private residence of Vittorio Emanuele III, is now the Egyptian embassy.
✉ Via Salaria 🚌 38, 310 🕘 dawn-dusk ♿ good

Martin Moos

Roma Gratis

The following sights won't burn a hole in your pocket – they're free:

- Roman Forum (p. 27)
- Pantheon (p. 24)
- Views from the Pincio, the Gianicolo and the Capitoline
- Trevi Fountain (p. 48)
- Bocca della Verità (p. 50)
- St Peter's Basilica (p. 30)
- Every church in Rome (pp. 41-5)
- Sistine Chapel & Vatican Museums (last Sun of the month; pp. 32-3)

Villa Borghese (3, D4) Scipione Borghese, a nephew of Pope Paul V, built a mansion (1605-14), for his huge art collection (now Galleria Borghese, p. 19) and employed top landscape designers to create impressive grounds with formal gardens, lakes, temples and summerhouses. This, Rome's most popular park, has been the property of the state since 1901. It's divided into different areas by avenues of trees, hedged walks, flower beds and gravel paths and includes art galleries, the **Bioparco** (p. 51) and **Piazza di Siena** (a shady amphitheatre c1792 used for equestrian and other events). ✉ **entrances at Porta Pinciana, Piazzale Flaminio, Pincio** 🚌 **52, 53, 56, 95, 116, 490, 495** 🕐 **dawn-dusk** ♿ **good**

Villa Celimontana (3, H6) When it's not overrun by newlywed couples seeking photo opps, this park is a peaceful haven a stone's throw from the Colosseum. Kids will enjoy the playground, and jazz aficionados flock to the outdoor festival in summer. ✉ **Via della Navicella** 🚌 **81, 673** Ⓜ **Colosseo** 🕐 **dawn-dusk** ♿ **good**

Villa Doria Pamphilj (3, H1) It's easy to find a quiet spot beside a Baroque fountain or under a parasol pine in Rome's largest park, laid out by Alessandro Algardi for Prince Camillo Pamphilj around 1650. Elegant Casino del Belrespiro, with its formal gardens, became state property in the late 1950s, the surrounding grounds a city park in '71. ✉ **Via di San Pancrazio** 🚌 **44, 870** 🕐 **dawn-dusk** ♿ **good**

QUIRKY ROME

Bocca della Verità (2, E9) The famous Mouth of Truth, a large disk in the shape of a mask, probably once served as the cover of an ancient drain. If you put your right hand into the mouth while telling a lie, it will snap shut. Or so they say. ✉ **Piazza della Bocca della Verità 18** 🚌 **23, 44, 81, 160, 175, 280, 628, 715** 🕐 **9am-6pm** ♿ **good**

Crypt of Santa Maria della Concezione (4, C13) Find out what *cappuccini* are really made of in the bizarre cemetery beneath the church of Santa Maria della Concezione. Between 1528 and 1870, the bones of some 4000 Capuchin monks were used to decorate the walls – in nice geometric patterns. ✉ **Via Veneto 27** ☎ **06 487 1185** Ⓜ **Barberini** 🕐 **Fri-Wed 9am-noon, 3-6pm** $ **compulsory donation**

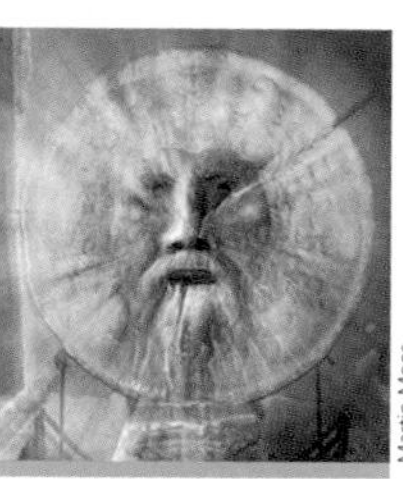
Martin Moos

Speak the truth drain mouth!

Museo delle Anime dei Defunti (4, D8) This museum, the weirdest in Rome, is devoted to dead souls trapped in purgatory who leave messages – in the form of hand and finger prints – for the living. ✉ **Lungotevere Prati 12** ☎ **06 68 80 65 17** 🚌 **70, 87, 186, 492** 🕐 **7.30-11am, 5-7.30pm** $ **free** ♿ **limited**

Piazza di Pasquino (6, D2) The weather-beaten statue in this square has quite a history. Under papal rule, there were few safe outlets for dissent. So when a local tailor, Pasquino, penned a caustic criticism of the authorities and stuck it to the statue in the dead of night, other Romans were quick to do the same. 'Pasquino' became the city's most active 'talking statue'; the messages or *pasquinade* still get left there today. ✉ **Piazza Pasquino** 🚌 **46, 62, 64, 116, J5** ♿ **good**

Scuola dei Gladiatori (3, K6) Don your tunic, sandals and helmet and a good dose of imagination and learn how to fight like a gladiator – under the watchful instruction of your *magister* from the Gruppo Storico Romano. Beware the *caronte* who'll finish you off with a mallet when you've had the thumbs down. Cynics not welcome. ✉ **Via Appia Antica 18** ☎ **0338 243 6678** e **digilander.iol.it/sergioiac** 🚌 **218** $ **€111 (2 day course)** ♿ **no**

ROME FOR CHILDREN

Some of the better hotels will have babysitters on their books, but when in Rome do like the Romans and take the children – of whatever age – out with you. Italians adore kids and yours will be spoiled to bits.

Bioparco (3, D5)
Rome's zoo is a long way from being one of the world's best but kids will enjoy it anyway. Laudable attempts are being made to phase out the caging of exotic animals and to 'conserve' only those creatures compatible with the ecosystem and climate of central Italy and Mediterranean animals in danger of extinction.
✉ Piazza San Pietro ☎ 06 321 65 64 🚌 40, 62, 64 ⏲ 8am-5.45pm (to 4.45pm Oct-Mar) $ L6000/€3.10

Dome of St Peter's
(4, D2) You can't beat this view of the city from the dome of St Peter's – the kids will love it. A small lift takes you half way but it's still a long climb to the top.
✉ ☎ 🚌 see p. 30
⏲ Apr-Sept 8am-5.45pm, Oct-Mar 8am-4.45pm $ L6000/€3.10

Gianicolo (4, J4)
The Gianicolo (Janiculum Hill) rises behind Trastevere and stretches to St Peter's. The panorama is fab, but kids might prefer the merry-go-round and pony rides, the puppet show and the cannon fired daily at noon.
✉ Piazza Garibaldi 🚌 870 ⏲ puppet show Mon-Fri 4-7pm, Sat & Sun 10.30am-1pm $ free (donation for puppet show) ♿ good

Museo della Civiltà Romana (1, C6)
Now you and the kids will know what Rome *really* looked like before everything fell into ruin. Mussolini established this museum in 1937 to glorify imperial Rome. There's an excellent model of the 4th century AD city, and plaster casts of monuments.
✉ Piazza G Agnelli 10, EUR ☎ 06 592 61 35 🚌 160 Ⓜ EUR Magliana ⏲ Tues-Sat 9am-7pm, Sun 9am-2pm $ L8000/€4.13 ♿ limited

Museo delle Mura
(3, J6) Step back in time and ramble along the ramparts of the city walls built by Aurelian (AD270-275) and his successor Probus. This unique museum within the well-preserved Porta San Sebastiano displays prints, drawings and models of the defensive walls.
✉ Via di Porta San Sebastiano 18 ☎ 06 70 47 52 84 🚌 218, shuttle bus to/from Colosseum (Sun only) ⏲ Tues-Sun 9am-7pm $ L5000/€2.58

Museo Nazionale delle Paste Alimentari
(4, E12) This well-organised museum traces the history of the nation's favourite dish and has old-fashioned pasta-making machinery on display. A portable CD player provides the commentary.
✉ Piazza Scanderberg 117 ☎ 06 699 11 19 🚌 62, 63, 81, 117, 119, 160, 492, 628 ⏲ 9.30am-5.30pm $ L12000/€6.19

Piazza Navona Christmas Fair (6, C3)
All things kitsch and garish take the place of Baroque elegance during the Christmas period as Piazza Navona is transformed into a festive marketplace, with merry-go-rounds and games, and stalls selling puppets, figures for nativity scenes and everything for the stocking.
✉ Piazza Navona 🚌 40, 46, 64, 70, 81, 87, 116, 186, 492, 628, J5 ⏲ early Dec-early Jan, 9am-2am ♿ good

Sally Webb

Roamin' Ragazzi

Some other things to keep visiting *bamibini* and *ragazzi* amused are:

- Colosseum (p. 15)
- Roman Forum (p. 27)
- Mercati di Traiano (p. 40)
- Castel Sant'Angelo (p. 38)
- Terme di Caracalla (p. 40)
- Vittoriano (p. 47)
- catacombs (pp. 38-9)

KEEPING FIT

Romans love their spectator sports but are not especially sporty. A few gyms in the historic centre accept casual visitors although not many of these are really well equipped by international standards, and they are usually small and crowded. Most luxury hotels now have small fitness rooms. You can walk or jog in any of the city's parks (Villa Doria Pamphilj and Villa Borghese being the most popular). Olympic-size swimming pools are thin on the ground, but some hotel pools allow paying guests in summer.

Cavalieri Hilton Hotel Pool (3, C1)
When the city sizzles and it's too hot to cope, the Hilton's stunning pool offers an urban oasis – at a price.
✉ Via Cadlolo 101 ☎ 06 350 91 🚌 907, 991 🕘 May-Sept 9am-7pm $ Mon-Fri L80,000/€41.31, Sat L95,000/€49.06

Circolo del Golf di Roma (1, C6)
You'll need a handicap and an existing membership of a golf club in your home country to play at Rome's oldest and most prestigious golf club (or on any course in Italy). Weekends are usually members only.
✉ Via Appia Nuova 716a ☎ 06 780 34 07

Game Tiber fishers near Ponte Vittorio Emanuele II

Bethune Carmichael

Romans take to their wheels at Villa Borghese.

🚌 650 Ⓜ Colli Albani 🕘 Tues-Sun 8am-8pm $ green fees L70,000/€36.15

Fitness Express (6, A1)
An American instructor runs this small but friendly gym in the heart of the historic centre. General classes include aerobic kickboxing, step, body sculpting and stretch. Yoga and tai chi courses are also available.
✉ Via dei Coronari 46 ☎ 06 686 5248 🚌 70, 81, 87, 116, 186, 492 🕘 Mon-Fri 9am-9pm, Sat 10am-4pm $ L30,000/€15.49

Olgiata Golf Club
(1, B5) The residential compound of Olgiata – about 30mins out of Rome along the Via Cassia, and hard to get to without a car – has a pretty 18 hole course open to visitors. Tee times are hard to get on weekends.
✉ Largo dell'Olgiata 15 ☎ 06 30 88 91 41 🚆 FM3 to Olgiata (then by car) 🕘 Tues-Sun 8am-7pm $ Tues-Fri L90,000/€46.48, Sat-Sun L120,000/€61.97

Piscina delle Rose
(1, C6) Romans tend to hang out at this pool for the whole day rather than popping in for a quick 20 laps – serious swimmers beware.
✉ Viale America 20 ☎ 06 54 25 21 85 Ⓜ EUR Palasport 🕘 May-Sept 9am-7pm $ L16000/12000, €8.26/€6.19 full/half day

Roman Sport Centre
(4, B12) Rome's largest and best equipped gym under Villa Borghese (near Piazza di Spagna) has a good weight room, aerobics classes, a 25m pool, spa, sauna and squash courts.
✉ Via del Galoppatoio 33 (entry also from Spagna metro) ☎ 06 320 16 67 🚌 88, 95, 116, 117, 119, 490, 495 Ⓜ Spagna 🕘 9am-10pm (to 3pm Sun) $ day pass L50,000/€25.82

out & about

WALKING TOURS

Getting to know the Ghetto

From the Area Sacra di Largo Argentina ❶ walk south to the Fontana delle Tartarughe ❷ and then to Via del Portico d'Ottavia. To your right is the Casa di Lorenzo Manilio ❸, built in 1468, or according to its inscription '2221 years after the foundation of Rome in 753BC' and the Forno del Ghetto ❹, which produces cakes to die for. Walk through Piazza delle Cinque Scole, then take Via Monte dei Cenci and Via dell'Arco dei Cenci, circumnavigating the Renaissance Palazzo Cenci ❺. Back in the piazza Sora Margherita ❻ is a great local spot for lunch. Return to Via del Portico d'Ottavia with its medieval houses (on the left) and head to the Portico d'Ottavia ❼ at the end of the street. Turn left and walk under the portico to Via di Sant'Angelo in Pescheria. Passing the church of the same name ❽, turn right at the drinking fountain for a splendid view of Teatro di Marcello ❾. Retrace your steps, turning left into Via del Portico d'Ottavia; the Museo della Comunità Ebraica & Synagogue ❿ is on your right about 50m further on. Cross the Lungotevere to the Isola Tiberina ⓫. On the other side of the island, the many delights of the Trastevere await ⓬.

distance 1.5km **duration** 1hr
start 46, 62, 63, 64, 70, 87, 186, 780, 810, H 8
end 23, 44, 75, 280, H 8

SIGHTS & HIGHLIGHTS

Area Sacra di Largo Argentina (p. 38)
Fontana delle Tartarughe (below; p. 47)
Forno del Ghetto (p. 89)
Sora Margherita (p. 79)
Portico d'Ottavia (p. 40)
Teatro di Marcello (p. 40)
Museo della Comunità Ebraica & Synagogue (p. 36)
Isola Tiberina (p. 47)
Trastevere (p. 31)

Tortoise Fountain built at hare speed

Amble through Villa Borghese

From Piazza del Popolo ❶ take either the road or the stairs up to the Pincio ❷, and its magnificent view towards St Peter's. Walk away from the panoramic terrace towards Piazza dei Martiri ❸, which marks the beginning of Villa Borghese park. Follow Viale delle Magnolie to a roundabout; cross over and go through the gates on the left, where Viale dell'Aranceria leads down to a pretty lake ❹. Follow the path back to Viale Pietro Canonica, past Piazza di Siena ❺ and the Museo Canonica ❻. Walk cross-country down a small track into a dip and back up the other side to the gates of the Bioparco (zoo) ❼, which is decorated with sculptured animals. Turn right and you'll reach the Galleria Borghese ❽ and its formal gardens. Viale del Museo Borghese leads back to the park entrance at Via Pinciana; the arches through the Aurelian walls lead to Via Veneto. Head downhill, past the US embassy and the Chiesa di Santa Maria della Concezione ❾. At the bottom of the street is Bernini's pretty Fontana delle Api (Fountain of the Bees) ❿, and in Piazza Barberini, his muscular Fontana del Tritone (Triton's Fountain) ⓫.

SIGHTS & HIGHLIGHTS

- Piazza del Popolo (p. 48)
- Pincio (p. 49)
- Villa Borghese park (p. 50)
- Piazza di Siena (p. 50)
- Museo Canonica (p. 36)
- Bioparco (p. 51)
- Galleria Borghese (p. 19)
- Chiesa di Santa Maria della Concezione (p. 50)
- Fontana del Tritone (p. 36)

Sally Webb

Duck into Villa Borghese for a lake view.

distance 3.4 km **duration** 2hrs
start Ⓜ Piazza del Popolo
end Ⓜ Piazza Barberini

Mosaic & Monumental Meander

Time this walk so that the churches are open; it's probably best started in the early morning, so that you can spend as long as you want gawping at the mosaics – the best examples in Rome of their respective periods. Start off at Piazza dell'Esquilino on the corner of Via Urbana. Head south-east for about 50m, to the church of Santa Pudenziana ❶ (below street level on your right) which has an early mosaic dating from AD390. Retrace your steps, crossing busy Via Cavour, and walk uphill alongside the Basilica di Santa Maria Maggiore to its entrance ❷. From there head south-west to Via Santa Prassede, to the inconspicuous Chiesa di Santa Prassede ❸ and its magnificent 9th century mosaics. Turn right leaving the church, and right again into Via di San Martino ai Monti and the piazza of the same name, then follow Via in Selci to Via Cavour. Avoiding the traffic fumes as best you can, walk downhill (about 250m) and carefully cross over to pretty Piazza Madonna dei Monti ❹ and the Osteria Gli Angeletti ❺ where you'll be served a good lunch. Continue down Via Cavour, cross Via dei Fori Imperiali to Via della Salaria Vecchia and past the entrance to the Roman Forum ❻ to the Chiesa di Santi Cosma e Damiano ❼. A right turn will lead you to the Colosseum ❽.

SIGHTS & HIGHLIGHTS

Chiesa di Santa Pudenziana (p. 45)
Basilica di Santa Maria Maggiore (p. 44)
Chiesa di Santa Prassede (p. 45)
Osteria Gli Angeletti (p. 83)
Chiesa di Santi Cosma e Damiano (p. 45)
Roman Forum (p. 27)
Colosseum (p. 15)

Martin Moos

Nun contemplates bun, Via dei Fori Imperiali

distance 2.2km **duration** 2-3hrs
start Ⓜ Cavour
end Ⓜ Colosseo

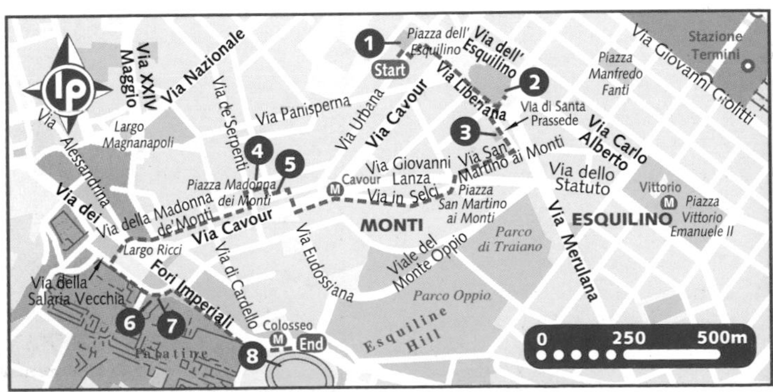

Along the Appia Antica

Known to ancient Romans as the *regina viarum* (queen of roads), the Via Appia Antica (Appian Way) extends from the Porta di San Sebastiano to Brindisi on the coast of Puglia. It was started around 312BC by the censor Appius Claudius Caecus, but didn't connect with Brindisi until around 190BC. Realistically, the only time to do this walk is on Sunday, when the road is traffic-free. Start at the Terme di Caracalla ❶; cross Piazzale Numa Pompilio, and follow the Via di Porta San Sebastiano (lined with villas behind high walls) south-east to the Porta di San Sebastiano and the Museo delle Mura ❷. Cross Viale di Porta Ardeatina and follow the Via Appia to a fork in the road and Chiesa Domine di Quo Vadis? ❸.

SIGHTS & HIGHLIGHTS

Terme di Caracalla (p. 40)
Museo della Mura (p. 51)
Chiesa di Domine Quo Vadis? (p. 41)
Catacombe di San Callisto (p. 38)
Basilica e Catacombe di San Sebastiano (p. 38)
Mausoleo delle Fosse Ardeatine (p. 46)
Circo Massenzio (p. 38)
Tomba di Cecilia Metella (p. 40)

Via Appia: way long, way old, way bumpy

Continuing along the left fork of the Appia, you'll reach the entrance to the Catacombe di San Callisto ❹ and beyond it a road to the right signposted to the Mausoleo delle Fosse Ardeatine ❺. Back on the Appia, pass the Basilica e Catacombe di San Sebastiano ❻ on the right and the Circo Massenzio ❼ on the left, finally reaching the grand Tomba di Cecilia Metella ❽, and some of the original Roman stone road just beyond it. The plant nursery opposite the tomb has a cafe, Garden Ristoro Cecilia Metella, for snacks and light meals.

distance 4km **duration** 2½hrs
start 🚌 628
end 🚌 218, 660; ATAC shuttle bus to/from Colosseum (Sun only)

EXCURSIONS

Ostia Antica (1, C2)

Founded in the 4th century BC at the mouth of the Tiber, Ostia was Rome's main port for 600 years. It was populated by merchants, sailors and slaves, and was a strategically important centre of defence and trade. Barbarian invasions and the outbreak of malaria led to the city's eventual abandonment and it slowly became buried under river silt, which explains the excellent state of preservation of the remains here.

The clearly discernible ruins of restaurants, laundries, shops, houses and public meeting places give a good impression of everyday life in a working Roman town. The main thoroughfare, the **Decumanus Maximus**, runs over 1km from the entrance to the city, the Porta Romana, to the Porta Marina which originally led to the sea. Behind the restored **theatre**, built by Agrippa and later enlarged to hold 3000 people, is the **Piazzale delle Corporazioni**, the offices of Ostia's merchant guilds, which display well-preserved mosaics depicting their different interests. The 2nd century **Casa di Diana** is a pristine example of ancient Rome's high-density housing, built when space was at a premium. Nearby the **Thermopolium** bears a striking resemblance to a modern Italian bar.

Ostia had several baths complexes, including the Baths of the Forum, which were also equipped with a roomful of stone toilets – the *forica* – still pretty much intact. Allow several hours to wander through the ruins and don't miss the superb Museo Ostiense which houses statuary and sarcophagi excavated on site.

INFORMATION

25km south-west of Rome

Ⓜ Piramide, then train from Porta San Paolo to Ostia Antica (25mins)

✉ Viale dei Romagnoli 717, Ostia Antica

☎ 06 563 58 099

ⓘ APT at Termini & Via Parigi 11; bookshop & ticket office onsite

🕘 Tues-Sun 9am-6pm, to 5pm Nov-Mar

$ L8000/€4.13

✕ restaurant/cafe on site

Sally Webb

The seats are always stone cold at Ostia.

Sally Webb

History has trodden lightly on Ostia Antica's incredible mosaics.

Villa Adriana (1, B5)

The summer residence built for Hadrian between AD118 and 134 was one of the largest and most sumptuous villas in the Roman empire. A model near the entrance gives you some idea of the scale of the massive complex, which you'll need several hours to explore.

Hadrian travelled widely and was a keen architect, and parts of the villa were inspired by buildings he had seen around the world. The massive Pecile, through which you enter, was a reproduction of a building in Athens, and the Canopo is was built as a homage to the sanctuary of Serapis near Alexandria, with a long canal of water, originally surrounded by Egyptian statues, acting as the 'Nile'.

Some of the highlights of the excavations include the fishpond encircled by an underground gallery where Hadrian took his summer *passeggiatas* (walks), and the emperor's private retreat, the **Teatro Marittimo**, on an island in an artificial pool, which could be reached only by a retractable bridge. There are also barracks, nymphaeums and temples and a museum displaying the latest discoveries from ongoing excavations. Archaeologists have found such features as a heated bench with steam pipes under the sand, and a network of subterranean service passages for horses and carts.

INFORMATION

24km north-east of Rome
Ⓜ Ponte Mammolo, then bus (1hr); local bus 4 from Tivoli
✉ Via di Villa Adriana, Tivoli
☎ 0774 53 02 03
ⓘ information office at entrance
🕘 9am to: 5pm Nov-Jan, 6pm Feb & Oct, 6.30pm Mar & Sept, 7pm Apr, 7.30pm May-Aug
$ L12,000/ €6.20
✕ Villa Esedra (☎ 0774 53 47 16), Via di Villa Adriana

Lauren Sunstein

On the starting blocks for the underwater balance the book on the head race.

Day-tripping in Tivoli

For a small place, there's lots to see and do in Tivoli. By the 1st century BC, it had become a holiday resort for Roman aristocrats who were attracted by the town's clean air and picturesque situation among olive groves. Tivoli's labyrinthine streets are definitely worth exploring, as are the gardens and artificial waterfalls of Villa Gregoriana park, and the two Republic-era temples perched on the edge of a ravine overlooking a deep valley at the edge of town. You can visit both the Villa d'Este and the Villa Adriana in a day – but start early. Go first to Tivoli town and Villa d'Este, then catch a local bus to Villa Adriana, 6km south-west of Tivoli, and return to Rome from there.

Villa d'Este (1, B5)

There's a sense of faded splendour about this former Benedictine convent, which Lucrezia Borgia's son Ippolito d'Este transformed in 1550 into a sumptuous pleasure palace with a breathtaking formal garden full of elaborate fountains and pools. From 1865 to 1886 the villa was home to Franz Liszt and inspired his composition *Fountains of the Villa d'Este.*

The Mannerist frescoes in the villa are worth a fleeting glance, but it's the garden you come here for – terraces with water-spouting grotesque heads, shady pathways and spectacular fountains, powered solely by gravitational force. One fountain once played the organ, another imitated the call of birds. Don't miss the Rometta fountain which features reproductions of the landmarks of Rome.

INFORMATION

30km north-east of Rome
- Ⓜ Ponte Mammolo, then bus (1hr)
- ✉ Piazza Trento, Tivoli
- ☎ 0774 31 20 70
- ⓘ tourist office (☎ 0774 31 12 49), Largo Garibaldi z
- 🕘 Tues-Sun 9am-7.30pm (to 5.30pm Oct-Mar)
- $ L8000/€4.13
- ✕ Trattoria L'Angolino, Via della Missione 3

Geoff Stringer

Cerveteri (1, B1)

Etruscan Cerveteri was one of the most important commercial centres in the Mediterranean from the 7th to the 5th century BC. The main attraction here is the **Banditaccia Necropolis** and its remarkable *tumoli* in which the Etruscans entombed their dead. Mounds of earth with carved stone bases are laid out as a town, with streets, squares and terraces of 'houses'. Perhaps the best example is the 4th century BC **Tomba dei Rilievi**, with its painted reliefs of cooking implements and other household items. Treasures taken from the tombs can be seen in the Vatican Museums and Villa Giulia in Rome, and also at the **Museo Nazionale di Cerveteri** in the town centre.

INFORMATION

45km north-west of Rome
- 🚌 from Lepanto (1hr10min)
- ✉ Necropoli di Banditaccia, Via del Necropoli, Cerveteri
- ☎ 06 994 00 01
- ⓘ Proloco tourist office (☎ 06 995 51 971), Piazza Risorgimento 19
- 🕘 necropolis Tues-Sun 9am-4pm (to 7pm in summer); museum Tues-Sun 9am-7pm
- $ necropolis L8000/€4.13; museum free
- ✕ Antica Locanda Le Ginestre, Piazza Santa Maria 5

Sally Webb

ORGANISED TOURS

Several tour companies offer free promotional tours of major monuments like the Colosseum or the Roman Forum. You'll see and hear the guides announcing their tours; you pay nothing but can choose to sign up for a paid tour by the same company. This is a good way to gauge the tone and nature of the tours on offer. Most tours have a central meeting point; call to check.

ATAC 110 (5, E2)
A hop on-hop off bus tour of the city's major monuments. You've got the flexibility to spend as much (or as little) time as you'd like at each sight. The full loop takes 1½hrs.
✉ **Piazza dei Cinquecento ☎ 06 469 52 252**
e www.atac.roma.it
$ L15,000/€7.75
⌚ 1/2hrly 9am-8pm

Ciao Roma (5, F3)
A small bus (painted to look like an old trolley car) zips you around Rome. Hop on/off at the Vatican, Colosseum, Piazza Venezia, Piazza Navona, Termini and Villa Borghese among other stops.
✉ **Via Giolitti 34**
☎ 06 87 40 64 81
$ L30,000/€15.49
⌚ 8.30 & 10.15am; 12, 2.30 & 4.15pm

Enjoy Rome (5, D4)
Designed for the budget traveller, 3hr walking tours cover ancient Rome (by day or night), the Vatican, or Trastevere and the Ghetto. Bike tours – 3½hrs with everything provided – are a huge hit, and include Bocca della Verità, the Colosseum and Villa Borghese.
✉ **Via Varese 39, Termini ☎ 06 445 18 43**
e www.enjoyrome.com, www.romebiketour.com
$ L30,000, €15.49/ L35,000,€18.08 walking/ bike tour ⌚ varies

Green Line Tours (5, F2) The various tours on offer (including Classical, Imperial and Christian Rome) have run-of-the-mill guides and are designed for lazy tourists. The illuminated Rome tour at night gives you a different perspective on the city.
✉ **Via Farini 5a**
☎ 06 482 74 80, 06 482 70 17
e www.greenlinetours.com $ L50,000/ €25.82 ⌚ 9am, 2.30pm

Scala Reale (5, D4)
For the discerning traveller, Scala Reale can plan custom-made private itineraries and thematic tours led by American graduate students specialising in art history and archaeology. Name your subject and time frame, they'll name their price.
✉ **Via Varese 52**
☎ 06 474 56 73
e www.scalareale.org
$ varies
⌚ by prior arrangement

Through Eternity Rome
Enthusiastic storytellers who are passionate about their subject (and native English speakers to boot) make Rome come alive. Twilight walking tours of Renaissance and Baroque Rome show the city arguably in its best light, and 'Feast of Bacchus' wine sampling tours combine aesthetic pleasures with gastronomic ones.
☎ 06 700 93 36, 0347 336 52 98 e www.througheternity.com
$ L30,000/€15.49
⌚ 10am, 2pm & 7pm

Vastours (4, B15)
Rome in all its incarnations – Ancient, Christian, Monumental and Artistic – is offered, but perhaps more interesting are the half-day/full-day trips to Ostia Antica and Tivoli respectively.
✉ **Via Piemonte 32-34**
☎ 06 481 43 09
e vastours@vastours.it $ Rome tours L50,000-68,000/ €25.82-35.12; Tivoli or Ostia L77,000/€39.77
⌚ 9am, 2.15pm

Walks of Rome (4, G15) Take your pick – ancient city, Renaissance Rome, Caesar's crawl or Vatican amble daily and catacombs on request – or if you've had enough of history, try the pub crawl instead. What the mainly British and American guides might lack in knowledge, they make up for in youthful enthusiasm.
✉ **Via Urbana 38**
☎ 06 484 853, 0347 795 51 75 e www.walksofeurope.com
$ L30,000-50,000/ €15.49-25.82 ⌚ 10am; 1, 6 & 8pm (varies)

shopping

Don't feel bad if you find that Rome's shop windows are competing with its monuments for your attention. It happens to everyone. Whether it's designer clothing, jewellery, books, homewares or antiques, chances are you'll find something that just *has* to be bought.

Shopping Areas

The area from **Piazza di Spagna** to **Via del Corso** (4, C11), including Via Condotti, Via Frattina and Via Borgognona, harbours most of the main designer shops for clothing, shoes, leather goods and accessories. Less expensive stores can be found there too. **Via Nazionale** (4, E14), **Via del Corso** (4, C10) and **Via dei Giubbonari** (2, A5) are full of reasonably priced clothing and shoe shops. For second hand clothes, visit the outlets along **Via del Governo Vecchio** (6, C1). If you're looking for antiques or an unusual gift, try **Via dei Coronari** (6, A1), **Via Margutta** or **Via del Babuino** (4, B10).

Sally Webb

Bag a designer buy on Via Borgognona.

Across the river, near the Vatican, is **Via Cola di Rienzo** (4, B5), where you'll find a good selection of clothing and shoe shops, as well as some excellent fine food outlets. Trastevere offers lots of interesting little boutiques and knick-knack shops tucked away in narrow medieval streets and lanes.

Rome's markets are a great place for bargain hunting and gift shopping. The best known is Trastevere's **Porta Portese** (p. 68), although there are several smaller, specialised markets worth a visit.

Tax Refunds

A value-added tax of around 19%, known as IVA, is slapped onto just about everything in Italy. If you are resident outside the EU and spend more than L300,000 in the same shop on the same day, you can claim a refund on this tax when you leave the EU. The refund only applies to purchases from affiliated retail outlets which display a 'Tax free for Tourists' sign. You have to complete a form at the point of sale, then get it stamped by Italian customs as you leave. At major airports you can then get an immediate cash refund.

Opening Hours

Shops usually open from 9.30am to 1pm and from 3.30 to 7.30pm (winter) or 4 to 8pm (summer), although a small boutique might not open until 10am and afternoon hours might be shortened. There is a trend towards continuous opening hours from 9.30am to 7.30pm but usually only larger shops and department stores do this. For a few out-of-hours options, see page 67.

CLOTHING

In addition to their designer boutiques, several of the top names also have more affordable diffusion ranges aimed at younger tastes and (slightly) lower budgets, and there are dozens of interesting boutiques where independent designers are making their mark. And remember: dress to impress (rightly or wrongly, the better dressed you are in Roman shops, the better service you'll get).

DIFFUSION RANGES

Emporio Armani
(4, B10) Roll up for Giorgio Armani's range of ready-to-wear suits and separates for men and women. **Armani Jeans** diagonally across the road at No 70a, carries the Armani jeans and sportswear collection.
✉ Via del Babuino 140
☎ 06 360 02 197
Ⓜ Spagna
🕘 Mon 4-7.30pm, Tues-Sat 10am-7.30pm

Fendissime (4, D10)
The third generation of the Fendi family runs this arm of the empire, selling clothes and accessories which err on the groovy side of classic.
✉ Via della Fontanella Borghese 56a ☎ 06 69 66 61 Ⓜ Spagna
🕘 Mon-Sat 10am-7.30pm, Sun 1-7pm

MaxMara (4, D11)
One of Italy's top labels, MaxMara only does ready-to-wear clothes, so it's somewhat more affordable (and usually a lot more wearable) than the 'big' designers. Trademark items include classic jackets, trousers and suits, and superb winter coats in luxurious cashmere blends. Other branches at Via Condotti 17 and Via Nazionale 28.
✉ Via Frattina 28
☎ 06 679 36 38
Ⓜ Spagna
🕘 Mon 3.30-7pm, Tues-Sat 10am-7pm

Versace vixens must visit!

Philosophy di Alberta Ferretti (4, D11)
Designer Alberta Ferretti's diffusion range carries the use of luxurious fabrics and embroidered pieces

Fashion Victims

Retail therapy can do serious damage to the plastic at the following designer stores:

- **Dolce e Gabbana** (4, C11) Piazza di Spagna 82-83 ☎ 06 679 22 94
- **Fendi** (4, C11) Via Borgognona 36-40 ☎ 06 69 66 61
- **Gianni Versace** (4, C10) Via Bocca di Leone 26 ☎ 06 678 05 21
- **Giorgio Armani Boutique** (4, C11) Via Condotti 77 ☎ 06 699 14 60
- **Gucci** (4, C11) Via Condotti 8 ☎ 06 678 93 40
- **Krizia** (4, C11) Piazza di Spagna 87 ☎ 06 679 37 72
- **Laura Biagiotti** (4, D10) Via Borgognona 43-44 ☎ 06 679 12 05
- **Missoni** (4, C11) Piazza di Spagna 78 ☎ 06 679 25 55
- **Prada** (4, C11) Via Condotti 92-95 ☎ 06 679 08 97
- **Roccobarocco** (4, C11) Via Bocca di Leone 65a ☎ 06 679 79 14
- **Salvatore Ferragamo** (4, C11) Via Condotti 73-74 ☎ 06 679 15 65
- **Trussardi** (men & women) (4, C10) Via Condotti 49-50 ☎ 06 678 02 80
- **Valentino Alta Moda** (4, C11) Piazza Mignanelli ☎ 06 679 58 62
- **Valentino Donna** (4, C11) Via Condotti 13 ☎ 06 678 36 56

The King & Queen of Roman Fashion

In the Roman fashion world two names stand out – Valentino Garavani and Laura Biagiotti. When **Valentino** set up his *alta moda* in 1959, his clientele included Jackie Kennedy, Sophia Loren and Audrey Hepburn. While his couture collections featuring superb evening gowns have always been inaccessible to all but the most wealthy of customers, his ready-to-wear lines for both men and women, introduced in the '70s, have become staples of the fashionable set.

The eternally elegant **Laura Biagiotti** is Rome's queen of fashion. Luxurious knitwear and silk separates, and lots of white and cream are her trademarks. Biagiotti is a generous philanthropist and has funded many restoration works in Rome. She has even named a perfume after the city.

through from the couture line. Original shoes, too.
✉ **Via Frattina 60**
☎ **06 679 77 28**
Ⓜ **Spagna**
🕘 **Mon 4-7.30pm, Tues-Sat 10am-7.30pm**

T'Store (4, C10)
Trussardi's *linea giovane* or diffusion range sells jeans, sportswear, chunky knits, jackets, casual trousers and more.
✉ **Via del Corso 477-478** ☎ **06 322 60 55**
Ⓜ **Spagna**
🕘 **Mon noon-8pm, Tues-Sat 10am-8pm, Sun 1-7.30pm**

Valentino Sport
(4, B10) The Roman designer's (slightly) more affordable range (formerly known as Oliver) is aimed at a younger market than his couture collections. Hipster jeans with embroidered or transparent panels were a big feature at the time of writing.
✉ **Via del Babuino 61**
☎ **06 360 01 906**
Ⓜ **Spagna**
🕘 **Mon 3-7pm, Tues-Sat 10am-7pm**

INDEPENDENT BOUTIQUES

Angelo di Nepi (4, B4)
Lovers of colour will adore this women's clothing store, selling beautifully made skirts, trousers, tops and scarves in stunning fabrics, including bright Indian silks, often embroidered.
✉ **Via Cola di Rienzo 267a** ☎ **06 322 48 00**
🚌 **23, 49, 81, 492**
Ⓜ **Ottaviano**
🕘 **Mon 12.30-8pm, Tues-Sat 9.30am-8pm**

Baullà (6, F2)
This gem of a shop between Campo de' Fiori and Piazza Farnese sells good-quality knits, original coats and jackets, skirts, tops, bags, scarves and accessories.
✉ **Via dei Baullari 37**
☎ **06 686 76 70**
🚌 **46, 62, 64, 116**
🕘 **Mon 4-7.30pm, Tues-Sat 9.30am-7.30pm**

Cenci (4, E9)
This Roman institution near the Pantheon stocks a big selection of top Italian and international labels for men, women and children and is a good bet if you prefer classic fashions on the conservative side (think English country squire and you get the idea).
✉ **Via Campo Marzio 1/7** ☎ **06 699 06 81**
🚌 **117, 119**
🕘 **Mon 4-7.30pm, Tues-Sat 9.30am-1.30pm, 4-7.30pm**

Lei (2, A5)
Bright young things pick up pretty dresses and elegant party outfits here. Most of the stock is by French designers, although they do have some Italian names.
✉ **Via dei Giubbonari 103** ☎ **06 687 54 32**
🚌 **46, 62, 64, 70, 81, 87, 186, 492, 628** 🚊 **8**
🕘 **Mon 3-7.30pm, Tues-Sat 10am-2pm, 3-7.30pm**

Marina Rinaldi (4, D10)
Italian women are small, so shops like this, offering classic clothes for the fuller-figured woman, are a rarity. Summer ranges are based on silk and linen, while winter sees luxurious woollens and cashmeres.
✉ **Via del Corso (cnr Largo Goldoni)**
☎ **06 692 00 487**
🚌 **81, 117, 119, 492, 628** Ⓜ **Spagna**
🕘 **Mon 4-7.30pm, Tues-Sat 10am-7.30pm**

Martin Moos

Loafing at Prada

Neil Setchfield

Rome is big on smalls.

LINGERIE

Brighenti (4, C11)
Absolutely luxurious lingerie and sensational, too-good-to-get-wet swimming costumes are what keeps generations of Italian women – including a fair proportion of television and film stars – coming back to Brighenti.
✉ **Via Frattina 7-10**
☎ **06 679 14 84**
Ⓜ **Spagna**
🕘 **Mon 3.30-7.30pm, Tues-Sat 10am-1.30pm, 3.30-7.30pm**

Fogal (4, C11)
You won't find better-quality hosiery, stockings and socks than at Fogal, and the skin-tingling fancy underwear is worth more than a passing glance.
✉ **Via Condotti 55**
☎ **06 678 45 66**
Ⓜ **Spagna**
🕘 **Mon 3.30-7.30pm, Tues-Sat 10am-1.30pm, 3.30-7.30pm**

La Perla (4, C11)
Satisfy your lingerie fantasies with Italy's most famous range. It's all absolutely luxurious, from the lace-trimmed silk bras, to the delicious negligees with matching dressing gowns and stiletto-heeled house slippers. Guaranteed to make you feel like a million dollars for less than a million Lire.
✉ **Via dei Condotti 78**
☎ **06 699 41 933**
Ⓜ **Spagna**
🕘 **Mon 3.30-7.30pm, Tues-Sat 10am-7.30pm**

Fashionable Men, Look No Further

- **Ermenegildo Zegna (4, C11)** Via Borgognona 7e ☎ 06 678 91 43
- **Ferre (4, C11)** Via Borgognona 6 ☎ 06 679 74 45
- **Gianni Versace (4, C11)** Via Borgognona 24-25 ☎ 06 679 50 37
- **Salvatore Ferragamo (4, C11)** Via Condotti 66 ☎ 06 678 11 30
- **Valentino Uomo (4, C11)** Via Bocca di Leone 15 ☎ 06 678 36 56

I Soliti Sospetti

You'll find certain chain stores in every large town in Italy. Rome is no exception. The Italian equivalent of a GAP, Next or Country Road, these shops sell up-to-the-minute wardrobe staples – casual T-shirts, shirts, trousers, skirts, jumpers and jackets – at accessible prices. Some of them include:

- **Benetton (4, G11)** Via Cesare Battisti 129 ☎ 06 699 24 010; **(4, B5)** Via Cola di Rienzo 197 and other locations
- **Stefanel (4, C11)** Via Frattina 31-32 ☎ 06 679 26 67
- **Sisley (4, C11)** Via Frattina 19a ☎ 06 699 41 787
- **Max & Co (4, C10)** Via Condotti 46 ☎ 06 678 79 46

SHOES & LEATHER GOODS

You don't have to look far in Rome for well made and well priced shoes or bags – after all leather (and new-wave imitations) is what Italy does best.

Calzatura Fausto Santini (4, F15)
The closest thing in Rome to an outlet store, this shoe shop near Basilica Santa Maria Maggiore is packed to the rafters with boxes of Fausto Santini shoes (see below) from past collections for half original prices. But don't tell anyone about it, or they'll all know.
✉ Via Santa Maria Maggiore 165 ☎ 06 488 09 34 Ⓜ Cavour ⏲ Mon 3.30-7pm, Tues-Sat 9.30am-1pm, 3.30-7.30pm

Fausto Santini (4, C11)
Italy's most original shoemaker is famous for his quixotic, colourful designs. No truly hip woman's wardrobe is complete without a pair of his peppermint-coloured patent leather mules and his flat boots with a coloured sock-like material (instead of leather) coming just under the knee. Good men's brogues too.
✉ Via Frattina 120 ☎ 06 678 41 14 Ⓜ Spagna ⏲ Mon 4-7pm, Tues-Sat 10am-7pm

Francesco Biasia (6, E5)
Bag ladies of the world are celebrating the opening of various Biasia boutiques in Rome. Incredibly soft leather wallets, funky patent leather bags in jewel-like colours, practical black evening bags and suit carriers and handbags in pony or leopard skin and fake fur are available at unbeatable prices.
✉ Via di Torre Argentina 7 ☎ 06 686 50 98 🚌 46, 62, 64, 70, 81, 87, 186, 492, 628 ⏲ Mon 3.30-7pm, Tues-Sat 10am-7pm

Furla (4, C11)
This outlet, right next to the Spanish Steps, is one of many in Rome and throughout Italy selling high quality leather bags and accessories, including wallets, belts, sunglasses, watches and costume jewellery at really affordable prices.
✉ Piazza di Spagna 22 ☎ 06 692 00 363 Ⓜ Spagna ⏲ 9am-7pm

Mandarina Duck
(4, D11) Who doesn't own a 'Duck' these days? This popular label features trendy handbags, backpacks, wallets and luggage in leather and a host of hard-wearing coloured fabrics and materials – even rubber.
✉ Via del Propaganda 1 ☎ 06 699 40 320 Ⓜ Spagna ⏲ Mon 3.30-7.30pm, Tues-Sat 9.30am-7.30pm

Nuyorica (6, F3)
Grrrrooooovy baby! Rome's never had a shoe shop as hip as this one, which sells shoes by international designers including Freelance, Ernesto Esposito, Rodolphe Menudier and Michel Perry. Exquisite but expensive.
✉ Piazza Pollarola 36-37 ☎ 06 688 91 243 🚌 46, 62, 64, 116 ⏲ Mon-Sat 10am-8pm, Sun 3-8pm

Sciú Sciá (6, E5)
The owner of this shop sources the best shoes from designers around Italy then gets them made up for his stock. The designs are both classic and contemporary, and the expertly crafted shoes last for years.
✉ Via di Torre Argentina 8-9 ☎ 06 688 06 777 🚌 46, 62, 64, 70, 81, 87, 186, 492, 628, J5 ⏲ Mon-Sat 10am-7.30pm

Tod's (4, C10)
Perhaps it's the practical rubber studs on the back of the heel (to reduce driving scuffs) that makes these men's and women's loafers so popular. The shoes are classic and costly, but aficionados swear they're the most comfortable you'll ever buy.
✉ Via Borgognona 45 ☎ 06 678 68 28 Ⓜ Spagna ⏲ Mon 3.30-7.30pm, Tues-Sat 10am-7.30pm

Neil Setchfield

Vamp it in Valentino: foot fashion for the well heeled.

ACCESSORIES & JEWELLERY

Andrew's Ties (4, D11) Top quality ties at bargain basement prices is what Andrew's does best. Rummage through the racks of silk ties – printed, woven or embossed – and ties in wool and cashmere. Just don't touch the window display. At these prices – from about L25,000/€12.91 up to about L50,000/€25.82 – you can take home a handful. There are also nice silk scarves for women.
✉ Via del Gambero 29
☎ 06 679 74 17
🚌 116, 117, 119
Ⓜ Spagna
🕐 Mon 3.30-7.30pm, Tues-Sat 10am-7.30pm

Better Late...

Rome's not great if you need to pick something up at an odd hour. However, there's good shopping at Fiumicino's new international terminal. Kiosks often open long hours and sell some tacky souvenirs and La Rinascente is open longer than most. For late-opening pharmacies, see page 117.

Bulgari (4, C11) Italy's most prestigious and famous jeweller is the Roman equivalent of Cartier in Paris or Tiffany & Co in New York. Large, colourful stones are set in both antique and chunky modern settings. Stunning single pieces are displayed under lights like museum exhibits, so even window shopping is a thrill.
✉ Via dei Condotti 10
☎ 06 679 38 76
Ⓜ Spagna
🕐 Mon 4-7.30pm, Tues-Sat 10am-7.30pm

La Cravatta su Misura (3, E7) For the man who has everything, how about a made-to-measure tie? Only the finest Italian silks and English wools are used in this tiny Trastevere *bottega* (shop). Choose your fabric, the width and length of the tie and, at a push, it can be ready in a few hours.
✉ Via Santa Cecilia 12
☎ 06 581 66 76
🚌 23, 280 🕐 Mon-Sat 10am-1pm, 4-7pm

Mondello Ottica (6, E1) Oh for astigmatism! Specs and sunnies have never looked this good. This is *the* place for the grooviest, quirkiest eyewear in town, with frames by leading European and international designers including Anne et Valentin, l.a.Eyeworks, Cutler and Gross, and the Belgian designer Theo. Prescription glasses can be ready the same day.
✉ Via del Pellegrino 97-98 ☎ 06 686 1955
🚌 46, 62, 64, 116
🕐 Mon 4-7.30pm, Tues-Sat 9am-1pm, 4-7.30pm

Moresco Ottica (2, A6) You won't beat the prices at this well-stocked eyewear shop – the owner *always* gives discounts. There are frames by all the major designers – Gucci, Chanel, Persol, Web and Luxottica to name a few – and prescriptions can be filled in a couple of hours.
✉ Via dei Falegnami 23a ☎ 06 688 05 079
🚌 46, 62, 64, 70, 81,

Roman jewellers nose their craft.

87, 186, 492, J5 🚋 8
🕐 Mon 11am-7.30pm, Tues-Sat 10am-7.30pm

Nicla Boncompagni (4, B10) This specialist shop sells vintage jewellery dating from the mid-19th century to the 1960s, including pieces by Van Cleef & Arpels and Cartier, and American jewellery of the 1940s and '50s.
✉ Via del Babuino 115
☎ 06 678 32 39
Ⓜ Spagna
🕐 Mon 4-7.30pm, Tues-Sat 10am-7.30pm

Rita Vallani (6, A1) Thou shalt not covet! The jewellery here is to die for – stunning antique (up to the 1950s) necklaces, earrings and brooches in gold and silver with precious and semi-precious stones.
✉ Via dei Coronari 149
☎ 06 687 88 70 🚌 70, 81, 116, 186, 492, 628
🕐 Mon 4-7.30pm, Tues-Sat 10.30am-1pm, 4-7.30pm

Sermoneta (4, C11) Gloves, gloves and more gloves: for men and women, in leather and suede, lined with cashmere, silk or angora, in the colours of the

rainbow and more besides.
✉ **Piazza di Spagna 61**
☎ **06 679 19 60**
Ⓜ **Spagna**
🕐 **Mon 3.30-7.30pm, Tues-Sat 10am-7.30pm**

Tempi Moderni (6, C1)
Vintage costume jewellery dating from 1880 to 1970 (with an emphasis on Art Nouveau and Art Deco) is the thing here: 19th century resin brooches, Bakelite from the '20s and '30s and costume jewellery by couturiers such as Chanel, Dior and Balenciaga.
✉ **Via del Governo Vecchio 108** ☎ **06 687 70 07** 🚌 **46, 62, 64, J5**
🕐 **Mon 3.30-7.30pm, Tues-Sat 9.30am-1.30pm, 3.30-7.30pm**

Troncarelli (6, D3)
For a little shop there are a lot of top brand hats for men and women here – bowlers, toppers, panamas, Borsalino and Florentine straw hats.
✉ **Via della Cuccagna 15** ☎ **06 687 93 20**
🚌 **46, 62, 64, 116**
🕐 **Mon-Sat 10am-7.30pm**

DEPARTMENT STORES

Rome has been slower than some of the northern Italian cities to adopt the trend towards department stores and malls. There is only one department store actually in the historic centre, but *centri commerciali* (large shopping centres) are popping up all over the place, mostly on the outskirts of town.

La Rinascente (4, E11)
It's hardly a Harrods or Macy's, but Rome's biggest department store has a good range of medium-quality clothing and accessories, as well as big name cosmetics.
✉ **Via del Corso 189**
☎ **06 679 76 91**
🚌 **52, 53, 62, 71, 85, 117, 119, 160, 175, 492, 850**
🕐 **Mon-Fri 9am-9pm, Sun 10.30am-8pm**

Retail giant La Rinascente

COIN (3, H7)
This compact store sells good-quality men's and women's clothing and accessories, cosmetics, and a good range of homewares. There's an excellent section of children's clothes. Branch also at Via di Cola di Rienzo 173 (4, B5).
✉ **Piazzale Appio 7**
☎ **06 708 00 91**
🚌 **81, 85, 87, 186, 810, 850, J3, J5**
Ⓜ **San Giovanni**
🕐 **9.30am-8pm**

UPIM (4, D12)
A budget store selling clothing, gifts and household goods. The quality of stock can be patchy, but good-value accessories can often be found. UPIM branch at Via Nazionale 211, Quirinale (4, E14).
✉ **Via del Tritone 172**
☎ **06 678 33 36**
Ⓜ **Barberini**
🕐 **Mon noon-8pm, Tues-Sat 9am-8pm, Sun 10.30am-8pm**

Selling Up

If you can time your visit to coincide with the sales, you'll pick up some marvellous bargains. Winter sales run from early January to mid-February and the summer sales run from July to early September. Look for the *saldi* signs.

MAS (5, G3)
This bargain hunter's paradise sells everything from cheese graters to leather jackets (some very good ones, too). Most of the stuff is dirt cheap and sometimes you can pick up quality stuff at low prices.
✉ **Via dello Statuto 11**
☎ **06 446 80 78**
🚌 **71** Ⓜ **Vittorio**
🕐 **Mon-Sat 9am-7pm**

MARKETS

Borgo Parioli (3, C6)
You'll have to venture into the 'burbs north of the centre for this market. On sale are original jewellery and accessories from the 1950s onwards – such as brooches, cigarette cases and watches – all in mint condition (but not always a bargain) as well as silverware, paintings, antique lamps and old gramophones.
✉ **Via Tirso 14** ☎ **06 855 27 73** 🚌 **63, 86, 92, 217** 🕘 **1st 3 weekends of the month, Sat & Sun 9am-8pm**

Mercato delle Stampe (4, D9)
This market is devoted exclusively to antique prints and second-hand books. Early music scores, architectural engravings, chromolithographs of fruit and flowers and views of Rome are among the stunning objects for sale. The cheap repros make fun souvenirs.
✉ **Largo della Fontanella di Borghese** 🚌 **70, 81, 117, 119, 186, 492, 628** Ⓜ **Spagna** 🕘 **Mon-Sat 8am-sunset**

Porta Portese (3, H3)
Rome's biggest and best-known flea market has a mishmash of new and old, from bags to bikes, frocks to furniture – everything including the kitchen sink. There's all manner of incredible deals, but if you don't bargain, it's boring! Watch out for pickpockets.
✉ **b/w Porta Portese & Piazza Ippolito Nievo, parallel to Viale Trastevere** 🚌 **23, 44, 75, 280** 🚋 **8** 🕘 **Sun 7am-1pm**

Underground (4, C12)
This monthly market has over 150 stalls selling antiques and collectables. There's a section for handmade goods and a children's section.
✉ **Ludovisi underground car park, Via Francesco Crispi 96** ☎ **06 360 05 345** 🚌 **116, 117, 119** Ⓜ **Barberini** 🕘 **2nd weekend of the month, Sat 3-8pm, Sun 10.30am-7.30pm**

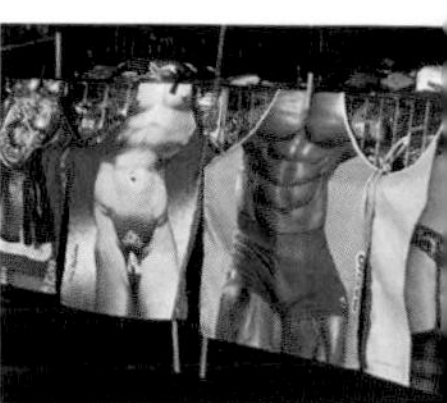
Aprons at Campo de Fiori

Via Sannio (3, H7)
If your life won't be complete without a full length leather coat, then this covered market's for you. Check out the leather in all shapes and shades, bargain shoes, retro jeans, fluffy fleeces, sports gear and more. Venture up the back for cheap second-hand clothing. How can pre-loved cashmere be in such mint condition?
✉ **Via Sannio** 🚌 **81, 85, 87, 810, 850, J3, J5** Ⓜ **San Giovanni** 🕘 **Mon-Sat 8am-1pm**

To Market, to Market...

Rome's fresh produce markets are treasured reminders of a more traditional way of life. There's generally a dazzling array of fresh fruit and vegetables, often meat and fish stalls, the usual delicatessen fare and sometimes stalls selling clothing, shoes or bric-a-brac. The most famous and picturesque of all is **Campo de' Fiori** (6, F2). In Trastevere, **Piazza San Cosimato** (2, E2) preserves the flavour of the traditional neighbourhood market. The huge market at **Piazza Vittorio Emanuele** (5, G3) is influenced by the various ethnic groups that have settled in the Esquiline area; it's great for closing bargains on Saturday afternoons. **Piazza Testaccio** (3, H4) has a local market with excellent quality produce, probably the best in Rome. Markets operate Mon-Sat 7am-1.30pm.

ARTS & ANTIQUES

The best antique shops are in and around Via dei Coronari (near Piazza Navona), Via Giulia, and Via del Babuino. Bargain furniture is a rare find in Rome, but a wander past the artisan workshops on Via del Pellegrino or Via dei Cappellari (near Campo de' Fiori) might unearth a gem.

Alberto Negri (6, A2)
Fancy an elaborate 18th or 19th century mirror or candlestick? Your passion for gilt is fully indulged in this specialist antique shop.
✉ Via dei Coronari 26 ☎ 06 688 069 14 🚌 70, 81, 116, 186, 492, 628 🕘 Mon 4.30-7.30pm, Tues-Sat 10am-1pm, 4.30-7.30pm

Alinari (4, B11)
The Alinari brothers were famous late 19th century photographers. The photographic prints (mostly views of Rome) and photography books on sale here are reproduced from the archives of their work, which contain more than a million glass plate negatives.
✉ Via Alibert 16a ☎ 06 679 29 23 Ⓜ Spagna 🕘 Mon 3.30-7.30pm, Tues-Sat 10am-1.30pm, 3.30-7.30pm

Animalier e Oltre (4, B10) It's not easy to define this antique/curio shop which stocks rustic furniture from northern Europe and North America, bric-a-brac and a huge selection of animal-shaped antiques (including French 19th century *animalier* sculptures). Among other things, you'll find exquisitely made porcelain dogs, animal-shaped salt & pepper sets and bedside lamps.
✉ Via Margutta 47 ☎ 06 320 82 82 Ⓜ Spagna 🕘 Mon-Sat 10am-2pm, 4-8pm

Antiquarius Stampe e Libri (6, C3)
The original prints sold here – by Dürer, Rembrandt, Piranesi et al – are for serious collectors, although the 18th and 19th century views of Rome make wonderful and affordable souvenirs. Antique maps will amuse the cartographically inclined.
✉ Corso di Rinascimento 63 ☎ 06 688 029 41 🚌 70, 81, 116, 186, 492, 628 🕘 Mon 3.30-7.30pm, Tues-Sat 9.30am-7.30pm

Art Deco Gallery (6, A2) As the name suggests, it's all Art Deco in here – ceiling lights, lamps, glassware, tables, statues and furniture (including simply upholstered, covetable chairs).
✉ Via dei Coronari 14 ☎ 06 686 53 30 🚌 70, 81, 116, 186, 492, 628 🕘 Mon 4.30-7.30pm, Tues-Sat 10am-1pm, 4.30-7.30pm

Bruno Verdini Antichità (6, A1)
Old Bruno's got the Biedermeier market wrapped up (in Via dei Coronari at least). Bureaux, tables, cabinets and bookcases are among the wares to tempt you.
✉ Via dei Coronari 224 ☎ 06 687 50 94 🚌 70, 81, 116, 186, 492, 628 🕘 Mon 3.30-7.30pm, Tues-Sat 9.30am-1pm, 3.30-7.30pm

Step Back in Time

In late May and again in late October the antiquarians of Via dei Coronari hold a *mostra-mercato* (antiques fair). The street is lit only by candles, red carpet runs its length, and the shops stay open late.

Martin Moos

Comics Bazar (4, F6)
This veritable warehouse of antiques is crammed with objects, lamps and furniture from the late 19th century to the 1940s, including a large selection of Viennese furniture by Thonet.
✉ Via dei Banchi Vecchi 127-128 ☎ 06 688 02 923 🚌 46, 62, 64, J5 🕘 Mon-Sat 9am-8pm

Lilia Leoni (4, C10)
Among the unusual objects and furniture here are collectable Murano drinking glasses and Art Nouveau (known as 'Liberty' in Italy) garden furniture, as well as pieces dating from the early 1900s to the 1950s.
✉ Via Belsiana 86 ☎ 06 678 32 10 🚌 117, 119 Ⓜ Spagna 🕘 Mon 4-8pm, Tues-Sat 10am-1.30pm, 4-8pm

Jon Davison

Picturesque Piazza Navona

Lumieres (2, C3)
Wind your way through the *vicoli* of Trastevere for these antique lamps, from Art Nouveau and Art Deco to the 1950s.
✉ **Vicolo del Cinque 48** ☎ **06 580 36 14** 🚌 **23, 280** ⌚ **Mon 4-7.30pm, Tues-Sat 10am-1.30pm, 4-7.30pm**

Marmi Line (6, A1)
Haven't you heard? No home is complete without a marble obelisk these days, so buy yours here. Among the antique and modern pieces are fabulous inlaid marble table tops, statues fit for a palazzo, and large marble eggs, the purpose of which is not immediately clear.
✉ **Via dei Coronari 143-5** ☎ **06 689 37 95** 🚌 **70, 81, 116, 186, 492, 628** ⌚ **Mon 3.30-7.30pm, Tues-Sat 9.30am-1pm, 3.30-7.30pm**

Nardecchia (6, B2)
This Roman landmark is only marginally less famous than Bernini's Fontana dei Fiumi opposite. It sells antique prints, including 18th century etchings of Rome by Giovanni Battista Piranesi, and more inexpensive 19th century views of the city.
✉ **Piazza Navona 25** ☎ **06 686 93 18** 🚌 **46, 62, 64, 70, 81, 87, 186, 492, 628, J5** ⌚ **Mon 4.30-7.30pm, Tues-Sun 10am-1pm, 4.30-7.30pm**

Yaky (2, B6)
It's got nothing to do with Italy, but will be right up your alley if you like antique Chinese furniture. The range of imported objects includes stunning wooden cabinets and lacquered bowls.
✉ **Via Santa Maria del Pianto 55** ☎ **06 688 07 724** 🚌 **23, 63, 280, 630, H** 🚋 **8** ⌚ **Mon-Sat 10am-8pm, Sun 10.30am-7.30pm**

DESIGN & HOMEWARES

Artemide (4, A10)
Have you ever wondered where those fabulous light fittings and lamps in those glossy designer mags originate? Chances are that they come from Artemide, which retails lamps and light fittings by Italian and international designers. Be aware that the plugs and bulbs are not universal.
✉ **Via Margutta 107** ☎ **06 360 01 802** 🚌 **117, 119** Ⓜ **Flaminio, Spagna** ⌚ **Mon 3-7pm, Tues-Sat 10am-1.30pm, 2.30-7pm**

Contemporanea (4, F7)
'Interior scenery' is what you pick up here, and it would not be difficult to spend a small fortune on weirdly stylish furnishings and fabulous fabrics by some of Italy's and Europe's top avant-garde designers.
✉ **Via dei Banchi Vecchi 143** ☎ **06 688 04 533** 🚌 **46, 62, 64, J5** ⌚ **Mon 3.30-8pm, Tues-Sat 10am-1.30pm, 3.30-8pm**

C.U.C.I.N.A. (4, C11)
Once upon a time C.U.C.I.N.A. was seriously avant-garde, selling groovy chrome everything and innovative modular shelf units on which to store it. The stainless steel look has become ubiquitous, but good quality kitchenware can still be snapped up here.
✉ **Via del Babuino 118a** ☎ **06 679 12 75** Ⓜ **Spagna** ⌚ **Mon 3.30-8pm, Tues-Sat 10am-1.30pm, 3.30-8pm**

De Sanctis (6, B3)
A good selection of Alessi products (including replacement parts) and other designer kitchenware and tableware can be found here. Of particular interest is the selection of Italian ceramics, including the colourful work of the Sicilian ceramicist De Simone.
✉ **Piazza Navona 82/84** ☎ **06 688 06 810** 🚌 **70, 81, 87, 186, 492, 628** ⌚ **Mon 4-7.30pm, Tues-Sun 10am-1pm**

Ecole De (4, G7)
'Frivolous' best describes the eclectic homewares, furnishings and gifts in this quirky shop, which sells everything from buttons to blow-up chairs, all with a strong dose of kitsch – and

not too expensive.
✉ **Vicolo della Moretta 10-11 ☎ 06 689 20 15 🚌 46, 62, 64, J5 🕐 Mon 3-8pm, Tues-Sat 10am-8pm**

Farnese (4, G8)
The stunning mosaic tables produced and sold here could be straight out of Pompeii. This artisan workshop and showroom is doing a good job conserving and continuing the great Italian tradition of ceramic tile making. It's *very* expensive, but then so is the Piazza Farnese rent.
✉ **Piazza Farnese 52 ☎ 06 687 47 92 🚌 23, 46, 62, 64, 116, 280, J4 🕐 Mon 4-7pm, Tues-Sat 10am-1pm, 4-7pm**

Flos Arteluce (4, C11)
More like a museum of lighting fixtures than a retail outlet, Flos 'exhibits' minimalist pieces in chrome and steel and simple colours like black and white.
✉ **Via del Babuino 84-85 ☎ 06 320 76 31 Ⓜ Spagna 🕐 Mon 4-7pm, Tues-Sat 10am-1.30pm, 4-7pm**

Home (6, E5)
Kitchen utensils, candles, glassware, vibrant crockery and haberdashery are among the homewares here (often big bargains). It also has some more upmarket stock: rustic antique-repro furniture and a large selection of oriental rugs.
✉ **Largo di Torre Argentina 8 ☎ 06 686 84 50 🚌 46, 62, 64, 70, 81, 87, 186, 492, 628, J5 🕐 Mon 3.30-7.30pm, Tues-Sun 10am-7.30pm**

A Special Shopping Species

While you shop, look out for a distinctive breed of Roman – the shop assistant. These curious creatures are imperious, grumpy and rude; they spend hours chatting to colleagues or talking on the phone and have developed a highly skilled art in ignoring customers. Scientists believe that the role of the shop assistant was originally to help shoppers part with their money; in Rome creatures exhibiting these behavioural traits are now virtually extinct.

Leone Limentani
(2, B7) This warehouse-style shop has an unbelievable choice of kitchenware and tableware. High-priced fine porcelain and crystal sit alongside bargain basement items. It also stocks plenty of Alessi (including replacement parts) and a good selection of quality pots and pans.
✉ **Basement, Via Portico d'Ottavia 47 ☎ 06 688 06 686 🚌 46, 62, 64, 70, 81, 87, 186, 492, 628, 630, H, J5 🕐 Mon 3.30-7.30pm, Tues-Sat 9.30am-1.30pm, 3.30-7.30pm**

Maurizio Grossi
(4, A10) If your idea of souvenirs is a repro bust of Marcus Aurelius, or an obelisk for the mantelpiece, then a visit to this marble emporium is a must. A novelty are the huge bowls of what looks like ripe figs and apricots; in fact they are heavy, sculpted marble, hand painted to resemble fruit.
✉ **Via Margutta 109 ☎ 06 360 01 935 Ⓜ Flaminio, Spagna 🕐 Mon-Sat 10am-7.30pm**

Spazio Sette (6, F5)
Hidden in a Renaissance palazzo is one of Rome's premier homewares stores. If you can manage to tear your attention away from the frescoed ceiling at the entrance, you'll find three levels of high-quality furniture, designer kitchen- and tableware and groovy gifts.
✉ **Via dei Barbieri 7 ☎ 06 688 04 261 🚌 46, 62, 64, 70, 81, 87, 186, 492, 628, 630, H, J5 🚋 8 🕐 Mon 3.30-7.30pm Tues-Sat 10am-1.30pm, 3.30-7.30pm**

Tad (4, B10)
Furniture, screens, vases, textiles and linens in trendy ethnic style are the features of this elegant interiors store.
✉ **Via di San Giacomo 5 ☎ 06 360 01 679 🚌 117, 119 Ⓜ Spagna 🕐 Mon 3.30-7.30pm, Tues-Sat 10am-7pm**

Damien Simonis

It's easy to find your cuppa.

FOOD & DRINK

Even the humblest neighbourhood *alimentari* can be a gourmet's paradise. Bottles of wine, olive oil or grappa, jars of preserved vegetables, or hunks of parmesan cheese make fabulous gifts or souvenirs (depending on your country's customs regulations). The following shops offer something extra special.

Castroni (4, B5)
Desperate Aussies have been spotted combing Castroni's well-stocked shelves for Vegemite while homesick Yanks make pilgrimages for cranberry juice and Betty Crocker cake mixes. Castroni boasts Rome's largest selection of international gourmet foods and food products. Here you'll find oils, vinegars, legumes, spices, aromatic herbs, dried fruit, jams, condiments, chocolates, tea and coffee – and that's just on the first shelf.
Via Cola di Rienzo 196-198 06 687 43 83 49, 81, 492 Lepanto, Ottaviano Mon-Sat 8am-8pm

'Gusto (4, C9)
The bookshop/cookshop at this New York-style eatery sells fabulous food and wine-related gifts: special olive oils, aged balsamic vinegars, sauces and condiments; wine, wine glasses, decanters and corkscrews; kitchen appliances and implements; and books on food and wine (including several English cookbooks).
Piazza Augusto Imperatore 9 06 322 62 73 81, 117, 119, 492, 628 10.30am-8pm

Superiore *drops (see p. 86)*

Moriondo & Gariglio (6, D7) The chocolates in this shop are displayed like jewels. But precious stones and metals never tasted this good. Moriondo and Gariglio were pastry chefs from Turin who brought their chocolate-making skills to Rome in 1886. The present owner's father learned his craft from them. With over 80 varieties of chocolate, pralines, toffee and jellied fruit, multiple visits are advised.
Via Piè di Marmo 21-22 06 699 08 56 46, 62, 64, 70, 81, 87, 186, 492, 628 8 Mon-Sat 9.30am-1.30pm, 3.30-7.30pm

Shaki (4, C11)
Food-related gifts such as bottled artichokes, peppers, anchovies and cheese, preserves and spreads are the speciality here. Cute gift ideas include parmesan cheese knives (in the shape of a mouse), pasta (in the shape of love hearts) and fun fridge magnets. It trades off its touristy position on Piazza di Spagna, so don't expect many bargains.
Piazza di Spagna 65 06 678 66 05 Spagna 9.30am-7.30pm

Say cheese at Volpetti.

Volpetti (3, H4)
Don't go shopping at Volpetti, Rome's pioneer gourmet deli, when you're hungry. You won't be able to resist the fantastic cheeses (including some unusual ones from other parts of Italy), hams and cured meats, *sott'aceti* (pickles) and *sott'olii* (grilled vegetables like eggplant and capsicum, preserved in oil). Oils, vinegar, wine, grappa and packaged pasta make good presents.
Via Marmorata 47 06 574 23 52 23, 75, 280, 716 Piramide Mon & Wed-Sat 9am-2pm, 4-8pm

FOR CHILDREN

Al Sogno (6, A3)
The mezzanine floor of this stunning toy shop is a wonderland of expensive dolls and stuffed animals of every shape and size. Even the fluffy sharks are cute. Go in with a child and you wallet is finished!
✉ **Piazza Navona 53**
☎ **06 686 41 98**
🚌 **70, 81, 87, 116, 186, 492, 628** 🕘 **9.30am-8pm (Sun from10am)**

Bertè (6, C3)
The patriarch of the family that runs this fabulous toy shop bears a striking resemblance to Pinocchio's Geppetto. So it's rather appropriate that the toys here include beautifully made wooden dolls and puppets, finely crafted scooters in wood and metal and high-quality educational games. Even 20- to 70-something kids will get a kick out of it.
✉ **Piazza Navona**
☎ **06 687 50 11**
🚌 **70, 81, 87, 116, 186, 492, 628**
🕘 **Mon 4-8pm, Tues-Sun 9.30am-1pm, 4-8pm**

Città del Sole (6, A4)
Some consider this to be Rome's best toy shop. When only the best quality educational and creative toys will do, this is the place for kids and adults alike.
✉ **Via della Scrofa 65**
☎ **06 688 03 805**
🚌 **70, 81, 87, 116, 186, 492, 628** 🕘 **Mon 3.30-7.30pm, Tues-Sat 10am-7.30pm, Sun 11am-1.30pm & 3.30-7.30pm**

Chicco (4, C11)
After the eye-popping price tags in some of the surrounding shops, Chicco's good-quality clothes and toys for babies, toddlers and young kids come as a welcome relief.
✉ **Via Frattina 146-147** ☎ **06 679 36 66**
Ⓜ **Spagna** 🕘 **Mon 3.30-7.30pm, Tues-Sat 9.30am-7.30pm**

La Cicogna (4, C11)
The fact that Italians spend such an inordinate amount of money on children's clothes is evident from the proliferation of these boutiques in Rome and around the country. There are fashionable children's clothes by top designers, as well as La Cicogna's own label.
✉ **Via Frattina 138**
☎ **06 678 69 77**
Ⓜ **Spagna** 🕘 **Mon 3.30-7.30pm, Tues-Sat 9.30am-7.30pm**

Mel Giannino Stoppani Librerie per Ragazzi (6, D10)
The best children's bookshop in Rome stocks mainly Italian books but one corner is devoted to French, Spanish, German and English books.
✉ **Piazza Santi Apostoli 59-65** ☎ **06 699 41 045** 🚌 **64, 70, 170, H** 🕘 **Mon-Sat 9.30am-7.30pm, Sun 10am-1pm, 4-7.30pm**

PréNatal (4, E14)
One of those reliable, reasonably priced shops selling well made wardrobe staples for kids up to 11 years old and for expecting mums too. Equipment such as bottles, prams, strollers, cradles and cots is also stocked.
✉ **Via Nazionale 45**
☎ **06 488 14 03**
🚌 **64, 70, 71, 170**
Ⓜ **Repubblica** 🕘 **Mon 3.30-7.30pm, Tues-Sat 9.30am-7.30pm**

Sotto una Foglia di Cavolo (4, B9)
This is where the beautiful children shop for classic and unusual clothing from Italy, France and the Netherlands. For babies and children up to eight years.
✉ **Via del Vantaggio 25** ☎ **06 360 02 960**
🚌 **117, 119, 628**
Ⓜ **Flaminio**
🕘 **Mon 3.30-7.30pm, Tues-Sat 9.30am-1.30pm, 3.30-7.30pm**

Zerododici di Benetton (4, C9)
It must be all that folding that makes the Benetton staff so grumpy. Never mind, the clothes here – exclusively for kids 12 years and under – are fun, hardy and well priced.
✉ **Via Tomacelli 137**
☎ **06 688 09 381**
🚌 **70, 81, 87, 186, 492, 628, 913** Ⓜ **Spagna**
🕘 **Mon 3.30-7.30pm, Tues-Sat 9.30am-7.30pm**

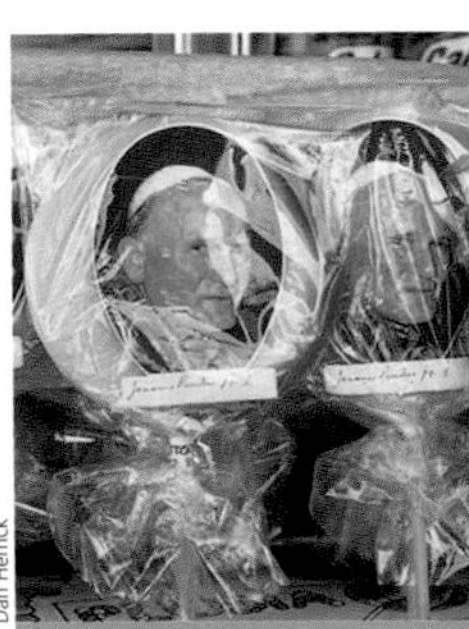
Dan Herrick

Papa Poppas: worship only in the very best of taste.

MUSIC & BOOKS

Anglo-American Bookshop (4, D11)
Novels, classics, reference books, literature and children's books – they're all here and all in English. Travel guides and maps are also available.
✉ **Via della Vite 27** ☎ **06 678 96 57** 🚌 **116** Ⓜ **Spagna** 🕘 **Mon 3.30-7.30pm, Tues-Sat 9am-1pm, 3.30-7.30pm**

Caro Vinile... Caro Cinema (6, F3)
More than a music shop, it's a collector's paradise. There are rare discs from the 1960s, a special section of Beatles memorabilia, plus film posters and photos.
✉ **Via del Paradiso 42** ☎ **06 687 40 05** 🚌 **46, 62, 64, 70, 81, 87, 116, 186, 492, 628** 🕘 **4-7.30pm**

Disfunzioni Musicali (3, F8) Located in the heart of San Lorenzo, Rome's university area, and popular with students, Disfunzioni Musicali specialises in alternative, non-commercial music, rare records and bootlegs. It also stocks second-hand records and CDs of everything from opera to rock, international to Italian artists.
✉ **Via degli Etruschi 4-14** ☎ **06 446 19 84** 🚌 **71, 492** 🕘 **Mon-Sat 10.30am-7.30pm**

Feltrinelli (6, E5)
If it's in Italian and in print, chances are Feltrinelli will have it. This well organised bookshop has a huge range of non-fiction books – art, photography, cinema, food and history among other subjects – as well as an extensive selection of Italian literature, travel guides and maps.
✉ **Largo di Torre Argentina 5a** ☎ **06 688 03 248** 🚌 **46, 62, 64, 70, 81, 87, 186, 492, 628** 🚋 **8** 🕘 **9am-8pm**

Feltrinelli International (4, D15)
Depending on your language, this multinational, multilingual shop stocks *livres, libros, livros, bücher, books* or *libri* in French, Spanish, Portuguese, German, English and Italian: contemporary literature and classics, fiction and non-fiction, plus lots of guidebooks for Rome, Italy, and the rest of the world (Lonely Planet included).
✉ **Via VE Orlando 84** ☎ **06 482 78 78** Ⓜ **Repubblica** 🕘 **Mon-Sat 9am-8pm, Sun 10am-1pm, 4-7.30pm**

Franco Maria Ricci (4, C11) It's odd to find a bookshop tucked in between high fashion boutiques, but the gems on sale here – splendidly produced and illustrated tomes on art and culture – are, arguably, as covetable as anything from Valentino or Versace. The superb glossy *FMR* magazine is also available here.
✉ **Via Borgognona 4d** ☎ **06 679 34 66** Ⓜ **Spagna** 🕘 **Mon 4-7pm, Tues-Sat 10am-1.30pm**

L'Allegretto (3, D3)
It's a bit out of the way, but opera and classical music fans will find what they want in this well-stocked shop in Prati (just north of Piazza Mazzini).
✉ **Via Oslavia 44** ☎ **06 320 82 24** 🚌 **186, 280** Ⓜ **Lepanto** 🕘 **Mon 4-7.30pm, Tues-Sat 9.30am-1.30pm, 4-7.30pm**

Libreria del Viaggiatore (6, E1)
This intimate bookshop is devoted to travelling and is crammed with travel guides (including Lonely Planet) and travel literature in various languages. It also has a huge range of maps for countries, regions and cities around the world, as well as hiking maps.
✉ **Via del Pellegrino 78** ☎ **06 688 01 048** 🚌 **46, 62, 64, J5** 🕘 **Mon 4-8pm, Tues-Sat 10am-2pm, 4-8pm**

Roman Recommended Readings

For more background into the city, stick your nose into:

- *The Agony and the Ecstasy* – Irving Stone
- *Cabal – An Aurelio Zen Mystery* – Michael Dibdin
- *Companion Guide to Rome* – Georgina Masson
- *Daily Life in Ancient Rome* – Jerome Carcopino
- *The History of the Decline and Fall of the Roman Empire* – Edward Gibbon
- *Rome: Biography of a City* – Christopher Hibbert
- *A Traveller in Rome* – HV Morton
- *A Woman of Rome (La Romana)* – Alberto Moravia

Ricordi Media Store (6, E10) Rome's largest music store (with other branches around the city) is well-stocked with CDs and music videos (from classical to cutting edge). In the shop next door there's a large selection of musical instruments, sheet music and scores, and books.
✉ Via Cesare Battisti 120d ☎ 06 679 80 22 🚌 64, 70, 170, H ⏲ Mon-Sat 9am-7.30pm, Sun 3.30-8pm

Rinascita (4, G10) This well-stocked music shop (adjacent to the bookshop of the same name) specialises in world and contemporary music and the latest trends. There's also a very good selection of jazz, soul, blues and classical music of all tastes.
✉ Via delle Botteghe Oscure 5 ☎ 06 699 22 436 🚌 46, 62, 64, 70, 87, 170, 492, H ⏲ 9.30am-7pm

The Corner Bookshop (3, C3) Piles of books, all in English, cover everything in this tiny corner shop. The well chosen stock includes best-sellers, contemporary literature, biography, history, travel guides, dictionaries and reference books. It's a bookworm's paradise where you'll want to buy it all.
✉ Via del Moro 48 ☎ 06 583 69 42 🚌 23, 280, 630, H 🚋 8 ⏲ 10am-1.30pm, 3.30-8pm (from 11am Sun)

SPECIALIST STORES

Ai Monasteri (6, B3) Step back in time. This impressive wood-panelled shop sells herbal essences, spirits, soaps, balms, deodorants, anti-wrinkle creams, bubble bath and various liqueurs. It's all made by monks in abbeys around Italy. The products must work – after all, God is on your side.
✉ Corso del Rinascimento 72 ☎ 06 688 02 783 🚌 70, 81, 87, 116, 186, 492, 628 ⏲ Mon-Sat 9am-1pm, 4.30-7.30pm (Thurs 9am-1pm only)

Officina della Carta (2, C2) Florence is more famous than Rome for hand-printed papers, but this tiny Trastevere workshop makes lovely things with it: storage boxes, photo albums, recipe books, notepads, photo frames and diaries. They produce superb merchandise and can make to order at short notice.
✉ Via Benedetta 26b ☎ 06 589 55 57 🚌 23, 280, 630, H 🚋 8 ⏲ 10am-1.30pm, 4-7.30pm

Papal Party Gear

Whether you're after papal party gear, nun's knickers, incense burners or a life-size painted wooden statue of the Virgin Mary, the streets around Via dei Cestari and Via di Santa Chiara (near the Pantheon) are where you'll find it. Anniable Gammarelli is the pope's official tailor, and has the responsibility to have a set of clothes ready for the new pope before anyone knows who it will be. So they make three different sizes – tall and thin, short and fat, and average – and hope that one fits.

Sally Webb

For when dressing is a bit of a habit.

places to eat

Eating is one of life's great pleasures for Romans and it should be a highlight of your trip. The historic centre is packed with eateries to satisfy all tastes and pockets. Monti boasts some interesting ethnic restaurants, as well as good pizzerias; across the river, Trastevere's pizzerias and trattorias are popular haunts for both Romans and foreigners. The Ghetto is the place for Roman Jewish cooking and Testaccio, near the former abattoir, is still known as *the* place to go for offal, the real *cucina romana.*

Eating, Italian Style

Italians rarely eat a sit-down *colazione* (breakfast). They tend to drink a cappuccino, usually *tiepido* (warm), and eat a *cornetto* (croissant) while standing at a bar. *Pranzo* (lunch) is traditionally the main meal of the day and many shops and businesses close for several hours to accommodate the meal and siesta which follows. *Cena* (evening meal) was traditionally a simple affair, but habits are changing because of the inconvenience of returning home for lunch.

A full meal consists of antipasto, which can vary from bruschetta to *prosciutto* (cured ham) with melon or figs, a *primo piatto*, pasta, soup or risotto, followed by the *secondo* of meat or fish. An *insalata* (salad) or *contorno* (vegetable) is ordered separately, and the meal is rounded off with *dolce* (dessert), *gelato* (see Sweet Treats, p. 89) or fruit and *caffè*.

Quanto Costa?

The price ranges used here indicate the cost for a two-course meal for one, excluding drinks:

$	under L25,000/€12.91
$$	L26,000-45,000/ €13.43-23.24
$$$	L46,000-79,000/ €23.76-40.80
$$$$	over L80,000/€41.32

Alan Benson

Where to Eat

The *trattoria* is usually a family-run concern serving unpretentious home-cooking. A *ristorante* is more formal, with a wider selection of dishes and a higher service standards. The *osteria* is a neighbourhood inn, usually with only a few dishes on offer, washed down with jugs of local wine; this is where you'll often experience the best cucina romana. *Pizzerias* can serve antipasto, pasta, meat and vegetable dishes as well as pizza. Look for the *forno a legna* sign, indicating a wood-fired oven. Rome's best fast food is *pizza a taglio* which is also known as *pizza rustica (*pizza by the slice, see p. 88). The *tavola calda* does cheap, pre-prepared meat, pasta and vegetable dishes in a self-service style and the *rosticceria* sells cooked meats, fried zucchini flowers, *supplì* and other takeaway fare.

Tourist Menus

Steer clear of restaurants in touristy parts of town which advertise a three-course *menu turistico* for a bargain price. Invariably the pasta is not freshly cooked and the food has been sitting around for too long, waiting to be microwaved.

Cucina Romana

The roots of Roman cuisine are in the diet of the poor. Historically, the ordinary folk ate the *quinto quarto* (fifth quarter) of the animal, which was all that was left after the rich had taken their pickings. **Offal** eaters shouldn't miss the opportunity to try *coda* (oxtail) or *trippa* (tripe) here, where they are done best. A local delicacy is *pajata,* the entrails of very young veal still containing the mother's milk, which are eaten roasted or tossed through rigatoni.

Deep frying, which has its origins in Jewish cooking, is another important feature of Roman cuisine. Deep-fried fillets of *baccalà* (salted cod), *fiori di zucca* (zucchini flowers) stuffed with mozzarella and anchovies, and *carciofi alla giudia* (whole deep-fried artichokes) are a must on any Roman gastronomic itinerary.

Fish is also an important fixture on the menus of Rome's better eateries. More often than not it is grilled whole and then filleted by the waiter at the table. **Antipasto** dishes in Rome are particularly good and many restaurants allow you to make your own mixed selection from a buffet.

Traditional Roman **pasta** dishes include spaghetti carbonara (with egg yolk, cheese and *pancetta,* or cured bacon) and *all'amatriciana* (with tomato, pancetta and chilli). Penne all'arrabbiata (literally 'angry' pasta) has a sauce of tomato and chilli. Another favourite Roman pasta dish is spaghetti *al cacio e pepe,* a deceptively simple dish of piping hot pasta topped by freshly grated pecorino romano, ground black pepper and a dash of good olive oil. Spaghetti *alla gricia* is similar but with the addition of pancetta.

Roman **meat dishes** to look out for are *saltimbocca alla Romana*, a thin fillet of veal topped with a slice of *prosciutto crudo* (cured ham), white wine and sage, and Easter favourite *abbacchio al forno,* spring lamb roasted with rosemary and garlic.

Although there are few exclusively **vegetarian** restaurants in Rome, vegetarians won't have any problems eating here. Vegetables are a staple of the Italian diet, and most eateries have a good selection of antipasti, contorni and salads in addition to vegetable based pastas and risottos. Vegetable dishes to try include: *carciofi alla romana,* artichokes stuffed with mint, parsley and garlic, *puntarelle,* a salad of curly Catalonian chicory tossed in a garlic, olive oil and anchovy dressing; and, in spring, freshly shelled *fave* (broad beans) served with a slice of pecorino romano cheese.

If you'd like to know more about Roman and Italian cuisine generally, pick up a copy of Lonely Planet's *World Food Italy.*

Alan Benson

CAMPO DE' FIORI

Take buses 23, 46, 62, 64 or 116, 280 for Campo de' Fiori.

Camponeschi
(4, G8) **$$$$**
ristorante
Position, position, position. A favourite with politicians, diplomats and the glitterati, Camponeschi enjoys one of the prettiest locations in the city. A few French dishes (such as soufflés) complement the creative Mediterranean menu.
✉ Piazza Farnese 50
☎ 06 687 49 27
🚌 see above 🕘 Mon-Sat 8pm-12.30am

Ditirambo (6, E2) **$$**
trattoria
There's a kind of rustic charm about Ditirambo. The food is traditional Italian with a dash of innovation (like tortelli with mint) and a good selection of vegetable-only dishes. The home-made bread and pasta add to its charms.
✉ Piazza della Cancelleria 72 ☎ 06 687 16 26 🚌 see above 🕘 12.30-3.30pm (Tues-Sun), 7.30-11.30pm daily ♿ V

Filetti di Baccalà
(4, G8) **$**
trattoria
Deep-fried baccalà is the main event in this quirky eatery. Paper-wrapped fish fillets are eaten with your fingers – the Romans swear it tastes better that way. Antipasti, salads and desserts are available for those who want more than the fish, the whole fish and nothing but the fish.
✉ Largo dei Librari 88
☎ 06 686 40 18
🚌 see above 🕘 Mon-Sat 5.30-10.30pm

Forno di Campo de' Fiori (6, F2) See p. 88.

Hostaria Giulio
(4, G7) ✱ **$$**
trattoria
Hunt down this good-value family-run place hidden in a quiet laneway off Via Monserrato. Vaulted ceilings top the cosy dining room; in summer ask for a table outdoors. Try the fresh porcini, celery and parmesan salad or the feather-light gnocchi, a home-made speciality.
✉ Via della Barchetta 19 ☎ 06 688 06 466 🚌 see above 🕘 Mon-Sat 12.30-3pm, 7.30pm-midnight ♿ V

Insalata Ricca
(6, E3) **$**
trattoria
Meal-in-themselves salads and (mainly veg-based) pasta dishes are on offer here. Insalata Ricca has become so popular with young Romans that new branches are sprouting up throughout the city.
✉ Largo dei Chiavari 85-86 ☎ 06 688 03 656 🚌 see above 🕘 12-3pm, 7pm-1am ♿ V

Guy Moberly
Farnese fans (see p. 88)

Ristorante Moserrato
(6, F1) **$$**
ristorante
This unassuming corner eatery does marvellous things with seafood and fish. The *spaghetti alle vongole* (with clams) and *risotto con scampi* (with prawns) are among the best in Rome. Shady outdoor tables and a great wine list (excellent north-east Italian whites) encourage long, relaxed summer lunches.
✉ Via Monserrato 96
☎ 06 687 33 86
🚌 see above
🕘 Tues-Sun 12.30-3pm, 7.30-11.30pm
♿ V

Sergio alla Grotta
(2, A4) **$**
trattoria/pizzeria
A menu-free zone – you decide your order by looking at pictures, then enjoy enormous helpings of Roman pasta (cacio e pepe, carbonara, amatriciana etc) and good meat and fish dishes. The pizza oven and grill cater to all tastes.
✉ Via delle Grotte 27
☎ 06 686 42 93
🚌 see above
🕘 Mon-Sat 12.30-3pm, 7.30-11.30pm ♿ V

Thien Kim (2, A3) **$$**
Vietnamese
Although the food here is really an Italian take on Vietnamese cooking, it's all pretty tasty, and lighter and more strongly flavoured than other local Viet options.
✉ Via Giulia 201
☎ 06 683 07 832
🚌 23, 116, 280, J4
🕘 Mon-Sat V

GHETTO & PALATINO

You have your choice of buses to access this area, including: 23, 44, 46, 62, 63, 64, 70, 81, 87, 95, 160, 170, 186, 280, 492, 628, 810, H, J4 or J5.

Benito (2, A6) **$**
tavola calda
Benito serves hungry workers fast. There are two pasta dishes daily, and a range of grilled meats, cheeses, vegetables and salads. Thursday's *gnocchi alla gorgonzola* is great. Be prepared to be shunted on as soon as you finish.
✉ Via dei Falegnami 14 ☎ 06 06 686 15 08 🚍 see above 🕘 Mon-Sat 8am-6pm ♿ V

Da Giggetto (2, B7) **$$$**
trattoria
You *have* to try the deep-fried artichokes at this local institution which has been serving Roman Jewish food for years. If you can, get a table on the footpath next to the ancient portico.
✉ Via del Portico d'Ottavia ☎ 06 686 11 06 🚍 see above 🕘 Tues-Sun 12-3pm, 7.30-11pm ♿ V

La Taverna degli Amici (2, A8) **$$$**
trattoria
With its charming, shaded terrace, this place is a hit with locals (especially Democratici di Sinistra politicians). Lunch service can be slow, but the antipasto, pasta and risotto dishes are worth the wait.
✉ Piazza Margana ☎ 06 699 20 637 🚍 see above 🕘 Tues-Sun 12-3pm, 8-11pm ♿ V

La Taverna del Ghetto (2, B7) **$$$**
kosher Italian
This is one of Rome's few kosher eateries. What the cave-like room lacks in atmosphere, the home-made pasta, grilled meats and fish make up for in taste. The *carciofi alla giudia* are fab. Try the puntarelle salad (laced with garlic and anchovy dressing) – it'll have you breathing fire.
✉ Via Portico d'Ottavia 8 ☎ 06 688 09 771 🚍 see above 🕘 Mon-Thurs & Sat-Sun 12-3pm, 8-11pm ♿

Piperno (2, B6) **$$$$**
ristorante
Deep frying is an art form at this famous eatery. House special is a mixed platter of deep-fried fillets of *baccalà*, stuffed zucchini flowers, veggies and mozzerella cheese. They also do great things with offal. Snag a table in the pretty courtyard.
✉ Via Monte de' Cenci 9 🚍 see above ☎ 06 688 06 629 🕘 Tues-Sat 12-3pm, 7.30-11pm, Sun 12-3pm ♿

St Teodoro (4, J12) **$$$$**
ristorante
One of Rome's best. Roman and Emilia-Romagnan dishes feature and there's a strong emphasis on fish. Pasta (made daily by the owner's mother) with seafood is divine. Save space for *gelatini di frutta* – divine fruit ice creams. The terrace is *the* place to be in summer.
✉ Piazza dei Fienili 49-50 ☎ 06 678 09 33 🚍 see above 🕘 Mon-Sat 12.45-3pm, 8pm-midnight ♿ V

Sally Webb
In the know Margherita

Sora Margherita (2, B6) **$$**
trattoria
So popular is this eatery that there's not even a sign above the door. Don't let the formica table tops put you off: you're here for the food – trad Roman and Jewish fare – and the bargain prices. Get here early to avoid a queue (especially for Thursday's fresh gnocchi).
✉ Piazza delle Cinque Scole 30 ☎ 06 686 40 02 🚍 see above 🕘 Mon-Fri 12-3pm ♿

Vecchia Roma (2, B8) **$$$$**
ristorante
With its pretty terrace Vecchia Roma is a summer delight. The pan-Italian menu is huge and changes seasonally. In summer there are imaginative salads, in winter lots of polenta based dishes, year-round good pasta and risotto.
✉ Piazza Campitelli 18 ☎ 06 686 46 04 🚍 see above 🕘 Thurs-Tues 12-3pm, 8-11pm ♿ V

Zì Fenizia (2, B6)
See p. 88.

PANTHEON

Gelateria della Palma (6, A5) & **Giolitti** (6, A6)
See reviews p. 89.

Mopping Up

Make the most of that rich pasta *sugo* (sauce) or juicy stew. Take a piece of bread and *fare la scarpetta* to mop up the last vestiges of flavour from your plate. After all, when in Rome...

Il Bacaro (4, E9) **$$**
ristorante
Miracles are performed in this tiny kitchen. Pasta and risotto dishes are artful and delicious and great things are done with beef and veal. In summer sit outside under a vine-covered pergola and soak up the vibe of this quiet, charming street. Bookings are essential.
✉ Via degli Spagnoli 27 ☎ 06 686 41 10 🚌 70, 81, 87, 116, 117, 119, 186 🕘 Mon-Sat 12.30-2.30pm, 8-11.45pm V

L'Angoletto (6, B5) **$$$**
ristorante
This eatery has a faithful clientele and trades off its long-standing reputation for good traditional food. If it's warm the terrace is *the* place to be. Try the spaghetti alla vongole (with clams, olive oil, garlic and chilli).
✉ Piazza Rondanini 55 ☎ 06 686 80 19 🚌 70, 81, 87, 116, 186 🕘 Mon-Sat 12.30-2.30pm, 8-11.30pm

La Rosetta (6, B5) **$$$$**
ristorante
The best fish restaurant in Rome? This is it. The menu features innovative combinations – how about shrimp, grapefruit and raspberry salad or fried *moscardini* (baby octopus) with mint? Owner-chef Massimo Riccioli is regarded as one of the best in Italy. Expensive but memorable.
✉ Via Rosetta 8-9 ☎ 06 686 10 02 🚌 70, 81, 87, 116, 186 🕘 Mon-Fri 12-3pm, 8-11.30pm, Sat 8-11.30pm

Oliphant (6, A4) **$$**
Tex-Mex
Rome's first 'Tex-Mex' is still one of its best and great for a meat fix. Go Tex with hot dogs or buffalo wings or Mex with tortillas and enchiladas. A good range of beers makes it a popular hangout.
✉ Via della Coppelle 31 ☎ 06 686 14 16 🚌 116 🕘 7-11.30pm

Osteria dell'Ingegno (6, A7) **$$**
ristorante
The designer decor inside contrasts with the antiquity of the piazza outside. On offer is central Italian cuisine with an international twist: warm goat's ricotta with grilled vegetables or farfalle with leeks and saffron. There's an emphasis on veggies (and some hearty salads) though turkey and Angus beef also feature.
✉ Piazza della Pietra 45 ☎ 06 678 06 62 🚌 62, 81, 85, 116, 117, 119, 160, 492, 628 🕘 Mon-Sat 12-3pm, 7.30pm-midnight V

Quinzi e Gabriele (6, A5) **$$$$**
ristorante
Q&G has cornered the market in simultaneously being plush and groovy, and it's a well-heeled crowd that peoples its tables. Fish and seafood are the main attractions. If it's any indication, many of Rome's top chefs dine here on their nights off.
✉ Via delle Coppelle 6 ☎ 06 687 93 89 🚌 70, 81, 87, 116, 186 🕘 Mon-Sat 8-11.30pm

They don't call it Piazza della Rotonda for nothing.

PIAZZA DI SPAGNA & PIAZZA DEL POPOLO

Al 34 (4, C11) **$$$**
ristorante
Dangerously close to the upmarket Via Condotti shopping area, and *always* busy, Al mixes Roman and regional cooking. Service can be haphazard and brusque – but the punters keep coming. Try rigatoni with pajata if you can stomach it, or linguini with lobster if you can't. Always book.
✉ Via Mario de'Fiori 34 ☎ 06 679 50 91 Ⓜ Spagna ⌚ Tues-Sun 12-3pm, 7-11pm ♿

Antico Forno (6, A10)
See p. 88.

Da Gino (4, D10) **$$**
trattoria
This old-fashioned trattoria is popular with politicians and journalists, especially at lunchtime. Try home-made fettuccine with peas and *guanciale* (cured pork) or rabbit in white wine, and save room for tiramisu. The old family retainer slumped over a table at the entrance isn't dead, he's just asleep.
✉ Vicolo Rosini 4 ☎ 06 687 34 34 🚌 81, 117, 119, 492, 628 ⌚ Mon-Sat 12.30-2.30pm, 7.30-11.30pm ♿

Edy (4, B10) **$$**
ristorante
Residents of upmarket Via del Babuino make up Edy's regular clientele – they know value in an area not known for it. Try house speciality, spaghetti *al cartoccio*, a silver-foil parcel of pasta and seafood. Fettuccine with artichokes is also worth writing home about.
✉ Vicolo del Babuino 4 ☎ 06 360 01 738 Ⓜ Spagna ⌚ Mon-Sat

'Gusto (4, C9) **$$**
pizzeria/ristorante
Warehousey 'Gusto is more New York than Rome. The pizzeria serves Napoli-style pizzas, the restaurant dishes like marinated sea bass and tuna with ginger rice, and eggplant and chickpea strudel in a goat's cheese and sesame-seed sauce. Who said Italian cooks aren't innovative?
✉ Piazza Augusto Imperatore 9 ☎ 06 322 62 73 🚌 81, 117, 119, 492, 628 ⌚ Tues-Sun 12.30-3pm, 7.30pm-1am ♿ (pizzeria) V

Margutta Vegetariana (4, A10) **$$**
vegetarian
Strangely decked out with black '70s-style love couches, this is one of Rome's few completely veg eateries. Stick with versions of Italian staples – pizza and pasta – and you'll eat well. The bland 'vegetarian specialities' will disappoint.
✉ Via Margutta 118 ☎ 06 326 50 577 🚌 117, 119 Ⓜ Spagna ⌚ Mon-Sat 12.30-3pm, 7.30-11pm ♿ V

Naturist Club – L'Isola (4, D11) **$$**
vegetarian
Also known as the Centro Macrobiotico Italiano, this eatery has a double life: at lunch it's a semi-self-service eatery dishing out veggie pies and wholegrain risottos; by night it's à la carte dining with fish as the speciality.
✉ 4th fl, Via delle Vite 14 ☎ 06 679 25 09 Ⓜ Spagna ⌚ Mon-Sat 12.30-2.45pm, 7.30-10.30pm V

Osteria Margutta (4, B11) **$$$**
trattoria
The artsy decor fits in well with the neighbouring antiques shops and artists' studios nearby. There's a good selection of veg antipasto and pasta with tasty sauces such as broccoli and sausage.
✉ Via Margutta 82 ☎ 06 323 10 25 Ⓜ Spagna ⌚ Mon-Sat 12-3pm, 7-11pm V

Otello alla Concordia (4, C11) **$$**
trattoria
The faithful following of local artisans and shopkeepers keeps Otello away from the tourist trap tag. Cannelloni and *pollo alla romana* (chicken with capsicum) are some of the dishes that they do well. A glassed-in courtyard makes an attractive winter garden – check out the fountain of fruit created daily.
✉ Villa della Croce 81 ☎ 06 679 11 78 Ⓜ Spagna ⌚ Mon-Sat 12.30-3pm, 7.30-11pm ♿ V

Pizzeria Il Leoncino (4, D10) **$**
pizzeria
It's cheap, it's hectic, it's not full of tourists, and best of all it serves up delicious, thin-crusted pizzas and it does it fast. A *centro storico* institution. Bring cash – no cards accepted.
✉ Via del Leoncino 28 ☎ 06 687 63 06 🚌 81, 117, 119, 492, 628 ⌚ Thurs-Tues ♿ V

San Crispino (4, E12)
See Sweet Treats p. 89.

Sogo Asahi
(4, D11) **$$$**
Japanese
The authentic flavours of classical Japanese food are alive and well here. A separate sushi bar, teppanyaki room and sakura (with tatami mats) preserve the ritual of Japanese dining. Tasting menus are excellent value, and sushi lovers shouldn't miss the Saturday evening buffet.
✉ **Via di Propaganda 22** ☎ **06 678 60 93** Ⓜ **Spagna** 🕘 **Mon-Sat 12.30-3pm, 7.30-11.30pm** ♿ **V**

Caffe Greco, a fave of Liszt, Wagner, Bizet, Casanova and others, is one of Rome's great cafes (see p. 88 for more).

PIAZZA NAVONA

Albistrò (4, F7) **$$**
international
If your tastebuds need a break, Albistrò is a nice alternative to Roman cuisine. The Swiss owner blends her heritage with regional Italian and oriental dishes with excellent results. The pretty interior features a tiny open courtyard. Reservations are essential on weekends.
✉ **Via dei Banchi Vecchi 140a** ☎ **06 686 52 74** 🚌 **46, 62, 64** 🕘 **Thurs-Tues 7.30-11.30pm** **V**

Il Primoli (6, E8) **$$**
ristorante
With its deep banquettes, designer lighting and minimalist white walls, Il Primoli wouldn't look out of place in London or Melbourne. But the food is definitely Italian – with pasta choices ranging from traditional to innovative and veal, lamb and beef featuring among the mains. The over solicitous staff is a drawback.
✉ **Via dei Soldati 22-23** ☎ **06 681 35 112** 🚌 **70, 81, 87, 116, 186, 492, 628** 🕘 **Mon-Sat 8-11.30pm** **V**

L'Orso 80 (6, F6) **$$**
trattoria
Nowhere does antipasto better than Orso. Bowls of it – vegetables, seafood, meat – just keep coming until you groan *'basta!'* (stop). The *primi* are not great but the char-grilled meats or wood-fired pizza are excellent. Foreigners love this place – just look at the signed photos on the walls: Tom & Nicole (in happier times), Brad Pitt and others.
✉ **Via dell'Orso 33** ☎ **06 686 49 04** 🚌 **70, 81, 87, 116, 186, 492, 628** 🕘 **Tues-Sun 12.30-3pm, 7.30-12.30pm** ♿ **V**

Osteria Bassetti
(6,C1) **$**
osteria
This tiny place doesn't have a name but it's made a big name for itself as one of Rome's best cheap eats. It doesn't have a menu either – you take your pick from the list the owner rattles off. A step back in time to the days when it was as cheap to eat out as eat in.
✉ **Via del Governo Vecchio 18** 🚌 **40, 46, 62, 64 , J5** 🕘 **Mon-Sat 7.30-11.30pm** ♿

Paladini (6, C1)
See p. 88.

Pizzeria da Baffetto
(6, D1) **$**
pizzeria
Baffetto's large pizzas would feed an army (or at least one hungry soldier) and deserve their reputation as among the best (and best value) in Rome. Expect to queue if you arrive after 9pm (expect to share a table). Sit downstairs to see the *pizzaiolo* at work.
✉ **Via del Governo Vecchio 11** ☎ **06 686 16 17** 🚌 **46, 62, 64, J5** 🕘 **7pm-1am** ♿ **V**

Quinto Bottega del Gelato (6, B2) & **Tre Scalini** (6, B3)
See reviews p. 89.

MONTI, ESQUILINO & CELIO

Agata e Romeo
(5, G2) **$$$$**
ristorante
This intimate and elegant eatery is the benchmark for Roman fine dining. Chef Agata Parisella serves innovative food combining the traditional and the unexpected. Try *raviolini* stuffed with eggplant in a goat's cheese sauce, or an aged pecorino tart with fig and honey sauce. Desserts, especially the legendary *millefoglie* (small puff pastry sheets filled with jam and cream), are exquisite.
✉ Via Carlo Alberto 45 ☎ 06 446 61 15 🚌 16, 70, 71, 75, 590 Ⓜ Vittorio Emanuele 🕘 Mon-Sat 1-3pm, 7.30-11pm

Al Giubileo (4, F14) **$**
pizzeria
Waiters dash around this high energy joint punching orders into computer handsets, pizza is piled onto wooden slabs and hungry punters dig in. Neapolitan pizza comes to Rome with Al Giubileo's *pizza verace* (real pizza), although the thin-crust Roman variety is also available. Don't fancy pizza? There's plenty of other stuff on the menu – melt-in-your-mouth *gnocchi alla sorrentina* (with tomato and mozzarella) for one.
✉ Via del Boschetto 44 ☎ 06 481 88 79 e www.algiubileo.com 🚌 64, 70, 71, 170 🕘 Tues-Sun 7.30-11.30pm 🚼 V

Baires (4, H13) **$$**
Argentinian
Baires is fun, funky and not at all Italian. Rome's first Argentinian eatery has taken the city by storm, serving up steaks as big as Sardinia, meat any which way and flavoursome soups based on legumes and pulses. Knock it all back with the excellent organic house wine. A good place for a rowdy, hungry group.
✉ Via Cavour 315 ☎ 06 692 02 164 e www.baires.it Ⓜ Cavour, Colosseo 🕘 12-3pm, 7.30pm-1am 🚼 V

Il Guru (4, G14) **$$**
Indian
Gurus in the know and those who just want a good meal make the pilgrimage here. On offer: tandooris, curries (of every strength) and great veggie choices. The decor will transport you eastwards and the friendly owner will steer you clear of too-hot-to-handle curries.
✉ Via del Cimarra 4-6 ☎ 06 474 41 10 🚌 64, 70, 117, 170 Ⓜ Cavour 🕘 7.30pm-midnight 🚼 V

Mexico al 104
(4, G15) **$$**
Mexican
It's hardly Acapulco but it's the closest you'll get in the centre of Rome. Tuck into tacos, burritos, chimichanga, flautas, tamales or enchiladas. There's not too much Mexican in the decor but the full gamut of Mexican flavour is on offer here in a L29,000/€14.39 set menu.
✉ Via Urbana 104 ☎ 06 474 27 72 🚌 75, 84, 117 Ⓜ Cavour 🕘 Tues-Sun 12-3pm, 7.30-11pm 🚼 V

Osteria Gli Angeletti
(4, G14) **$$**
trattoria
Consistently good food and outdoor seating on atmospheric Piazza Madonna dei Monti make this a fine choice. Service can get a bit slow when they're busy, but the prices are reasonable. It caters well to both carnivores and vegetarians, with a cluster of fail-safe pasta dishes to satisfy the fussiest of eaters.
✉ Via dell'Angeletto 3 ☎ 06 474 33 74 🚌 75, 84, 117 Ⓜ Cavour, Colosseo 🕘 12-3pm, 7.30pm-1am; closed in Dec 🚼 V

Pasqualino (4, K15) **$$**
trattoria
Reliable food at honest prices is the trademark of this down-to-earth local place. Grilled fish is usually good, the calf's liver a speciality and the pasta with seafood in a creamy tomato sauce excellent. Grab an outdoor table for a glimpse of the Colosseum.
✉ Via dei Santi Quattro 66 ☎ 06 700 45 76 🚌 75, 85, 87, 117, 175, 810, 850 Ⓜ Colosseo 🚋 3, 8 🕘 Tues-Sun 12.30-3pm, 7.30-11pm 🚼

Shawerma (4, K15) **$**
Egyptian
Half pub, half informal eatery, Shawerma serves Egyptian-style comfort food to soak up the lagers – all within a stone's throw of the Colosseum. House specialities are vegetable couscous, vegetable tajine, kebabs, tabouli and felafels. Friday and Saturday are belly-dancing nights.
✉ Via Ostilia 24 ☎ 06 700 81 01 🚌 81, 85, 87, 117, 186, J4, J5 Ⓜ Colosseo 🚋 3 🕘 Tues-Sun V

TRASTEVERE

For Trastevere, take buses 23, 44, 75, 280, 630 or H, or tram 8.

Akropolis (4, K8) **$**
Greek
Classic Greek dishes – moussaka, dolmades, tzatziki, taramasalata, Greek salad – are served here to eat in or take away, plus those sweet, sticky cakes for which the Greeks are deservedly famous.
✉ Via San Francesco a Ripa 103 ☎ 06 582 22 600 🚌 🚊 see above 🕘 Tues-Sun, 7-11pm (to midnight Sat) ♿ V

Alberto Ciarla (4, K7) **$$$$**
ristorante
Ciarla knows its top-quality fish and seafood. The decor is 30 years out of date, but so what, you're meant to be concentrating on the food: platters of raw, smoked and marinated fish, herb-scented *spigola* (sea bass), or *mazzancolle al coccio* (king prawn terrine).
✉ Piazza San Cosimato 40 ☎ 06 581 86 68 🚌 🚊 see above 🕘 7.30-11.30pm

ATM Sushi Bar (4, H6) **$$**
Japanese
The quiet Trastevere backstreets is an odd place to find a Japanese eatery, especially one this good. Chill out amid the minimalist decor, soft lighting and relaxed music and chow down on excellent sushi, sashimi, nori rolls, tempura and other Japanese classics.
✉ Via della Penitenza 7 ☎ 06 683 07 0053 🚌 23, 280 🕘 Tues-Sun 7.30-11pm V

Bar San Calisto (2, E3) See p. 89.

Casetta di Trastevere (2, D3) **$$**
trattoria
There's nothing fancy about this local tratt – except that it always seems to be serving just what you fancy, like steaming bowls of *pasta e fagioli* (thick borlotti bean soup) or piquant mounds of penne amatriciana. When it's warm the outdoor tables cram up and service slows.
✉ Piazza de'Renzi 31a ☎ 06 580 01 58 🚌 🚊 see above 🕘 Mon-Sat noon-3.30pm, 7.30-11pm ♿

Da Augusto (2, D3) **$**
trattoria
One of Trastevere's favourite mamma's kitchen dishes up honest fare at prices you only read about. Enjoy home-made fettuccine or *stracciatella* (clear broth with egg and parmesan) at rickety tables that spill out onto the piazza in summer.
✉ Piazza de'Renzi 15 ☎ 06 580 37 98 🚌 🚊 see above 🕘 usually Mon-Sat 12.30-3pm, 8-11.30pm ♿

Da Lucia (2, D1) **$**
trattoria
Once upon a time Roman trattorias were all like this. As well as fab antipasto and pasta, there are Roman specialities: *pollo con peperoni* (chicken with peppers) and *trippa all romana* (tripe with ragù or tomato sauce). Sit outside under the neighbours' washing in summer.
✉ Vicolo del Mattinato 2 ☎ 06 580 36 01 🚌 🚊 see above 🕘 Tues-Sun 12.30-3.30pm, 7.30-11pm ♿

Ferrara (2, C3) **$$$**
ristorante
This former *enoteca* (wine seller), decorated with whitewashed walls and old casks, is a compulsory stop on any foodie itinerary for dishes like *orecchiette* (shell pasta) with zucchini and ginger-scented prawns or warm rabbit salad with spicy couscous. Expert advice is on tap for choosing wine from the encyclopedic lists. Book a courtyard table.
✉ Via del Moro 1a ☎ 06 580 37 69 🚌 🚊 see above 🕘 Mon & Wed-Sat 8pm-midnight, Sun 1-3.30pm, 8pm-midnight V

Fonte della Salute (2, E4) & **Forno la Renella** (2, C3) See reviews pp. 88-9.

La Botticella (2, D2) **$$**
trattoria
Could this be Rome's best spaghetti amatriciana? While you're testing the theory, go *romana* with tripe, oxtail or lamb, or *fritto alla botticella* – a tempura-like dish of deep-fried

Watch for drips as you dine.

vegetables and apple slices. In summer, eat outside beneath the neighbours' washing, and listen in on their arguments as well.
✉ **Vicolo del Leopardo 39a ☎ 06 581 47 38 🚌 🚋 see above 🕘 Wed-Mon 12.30-3.30pm 🚼**

La Tana di Noantri (2, D2) **$$**
trattoria/pizzeria
A great position, extensive menu, good food and professional staff make this local institution a year-round hit. It's cosy and welcoming in winter, and in the warmer months outdoor shaded tables make an excellent spot to watch the passing parade. Kids can tuck into a pizza while parents enjoy more sophisticated fare.
✉ **Via Paglia 1 ☎ 06 580 64 04 🚌 🚋 see above 🕘 Wed-Mon 12.30-3pm, 7.30-11.30pm 🚼 V**

Panattoni (2, E5) **$**
pizzeria
Eating at a place dubbed *l'obitorio* (the morgue) might put some people off, but those in the know (and there are many) take the ice-cold marble tables in their stride and tuck into top notch pizza. The simple, thin-crusted Margherita is to die for – though it's probably not wise to expire here!
✉ **Viale di Trastevere 53 ☎ 06 580 09 19 🚌 🚋 see above 🕘 Thurs-Tues 7pm-2am 🚼 V**

Paris (2, E3) **$$$**
ristorante
Outside the Ghetto, old-fashioned Paris is the best place for true Roman Jewish cuisine: try *fritto misto con baccalà* (deep-fried vegetables and salt cod), *pasta e ceci* (thick chickpea soup) or fresh grilled fish. Dine on the piazza for added romance.
✉ **Piazza San Calisto 7 ☎ 06 581 53 78 🚌 🚋 see above 🕘 Tues-Sat 12-3pm, 8-11.30pm, Sun 12-3pm**

Pizzeria Ivo (4, K7) **$**
pizzeria
Ivo is all class: the cheap wood-panelled walls are plastered with photos of victorious soccer teams and TV stars, the house wine could double as diesel fuel and you could get asphyxiated at its outdoor tables. Despite all that it's always packed and the pizzas, though small, are really tasty.
✉ **Via San Francesco a Ripa 158 ☎ 06 581 70 82 🚌 🚋 see above 🕘 Wed-Mon 7.30pm-1am 🚼 V**

Pizzeria Popi-Popi (4, K8) **$**
pizzeria
It's hardly surprising that Popi-Popi is a popular haunt for Rome's youth – its pizzas are good, big and cheap. Dodge those garlands of garlic inside. The outdoor tables that spill into the piazza opposite are a big attraction in summer.
✉ **Via delle Fratte di Trastevere 45 ☎ 06 589 51 67 🚌 🚋 see above 🕘 Fri-Wed 7.30pm-1am 🚼 V**

Pizzeria San Calisto (2, E3) **$**
pizzeria
Big is beautiful at San Calisto, and these pizzas are so large they fall off your plate. Dine at one of the outdoor tables in summer and watch the passing parade. The muralled front dining area is also pleasant, but avoid the basement.
✉ **Piazza di San Calisto 9a ☎ 06 581 82 56 🚌 🚋 see above 🕘 Tues-Sun 7.30pm-1am 🚼 V**

Other Eats

Fed up with pasta? Pizza'd out? Rome's not strong on ethnic eats, with a few exceptions:

ATM Sushi Bar (p. 84)
Sogo Asahi (p. 82)
Thien Kim (p. 78)
Baires (p. 83)
Surya Mahal (p. 85)
Mexico al 104 (p. 83)
Il Guru (p. 83)

Ripa 12 (3, H4) **$$$**
ristorante
This Calabrian family restaurant serves original pasta, fish and seafood dishes and is credited by some with having invented *carpaccio di spigola* (very fine slices of raw sea bass). There are some tables on the street, but unless you want your fish smoked by traffic fumes, sit inside.
✉ **Via San Francesco a Ripa 12 ☎ 06 580 90 93 🚌 🚋 see above 🕘 Closed Sun 🚼**

Surya Mahal (4, K7) **$$$**
Indian
For those who appreciate aesthetics as well as culinary expertise, this top-notch restaurant has a delightful garden terrace beside the fountain on Piazza Trilussa. Set menus – vegetarian, meat or fish – provide an opportunity to try it all.
✉ **Piazza Trilussa 50 ☎ 06 589 45 54 🚌 🚋 see above 🕘 Mon-Sat 7.30-11.30pm V**

PRATI

Da Cesare (4, C7) **$$**
ristorante
Wood panelling and sombre fabrics gives this restaurant a clubby feel. Young and groovy it ain't, but it's popular with foodies in autumn and winter, when the menu offers game, truffles, porcini mushrooms and wonderful soups made from lentils, chickpeas, borlotti and cannellini beans. Good for a post-Vatican lunch.
✉ Via Cresenzio 13 ☎ 06 686 12 27 🚌 49, 70, 87, 280, 492, 913 ⏱ Tues-Sat 12.30-3pm, 7.30-11pm, Sun 12.30-3pm 🚸 V

Il Simposio (4, C7) **$$$**
enoteca
What was once a simple enoteca eatery (attached to Costantini, one of Rome's best-known winesellers) has metamorphosed into a top restaurant, with a menu as impressive as the enoteca's Art Nouveau vine decoration and magnificent cellar area.
✉ Piazza Cavour 16 ☎ 06 321 15 02 🚌 49, 70, 87, 280, 492, 913 ⏱ Mon-Fri 12-3pm, 8-11pm, Sat 8-11pm

Osteria dell'Angelo (4, A3) **$$**
trattoria
In an area not renowned for culinary choices, seats at these basic wooden tables fill up fast. Locals return time and again for tripe, braised oxtail, or bowls of *picchiapò*, a meaty stew with not a lot of meat in it. The *tonnarelli cacio e pepe* is legendary.
✉ Via G Bettolo 24 ☎ 06 372 97 40 🚌 23, 70, 913, 990 Ⓜ Ottaviano ⏱ Mon-Wed, Fri & Sat 7.30-11pm, Tues & Fri 12.30-2.30pm 🚸 V

QUIRINALE

Colline Emiliane (4, D13) **$$**
trattoria
This homely tratt brings the rich cuisine of Emilia-Romagna to Rome. Home-made pasta parcels stuffed with pumpkin and the slow-cooked veal with mashed potatoes are specialities, best washed down with a good Emilian wine. Definitely a wintry type of place.
✉ Via degli Avignonesi 22 ☎ 06 481 75 38 Ⓜ Barberini ⏱ Sat-Thurs 12.45-2.45pm, 7.45-10.45pm 🚸

Da Ricci (4, F14) **$**
pizzeria
Reputed to be Rome's oldest pizzeria, Da Ricci began life as a wine shop in 1905 and has been run by the same family ever since. Pizzas here have thicker crusts than the Roman norm, and some say it's the best in town. Good salads and home-made desserts too.
✉ Via Genova 32 ☎ 06 488 11 07 🚌 64, 70, 71, 170 Ⓜ Repubblica ⏱ Tues-Sun 7.30-11.30pm 🚸 V

Tullio (4, C14) **$$$**
ristorante
A little piece of Tuscany in the heart of Rome. Start with tasty paté-smeared crostini, warm up with hearty *ribollita* bean soup, tuck into the classic char-grilled *fiorentina* (thick T-bone steak) or a herby ossobuco and dunk *tozzetti* (almond biscuits) in a glass of *vin santo* (dessert wine) to round if off.
✉ Via San Nicola da Tolentino 26 ☎ 06 474 55 60 Ⓜ Barberini ⏱ Mon-Sat 12.30-2.30pm, 7.30-11pm

In Vino Veritas

Wine buffs would argue that the Lazio region is the poor relation as far as Italian wine production is concerned, although some good white wines – notably Frascati Superiore – are produced in the Castelli Romani area (south-east of the city). You can taste local and not-so-local wine in Rome's *enoteche* (wine shops). Most mid-range trattorias stock only a limited selection of bottled wines, as customers often order the house wine *(vino della casa)* or the local wine *(vino locale)*.

Alan Benson

TESTACCIO

Take buses 23, 75, 95, 170, 280, 716 or 781, or tram 3 or 8 for these eateries.

Augustarello (3, J4) **$$**
trattoria
If sweetbreads and oxtail aren't your thing, then stay away, as this is the food that they do best. Virtually every dish (other than pasta) in this old-fashioned tratt has some visceral connection.
✉ **Via G Branca 98** ☎ **06 574 65 85** 🚌 🚊 **see above** 🕐 **Mon-Sat 12-3.30pm, 7.30-11.30pm**

Cecchino dal 1887 (3, J4) **$$$**
ristorante
Family-run Cecchino provides constant fodder for travel magazines seeking the best places for traditional Roman dining. Its location near the former abbatoir (now a social centre) is appropriate, given that offal – from calf's head to pig's trotters and sweetbreads – is its trademark. The great wine cellar is a bonus.
✉ **Via di Monte Testaccio 30** ☎ **06 574 63 18** 🚌 🚊 **see above** 🕐 **Tues-Sat 12-3pm, 8-11.30pm**

Da Felice (3, H4) **$**
trattoria
Shoppers and stallholders from the nearby Testaccio market frequent this popular local institution, especially for lunch. Ask nicely for a table as the proprietor will only let you sit down if he likes the look of you. If you pass muster, you'll enjoy true Roman fare for a bargain price. Definitely try the spaghetti al cacio e pepe.
✉ **Via Mastro Giorgio 29** ☎ **06 574 68 00** 🚌 🚊 **see above** 🕐 **Mon-Sat 12.30-3pm, 8-10.30pm** 🚼

Remo (3, J4) **$**
pizzeria
Remo's thin-crusted pizzas vie for our vote as the best in Rome. You won't find a noisier, more popular pizzeria than this – think of the obligatory queues as part of the local colour. Make your order by checking the appropriate box on a slip of paper, and ensure it includes some *supplì*.
✉ **Piazza Santa Maria Liberatrice 44** ☎ **06 574 62 70** 🚌 🚊 **see above** 🕐 **Mon-Sat 7.30pm-1am** 🚼 **V**

Trattoria da Bucatino (3, H3) **$**
trattoria
There's nothing fancy about this popular neighbourhood eatery, decorated with the ubiquitous garlands of garlic and empty chianti bottles. The large antipasto buffet is excellent, and there's a good variety of pasta and meat mains. Save room for the desserts which exceed normal tratt standards.
✉ **Via Luca della Robbia 84** ☎ **06 574 68 86** 🚌 🚊 **see above** 🕐 **Tues-Sun 12.30-3.30pm, 8-11.30pm** 🚼 **V**

WORTH A TRIP

Antico Arco (4, K4) **$$$**
ristorante
Gourmets-in-the-know tip this as the next big hit. Tradition meets innovation here: cacio e pepe with zucchini flowers; tagliatelle with guinea fowl ragù, tomato and rosemary. Veal cutlets with pear is an enticing main, and ricotta cheese timbale with chocolate and orange a divine dessert.
✉ **Piazzale Aurelio 7, Gianicolo** ☎ **06 581 52 74** 🚌 **710, 870** 🕐 **Mon-Sat 7.30-11.30pm, Sun 12.30-3pm**

Cacio e Pepe (3, D3) **$**
trattoria
You won't find better home-made pasta in the entire city than at this hole in the wall. Spaghetti carbonara and namesake cacio e pepe are sublime. In summer, tables spill onto the street, and in winter hungry Romans will sit outside, wrapped in overcoats and scarves, rather than have to wait for a table indoors.
✉ **Via Avezzana 11, Prati** ☎ **06 321 72 68** 🚌 **186, 280** 🕐 **Mon-Sat 7.30-11.30pm** 🚼

La Pergola (3, C1) **$$$$**
ristorante
As far as international haute cuisine is concerned La Pergola's had the awards wrapped up for years. If you like silver lids on your food, side-tables for your handbags and faultless service then La Pergola's for you. The food really is incredible, and the view is alone worth the short trip.
✉ **Cavalieri Hilton Hotel, Via A Caldolo 101, Balduina** ☎ **06 35 091** 🚕 **take a taxi** 🕐 **Tues-Sat 7.30-11.30pm** **V**

ON THE RUN

Antico Forno (6, A10) **$**
pizza a taglio
Your wishes won't necessarily come true by throwing a coin into the Trevi Fountain but a few coins spent in this famous bakery opposite will assure you of a delicious slice of pizza or a hearty filled panino.
✉ **Via delle Muratte 8**
☎ **06 679 28 66**
🚌 **23, 280, 630**
🕘 **9am-9pm** ♿ **V**

Sally Webb
Motoring in from all over.

Forno di Campo de' Fiori (6, F2) **$**
pizza a taglio
People come from all over Rome for the *pizza bianca* here. Drizzled with extra virgin olive oil and sprinkled with crunchy grains of sea salt, it proves the maxim that less is more. The *pizza rossa* with a thin layer of tomato paste is just as good. Buy it by the metre.
✉ **Campo de' Fiori 22**
☎ **06 688 06 662**
🚌 **46, 62, 64, 116**
🕘 **Mon-Wed, Fri & Sat 7am-1.30pm, 5.30-8pm, Thurs 7am-1.30pm** ♿ **V**

Forno la Renella (2, C3) **$**
pizza a taglio
This bakery has been producing Rome's best bread for decades. As the embers die down in the wood-fired ovens, the bakers turn their hand to slabs of thick, doughy pizza with toppings like tomato, olives and oregano, or potato and rosemary. Pizza by the slice – worth crossing rivers for.
✉ **Via del Moro 15-16**
☎ **06 581 72 65**
🚌 **23, 280, 630, H**
🕘 **9am-9pm** ♿ **V**

Paladini (6, C1) **$**
sandwiches
The staff are glum, there's nowhere to sit and you can wait for ages to be served, but the continuous mass of customers affirms its position as Rome's best sandwich shop. Fill your piping-hot pizza bianca with cured meats, cheese, artichokes and more.
✉ **Via del Governo Vecchio 29**
☎ **06 688 06 662**
🚌 **46, 62, 64, 116, J5**
🕘 **Mon-Wed, Fri & Sat 7am-1.30pm, 5.30-8pm, Thurs 7am-1.30pm**
♿ **V**

Zì Fenizia (2, B6) **$**
pizza a taglio
Better known as the kosher pizzeria (Rome's one and only) Zì Fenizia makes, arguably, the city's best pizza by the slice. There's no cheese on this kosher variety but you don't miss it. The toppings are not the usual suspects either.
✉ **Via Santa Maria del Pianto 64** 🚌 **23, 46, 62, 63, 64, 70, 81 87, 186, 280, 492, 628, 810, H, J4, J5** 🚊 **8** 🕘 **Sun-Thurs 8am-8pm, Fri 8am-3pm, closed Jewish holidays** ♿ **V**

Café Crawl

Pick your bar or cafe to suit your mood. Fabulous coffee? Try **Sant'Eustachio** or **Camilloni**, both in Piazza Sant'Eustachio (6, C4). Picturesque outlook? Take a seat at **Bar Marzio** (2, D3; Piazza Santa Maria) or Piazza Farnese's **Caffè Farnese** (6, F2). A bit of literary history? Head for Keats, Byron and Goethe's favourite haunt **Caffè Greco** (4, C11), Via Condotti 86 (p. 82). Communism with your Coffee? **Vezio's** bar (2, A8; Via dei Delfini; at right) is the watering hole for *compagni* from the nearby Democratici di Sinistra party HQ. Start talking politics or football with owner Vezio Bagazzini (as much a local legend as the bar itself), and you'll be there a while.

Sally Webb

SWEET TREATS

Roman diners will often leg it to the nearest *gelateria* after dinner.

Bar San Calisto (2, E3) **$**
bar/gelateria
There's nothing fancy about this local bar but this author's ongoing research suggests that the chocolate gelato – soft and creamy and almost like a mousse – is the best in town. The coffee flavour's not bad either.
✉ Piazza San Calisto ☎ 06 583 58 69 🚌 75, 630, H 🕘 Mon-Sat 6am-1.30am ♿

Fonte della Salute (2, E5) **$**
gelateria
Whether this place really is a fountain of health (as its name translates) is debatable, although the soy and yoghurt-based gelati support the theory. Fruit flavours are superb and the *marron glacé* so delicious that it *has* to be good for you. Scoops are more generous than more central places.
✉ Via Cardinal Marmaggi 2-6 ☎ 06 589 74 71 🚌 23, 75, 280, 630, H 🕘 10am-1.30am (to 2am Fri-Sat) ♿

Gelateria della Palma (6, A5) **$**
gelateria
You could be forgiven for thinking you'd stumbled into Willy Wonka's factory here, and choosing from the 100 flavours is tough. House specialities are extra creamy (and rich) mousse gelati and the *meringata* varieties with bits of meringue throughout.
✉ Via della Maddalena 20-23 ☎ 06 688 067 52 🚌 70, 81, 87, 116, 492, 628 🕘 8am-1am ♿

Giolitti (4, E9) **$**
gelateria
Giolitti still trades off its reputation as Rome's best gelateria, and at one time it regularly delivered tubs of Pope John Paul II's fave, *marrons glacé*, to his summer residence. The 70-odd flavours on offer will satisfy less pious sweet tooths.
✉ Via degli Uffici del Vicario 40 ☎ 06 699 12 43 🚌 70, 81, 87, 116, 492, 628 🕘 7am-2am ♿

Quinto Bottega del Gelato (6, B2) **$**
gelateria
Milkshakes, smoothies and fruit salad complement the many flavours of gelato available here at this 'ice-cream boutique', a stone's throw from Piazza Navona.
✉ Via di Tor Millina 15 ☎ 06 686 56 57 🚌 70, 81, 87, 116, 492, 628 🕘 12.30pm-2.30am ♿

San Crispino (4, E12) **$**
gelateria
They say you've never tasted real gelato until you've been to San Crispino. Fruit flavoured sorbets change according to season but it's the cream-based flavours – ginger, whisky and pistacchio to name a few – that are the real winners. The cinnamon is divine.
✉ Via della Panetteria 42 ☎ 06 679 39 24 Ⓜ Barberini 🕘 noon-12.30am (to 1.30am Fri-Sat) ♿

Martin Moos
Sweet old lady

Tre Scalini (6, B3) **$**
gelateria
You can't walk through Piazza Navona and not stop for a *tartufo* here. It's a rich ball of chocolate gelato, filled with huge chunks of pure chocolate, squashed flat and served with mountains of whipped cream. Bernini's achievements in the piazza fade into insignificance in comparison!
✉ Piazza Navona 30 ☎ 06 688 01 996 🚌 70, 81, 87, 116, 492, 628 🕘 Thurs-Tues 8am-1.30am ♿

Or Perhaps a Pastry?

Gelato ain't enough? Try the wares at one of these:

Bella Napoli (4, F7) Corso Vittorio Emanuele 246
Bernasconi (4, H9) Piazza B Cairoli 16
La Dolceroma (2, B7) Via del Portico d'Ottavia 20
Forno del Ghetto (2, B6) Via del Portico d'Ottavia 2
Ruschena (4, C8) Lungotevere Mellini 1
Sacchetti (4, K7) Piazza San Cosimato 61

entertainment

You don't have to look far to be entertained in Rome. Whether it's opera or soccer, dance or drinking, the Eternal City has something for everyone. Most of the activity is in the historic centre *(centro storico)*. Campo de' Fiori is especially popular with younger crowds, while the alleyways near Piazza Navona hide some interesting late-night hangouts. Trastevere, Monti and the Esquiline are also full of bars, pubs and gay venues.

The pub and bar scene isn't huge – basically because Romans (and Italians in general) don't consume a lot of alcohol. However the past few years have seen dozens of new 'theme' pubs set up, which cater to the growing numbers of young travellers and students. The clubbing scene is less active in Rome than in other European capitals. Still, there's something for all tastes, with some clubs retaining a certain sophisticated glamour and others priding themselves on being the latest in hip and groovy.

Rome comes alive in summer with the many festivals of dance, music, opera, theatre and cinema. Many of these performances take place under the stars, in parks, gardens and church courtyards, with classical ruins and Renaissance villas as the backdrop. Catch one of these productions and it will undoubtedly be the highlight of your trip. Autumn is also full of cultural activity with specialised festivals dedicated to dance, drama and jazz.

And if you tire of all of the above, follow the lead of the Roman youth who have made doing nothing into an art form.

Festival Hotlines

It's hard to keep track of all the festivals in Rome. Venues vary – check the daily or listings press – or contact the organisers, some of whom include:

- Concerti a Villa Giulia ☎ 06 68 80 10 44
- Cosmphonies ☎ 06 373 52 205
- Invito alla Danza ☎ 06 44 29 23 23
- Isola del Cinema ☎ 06 583 31 13
- New Operafestival ☎ 06 561 15 19
- Notti di Cinema a Piazza Vittorio ☎ 06 445 12 08
- OperaEstate ☎ 06 86 80 01 25
- Roma incontra il mondo ☎ 06 418 03 69
- Roma Jazz Festival ☎ 06 54 39 63 61
- Teatro dell'Opera Summer Season ☎ 06 48 16 01
- Villa Celimontana Jazz ☎ 06 589 78 07

Sally Webb

What's On

Roma C'è is the most comprehensive entertainment guide and has a small section in English. It is published every Thursday. *Wanted in Rome,* published on alternate Wednesdays, contains listings and reviews of the most important festivals, exhibitions, dance, classical music, opera and cinema. Both magazines are available from newsstands. The daily newspapers *Il Messaggero* and *La Repubblica* have listings of theatre, cinema and special events.

Special Events

January/February *Carnevale* – children in fancy dress parade the streets and greedy adults eat *bigné* and *fritelle* pastries

March/April *Festa della Primavera* – Spanish Steps are filled with azaleas making for a perfect photo opportunity

April *Natale di Roma* – 21 April; the Eternal City celebrates her birthday (she was 2754 in 2001); bands and standard bearers perform in Piazza del Campidoglio

May *Primo Maggio* – 1 May; Rock concert in Piazza di Porta di San Giovanni
Italian Open – tennis at the Foro Italico
Via dei Coronari Mostra-Mercato – antiques fair (mid-end May)

June *Cosmphonies* – until early July; season of theatre, music and dance in the Roman theatre at Ostia Antica
Accademia Nazionale di Santa Cecilia – concert series in Villa Giulia gardens
Estate Romana – until Sept; dozens of events, supported and promoted by the city authorities, come under this festival
Villa Celimontana Jazz – until September; Rome's most atmospheric jazz festival, under the stars in grounds of the Renaissance Villa Celimontana
San Pietro e San Paolo – 29 June; religious celebrations and processions for Rome's patron saints Peter & Paul; the city gets a public holiday

July *OperaEstate* – opera concerts and recitals in at Sant'Ivo alla Sapienza
Festa di Noantri – mid-end July; Trastevere's residents celebrate over local wine and *porchetta* (roasted suckling pig cooked on the spit)
Rome Pride – festival celebrating gay rights and culture
Isola del Cinema – until mid-Aug; international film festival
Massenzio – until August; screen under the stars on the Celian hill (opposite the Colosseum); one of Rome's most popular festivals for decades
Teatro dell'Opera Summer Season – until early Aug; opera house (orchestra, singers and ballet dancers) goes to the football stadium

August *Ferragosto* – 15 August; everything shuts down, and the only thing you can eat in the few places still open is *pollo con peperoni*
Notti di Cinema a Piazza Vittorio – until early Sept; open air cinema in the most multicultural part of town

September *Venezia a Roma* – films screened at the Venice Film Festival get a quick pre-release showing in Rome
Via dell'Orso Craft Fair – artisans in and around this charming street near Piazza Navona open their studios and workshops

October/November *ETI*: *Percorsi Internazionali* – theatre festival
Romaeuropa Festival – city's most with-it festival of theatre, dance and opera
Roma Jazz Festival – top jazz performers come to Rome to do their thing
Via dei Coronari Mostra-Mercato – antiques fair

December *Piazza Navona Christmas Fair* – early Dec-6 Jan; gaudy stalls and kitsch souvenirs get tackier each year but they keep coming back
Presepi time – churches around Rome set up their nativity scenes

BARS & PUBS

You've really got three options here: Italian style bar/cafe (where all ages are welcome), wine bars (*enoteche*) or pubs (*birrerie*). Pubs, not traditionally part of local culture, have taken off with a bang since the early '90s.

Antica Enoteca (4, C10)
Local shopkeepers and shoppers keep this Roman institution going. The original fittings include an impressive cash desk and a polished wood and brass counter where you can perch to sample a glass or two of the Italian and international wines available. Move from the bar to the restaurant when hunger hits – the food is fab.
✉ **Via della Croce 76b**
☎ **06 679 08 96**
🚌 **117, 119 Ⓜ Spagna**
🕘 **Mon-Sat 11am-1am**

Bar del Fico (6, B1)
Want some Roman atmosphere? For some unexplained reason this bar buzzes more than any other in town. The place, popular with local actors and artists, is packed until the early hours and crowds spill out the door and block the neighbouring streets.
✉ **Piazza del Fico 26**
☎ **06 686 52 05**
🚌 **46, 62, 64, 70, 81, 87,116, 186, 492, 628**
🕘 **8am-2am**

Sally Webb

Sharing hair of the dog at Bar San Calisto

Bar della Pace (6, B2)
Bring some serious attitude with you to this 'in' crowd locale. Drowning in ivy and with a superb wood panelled interior, this gorgeous corner bar is as good for an early evening aperitif outside in summer as it is for a leisurely nightcap (or a light meal) inside in winter.
✉ **Via della Pace 5**
☎ **06 686 12 16**
🚌 **46, 62, 64, 70, 81, 87,116, 186, 492, 628**
🕘 **10am-2am**

Baronato Quattro Bellezze (4, E7)
On Thursdays, drag queen owner Dominot dons gown and wig and performs Piaf songs to piano accompaniment in this unique, dimly lit bar, decorated with bizarre features such as a rocking horse. Tunisian meals and snacks will sustain you through your tipplings of cocktails, *vin chaud* or *amaro*. Reserve a table for the Piaf show.
✉ **Via di Panico 23**
☎ **06 687 28 65**
🚌 **46, 62, 64**
🕘 **Tues-Sun 8pm-2am**

Bar San Calisto (2, E3)
Seedy and cheap, the perennially popular but decidedly unglamorous San Calisto attracts well-heeled locals, the arty set, people doing dodgy deals and a few well-known winos. It is famous for its to-die-for hot chocolate in winter and chocolate gelato (the best in town; p. 89) in summer.
✉ **Piazza San Calisto**
☎ **06 583 58 69**
🚌 **75, 630, H**
🕘 **Mon-Sat 6am-1.30am**

Bartaruga (2, A7)
Named – in a fashion – after the Fontana delle Tartarughe opposite, this combo cocktail bar/tea room/pub is quirky and original. Decked out in bright colours with oriental furniture, velvet cushions and a Turkish harem feel, it's the type of place where you can spend hours sipping tea or quaffing wine.
✉ **Piazza Mattei 9**
☎ **06 689 22 99**
🚌 **46, 62, 64, 70, 81, 87,116, 186, 492, 628, H**
🕘 **Mon-Sat 10am-2am**

Four XXXX (3, J4)
Homesick Aussies originally came here for the beer. However this eclectic Testaccio haunt has undergone a bit of 'latinisation' and now has something for everyone: Castlemaine XXXX beer on tap; tequila cocktails if you want something stronger; tasty South American food; and good live jazz or a DJ most nights.
✉ **Via Galvani 29**
☎ **06 575 72 96**
🚌 **23, 75, 170, 280, 716**
Ⓜ Piramide 🕘 **7pm-2am**

Fiddler's Elbow (5, G1)
The Guinness, darts and chips formula has been working well here for over 20 years and it doesn't look set for change. One of the first Irish pubs to hit Rome, it's still popular with foreigners and locals.
✉ **Via dell'Olmata 43**
☎ **06 487 21 10** Ⓜ **Cavour** 🕘 **4.30pm-1am**

Il Goccetto (4, F6)
Most of the customers of this club-like *enoteca* are regulars who live nearby and drop in for a drink after work. Wines from all over the world share shelf space with the top Italian drops, and there's a choice of around 20 by the glass.
✉ **Via dei Banchi Vecchi 14** ☎ **06 68 64 268** 🚌 **46, 62, 64**
🕘 **Mon-Sat 5.30-10pm**

Jonathan's Angels (6, B1) Rome at its quirky best is on display here. Run by an artist, the whole bar – even the loo – is covered with pictures and decorations. It's a relaxed place for a late night drink.
✉ **Via della Fossa 18**
☎ **06 689 34 26**
🚌 **46, 62, 64, 70, 81, 87, 116, 186, 492, 628**
🕘 **1pm-2am**

L'Angolo Divino (4, H8) For many years this charming place with wooden beams and terracotta floors was a simple *vini e oli* (wine and oil) outlet but it's been spruced up and is a lovely place for a quiet glass of wine – chosen from the selection of a dozen or so bottles. An excellent selection of cheeses complements the wines and light meals are available.
✉ **Via dei Balestrari**

Sally Webb

Baristas sling many a treat at Sacchetti (p. 89).

☎ **06 686 44 13**
🚌 **46, 62, 64, 116**
🕘 **Mon-Sat 12.30-2.30pm, 6.30-10pm**

Marconi (5, G2)
Regulars come here as much for the food as the booze. It's a bit of an international smorgasbord, with Irish breakfasts alongside stodgy English fish and chips and Hungarian goulash. Oh, and then there's the beer...
✉ **Via Santa Prassede 9**
☎ **06 486 636**
🚌 **16, 71, 75, 84**
🕘 **12pm-1.30am**

Ned Kelly (6, A5)
As the name might suggest, this bar has an Aussie theme and serves Foster's Lager among other brews. Bushrangers from far and wide flock to see coverage of sports events on the satellite TV screens.
✉ **Via delle Coppelle 13**
☎ **06 683 22 20**
e **www.nedkelly.it**
🚌 **62, 64, 70, 81, 87, 116, 186, 492, 628**
🕘 **6.30pm-2am**

Sloppy Sam's (6, F2)
A cross between an Italian bar and an English pub, Sloppy Sam's is friendly and relaxed. Sit down on a comfortable wooden chair (repro antique), choose your beer from the selection on tap, grab a plate of nachos, and take it from there.
✉ **Campo de' Fiori**
🚌 **46, 62, 64, 116**
🕘 **6pm-2am**

Stardust Live Jazz Bar (2, C3) You can be lucky and stumble into Stardust to find musicians playing jazz or happen across an all-night jam session – it's a local place that tends to close when the last customers fall out the door. On Sunday the 'American brunch' features bagels and American coffee.
✉ **Vicolo dei Renzi 4**
☎ **06 583 20 875**
🚌 **23, 75, 280, H**
🕘 **varies**

The Drunken Ship (6, F2) Foreign students (especially Americans) seem to make the Drunken Ship their second home in Rome. Perhaps it's the welcoming atmosphere or the daily happy hour (7-9pm).
✉ **Campo de' Fiori 20**
☎ **06 683 00 535**
🚌 **46, 62, 64, 116**
🕘 **6pm-2am**

Taverna del Campo (6, F2) Come for breakfast, stay for lunch, have an afternoon beer and then rock on into the night. You can do it all here and judging from the constant crowds spilling out into the

piazza at all times of the day, a lot of people do.
✉ **Campo de' Fiori 16** ☎ **06 687 44 02** 🚌 **46, 62, 64, 116** 🕘 **8am-2am**

Trinity College (6, C8)
There's a good selection of imported beers, great food and an easy-going ambience in this stalwart of the pub scene. It gets packed to overflowing on Fridays and weekends.
✉ **Via del Collegio Romano 6** ☎ **06 678 64 72** 🚌 **63, 81, 85, 95, 117, 119, 492, 628** 🕘 **11am-3am**

Vineria (6, F2)
This charming place is also known as Da Giorgio. At the heart of Campo de' Fiori, the Vineria was once the gathering place of the Roman literati. Today, the crowd that spills out noisily into the piazza are decidedly less bookish, but it is still a good place to drink. Take your pick from a wide selection of wine and beers.
✉ **Campo de' Fiori** ☎ **06 688 03 268** 🚌 **46, 62, 64, 116** 🕘 **9am-1am, from 5pm Sun**

Veni, vidi, vici ... Vineria

DANCE CLUBS

In terms of dance clubs – discos to the locals – Rome rates way behind the Berlin or London scenes. However, there's still plenty of choice: from grungy clubs with hip DJs or live music to upmarket clubs full of jet-set types. Entry to the latter can be up to L40,000/€20.66 – which can include one drink. In summer they all close down and move to the beach.

Alien (3, D6)
The distinctive decor of Alien is like something out of sci-fi film. Dancers on raised platforms groove to the rhythm of house, techno and hip-hop. For the retros among us, one of the two dance areas features '70s and '80s revivals. Dress smart, but casual.
✉ **Via Velletri 13** ☎ **06 841 22 12** 🚌 **38, 313** 🕘 **10.30pm-4am** $ **from L30,000/€15.49**

Goa (3, L4)
The far-from-central location hasn't affected the popularity of Goa. It's decked out in ethnic style, with comfy couches to sink into when your feet need a break from the dance floor. The bouncers rule – you mightn't get in if they don't like the look of you. Tuesday is 'Gorgeous Goa Gay' night.
✉ **Via Libetta 13** ☎ **06 574 82 77** Ⓜ **Garbatella** 🕘 **Tues-Sat 11pm-3am** $ **L30,000/€15.49**

Black Out Rock Club (3, J7) Known as *the* club to dance to punk, rock and indie music, Black Out occasionally has gigs by British (and American) punk and rock bands.
✉ **Via Saturnia 18** ☎ **06 704 96 791** 🚌 **81, 85, 87, 186, 810, 850, J3, J5** Ⓜ **San Giovanni** 🕘 **10.30pm-2.30am** $ **L15,000/€7.75**

Bush (3, J4)
This Testaccio club has a reputation for excellent DJs, especially on Thursday which is hip-hop, R&B and soul night.
✉ **Via Galvani 46** ☎ **06 572 88 691** 🚌 **23, 30, 75, 280, 716** Ⓜ **Piramide** 🕘 **Tues-Sun 11pm-4am** $ **L20,000/€10.33**

Gilda (4, D11)
Appealing to a slightly older, wealthier and – some might say – less than cool clientele, Gilda has plush decor, state-of-the-art lighting and a huge dance floor. Despite all this effort, it has a sterile, formal atmosphere – not helped perhaps by the dress code which requires jackets for men and smart casual for women.
✉ **Via Mario de' Fiori 97** ☎ **06 678 48 38** Ⓜ **Spagna** 🕘 **10pm-4am** $ **L30,000/€15.49**

LIVE MUSIC VENUES

Alexanderplatz (4, A2)
Rome's leading jazz and blues club hosts top international (especially American) musicians and well known Italian artists from October to June. Book a table. In July-August the club moves to the grounds of the Renaissance Villa Celimontana, Celian Hill for **Villa Celimontana Jazz** festival.
✉ Via Ostia 9 ☎ 06 397 42 171 Ⓜ Ottaviano 🕐 Mon-Sat 8.30pm-2.30am $ L15,000/€7.75

Big Mama (4, K8)
This basement Trastevere club has branded itself the 'home of the blues', although it also plays host to rock and jazz artists, both Italian and international.
✉ Vicolo di San Francesco a Ripa 18 ☎ 06 581 25 51 🚌 44, 75, H 🚋 8 🕐 9pm-1.30am $ L10,000/€5.16 (monthly subscription)

Black Out Rock Club
(2, J7) See listing p. 94.

Fonclea (4, C4)
Don't let the English country pub decor put you off. This great little venue has jazz, soul, funk and rock music (including cover bands) most nights.
✉ Via Crescenzio 82a ☎ 06 689 63 02 🚌 23, 49, 81, 492 🕐 7pm-2am $ free (Sat L10,000/€5.16)

Il Controlocale (4, K15)
This small club, not far from the Colosseum, showcases a variety of live music from Italian folk to blues (Wed-Sat). The 'unplugged' jam sessions (Mon) are popular and lots of fun.
✉ Via dei Santi Quattro 103 ☎ 06 700 89 44 🚌 81, 85, 87, 117, 810, 850 Ⓜ Colosseo 🕐 9pm-2am $ L10,000/€5.16

Testaccio Village (3, J4)
The things you can do with an open street if you try! The summer months see part of Via di Monte Testaccio transformed into an outdoor entertainment complex with bars, several dance areas and live music – international acts, Italian performers, rock, pop, jazz, ethnic sounds.
✉ Via di Monte Testaccio 🚌 23, 75, 280, 716 Ⓜ Piramide 🕐 June-Sept 7pm-2am $ L15,000/€7.75 (weekly ticket, unlimited entry; extra charge for some concerts)

Villaggio Globale
(3, J3) Testaccio's former slaughterhouse has become a grungy but popular alternative meeting place and stand-up venue for concerts, lectures and other events. Facilities are fairly basic but many quality acts play here.
✉ Lungotevere Testaccio ☎ 06 573 00 39 🚌 23, 95, 170, 280, 781 Ⓜ Piramide 🕐 varies $ from L5000/€2.58

Martin Moos
Castel Sant'Angelo rock fest

CLASSICAL MUSIC & OPERA

Accademia Nazionale di Santa Cecilia (4, D5)
The year-round program features world class performers together with the highly regarded Santa Cecilia orchestra directed by Myung-Whun Chung. Short festivals dedicated to a single composer are a feature of the autumn calendar. In June the orchestra and its guest stars move to the Villa Giulia gardens for the summer concert series.
✉ Via della Conciliazione 4 ☎ 06 688 01 044 e www.santacecilia.it 🚌 23, 62, 64 🕐 varies $ L20,000-L60,000/ €10.33-30.99 ♿

Accademia Filarmonica Romana
(3, B2) Founded in 1821, Rome's music academy members have included Rossini, Donizetti and Verdi. The program (October-May) features mainly chamber and choral music, with some contemporary concerts and multi-media events.
✉ ☎ see Teatro Olimpico p. 97 e vivaldi.nuovo.nexus .it/filarmonica 🚋 2 🕐 varies $ L30,000-L60,000/€15.49-30.99 ♿

Associazione Musicale Romana
(4, F6) This group organises recitals and concerts throughout the year as well as two prestigious events held in churches around the city: an international organ festival in September and a harpsichord festival during spring.
✉ Via dei Banchi Vecchi 61; concerts in various locations ☎ 06 39 36 63 22 🚌 46, 62, 64 🕐 varies $ L15,000-L40,000/€7.75-20.66

Istituzione Universitaria dei Concerti (3, F7)
The recitals and chamber music concerts held in the Aula Magna of La Sapienza university range from classical to contemporary: it could be Mozart or Beethoven one week, and Miles Davis the next.
✉ Piazzale Aldo Moro 5 ☎ 06 361 00 51 e www.concertiiuc.it 🚌 492 Ⓜ Castro Pretorio $ 🕐 varies

Teatro dell'Opera di Roma (4, E15)
The functional fascist-era exterior of Rome's opera house doesn't prepare you for the elegance of the 19th century interior which is all plush red velvet and gilt. Although the company has a reputation as the poor cousin of Milan's La Scala or San Carlo in Naples due to inconsistent artistic direction, a night at the opera is a night to remember.
✉ Piazza Beniamino Gigli 8 ☎ 06 481 60 255, toll free 800 01 66 65 Ⓜ Repubblica 🕐 varies; season Dec-June $ L40,000-200,000/€20.66-103.29

Teatro Ghione (4, F3)
This long-standing Roman theatre near St Peter's has an eclectic program of recitals, often featuring major international opera singers.
✉ Via delle Fornaci 37 ☎ 06 637 22 94 e www.ghione.it 🚌 62 $ 🕐 varies

First Night in Rome
The operas *Cavalleria Rusticana* by Mascagnai and (appropriately) Puccini's *Tosca* had their world premieres at the Teatro dell'Opera di Roma. Rossini's operas *Il Barbiere di Siviglia* (Barber of Seville) and *La Cenerentola* both premiered in Rome, at Teatro Argentina.

Ostia Antica's theatre is still used for performance *(p. 57)*

Voices of Angels
Listening to sacred music in a Roman church can be an ethereal experience. Free concerts are held in many of Rome's churches, especially at Easter and around Christmas and New Year, with seats available on a first-come-first-served basis. Sant'Ignazio in Loyola is a popular venue for choral masses as is the Pantheon and San Giovanni in Laterano. San Paolo Fuori le Mura hosts an important choral mass on 25 January and a *Te Deum* is sung at the Chiesa del Gesù (pictured at right) on 31 December.

THEATRE & DANCE

If you understand Italian there's a wealth of theatre to enjoy, although Italian stage productions are often more melodramatic than dramatic. Many of the city's theatres are worth visiting for the architecture and decoration alone. Rome is a regular stop on international dance company itineraries.

Teatro Argentina
(6, F5) This state-funded theatre is the official home of the Teatro di Roma and stages major theatre and dance productions. Book early for the dance productions, which often sell out.
✉ **Largo di Torre Argentina 52 ☎ 06 688 04 601 e www.teatrodiroma.it 🚌 46, 62, 64, 70, 81, 87, 186, 492, 628 🚋 8 $ 🕘 varies**

Teatro dell'Opera di Roma (4, E15)
Each season the opera theatre lists a few classical ballets in its program. These productions are generally worth seeing only if there are guest stars as the opera's *corps de ballet* has been in a sorry state for years and couldn't pirouette its way out of a pantomime. Dress smart casual to formal.
🚌 ☎ ✉ Ⓜ see p. 96 🕘 varies; season Dec-June $ L25,000-L100,000/€12.91-51.65

Teatro Olimpico
(3, B2) Rome's leading dance stage often hosts world-class dance troupes, ranging from classical ballet to dance theatre, from ethnic dance to avant-garde performances. Momix, Moses Pendleton, Daniel Erzalow, Pina Bausch, Jiri Kylian and Lindsay Kemp are among the many choreographers and companies to have performed in recent years.
✉ **Piazza Gentile da Fabriano 17 ☎ 06 320 17 52, 06 326 59 91 e www.teatroolimpico.com/english.htm 🚋 2 $ 🕘 varies**

Teatro Quirino (6, A9)
Classical Italian works such as *Commedia dell'Arte* are regularly featured here.
✉ **Via M Minghetti 1 ☎ 06 679 45 85 🚌 62, 64, 70, 81, 85, 87, 117, 119, 186, 492, 628 $ 🕘 varies**

Teatro Sistina (4, C12)
This is Rome's principal theatre for big-budget (but not always top-quality) musicals and theatre spectaculars.
✉ **Via Sistina 129 ☎ 06 482 68 41 e www.ilsistina.com Ⓜ Barberini $ 🕘 varies ♿**

Teatro Valle (6, D4)
This perfectly proportioned theatre is like a mini opera house, with three levels of private boxes. The variable program often includes contemporary English-language works with subtitles or translated into Italian.
✉ **Via del Teatro Valle 23a ☎ 06 688 03 794 🚌 30, 70, 81, 87, 116, 186, 492, 628 $ 🕘 varies**

Teatro Vascello (3, H2)
Fringe theatre, experimental dance and workshops of various kinds are the staple fare at this well designed modern theatre in the Monteverde area south east of Trastevere.
✉ **Via Carini 72 ☎ 06 588 10 21 🚌 44, 75 $ 🕘 varies**

Teatro Inglese

English theatre in Rome is thriving, thanks to the large population of expat and bilingual thespians in town. These are usually weekly fixtures or short seasons, and details (even theatres) can change at short notice. Call for information or check the listing press.

- **Off Night Repertory Theatre** (☎ 06 444 13 75, e www.porticus.com/offnight) stages productions of contemporary and classic one-act and full-length plays. Friday performances also at **Arte del Teatro** (4, F15; Via Urbana 107; ☎ 06 488 5608).
- **The Miracle Players** (☎ 06 446 98 67, e www.miracleplayers.org) has free open-air summer plays in historic settings (eg *Julius Caesar* at the Roman Forum).
- **Teatro Agora** (4, H6; Via della Penitenza 33; ☎ 06 687 41 67) has short-run works in European languages.

CINEMAS

Rome has more than 80 cinemas where you can catch a film for around L13,000/€6.71. Outdoor cinema is popular during the summer: arty **Isola del Cinema** international film festival takes place on the Isola Tiberina; and the **Massenzio** festival mixes current release and old classics at nightly screenings in Parco del Celio (4, K14). Check the listings press for details.

Barberini (4, D13)
Grab your tub of popcorn and your Coca-Cola and settle in for a Hollywood latest release – dubbed into Italian, of course.
✉ **Piazza Barberini 52**
☎ **06 482 77 07**
🚌 **62, 95, 175, 492**
🕘 **3pm-2am** ♿

Intrastevere (2, B2)
This intimate triple-screen cinema plays mainstream Italian movies and international art-house releases.
✉ **Vicolo Moroni 3a**
☎ **06 588 42 30** 🚌 **23, 280** 🕘 **3-11.30pm**

Pasquino (2, D3)
Among the expat set, the Pasquino is a Roman institution. Current major release films and the odd art house choice (all in English) are screened every day. There's also an Internet cafe.
✉ **Piazza Sant'Egidio 10** ☎ **06 580 36 22**
🚌 **23, 280, H** 🚋 **8**
🕘 **3pm-midnight**

Warner Village Moderno (5, D1)
The five screens in this state-of-the-art complex show Hollywood blockbusters and major release Italian films.
✉ **Piazza della Repubblica** ☎ **06 47 77 92 02** Ⓜ **Repubblica**
🕘 **3pm-2am** ♿

Hollywood on the Tiber

Rome has always played a major role in Italian cinema, both as a subject and as a production centre. The Cinecittà film studio (1, C3) was set up in 1937 and in its heyday was labelled 'Hollywood on the Tiber'.

In the '50s and '60s major American movies made there included *Ben Hur, Cleopatra* and *Spartacus*. By the early '60s, however, this icon of Italian cinema began to wane as location shooting became the norm.

After many lean years, the future for Cinecittà looks rosy with increased investment in digital technology. Cheaper production costs mean that many Hollywood producers are again filming here. Recent movies such as *U571, Tea with Mussolini* and *Gangs of New York* were partially filmed at Cinecittà.

Other great films that have been partially or fully set in Rome include: *Caro Diario, La Dolce Vita, Ladri di Biciclette* (Bicycle Thieves), *Roma Città Aperta* (Rome Open City), *Roman Holiday, The Talented Mr Ripley* and *Three Coins in the Fountain*.

Neil Setchfield

Films in English

Most foreign films are dubbed into Italian; those screened in the original language (with Italian subtitles) are indicated in listings by *versione originale*.

Cinemas regularly screening current releases in English or original language include:

- **Quirinetta** (6, B9)
Via Minghetti 4
☎ 06 679 00 12
(in English daily)
- **Alcazar** (4, K8)
Via Merry del Val 14
☎ 06 588 42 30
(in English Mon)
- **Nuovo Sacher** (2, H3)
Largo Ascianghi 1
☎ 06 581 81 16
(original language Mon & Tues)

GAY & LESBIAN ROME

You'll need to do some research to track down the happening gay and lesbian scene, which tends to be nocturnal and a bit sleazy (dark rooms are still a feature of some clubs). For bars and clubs listings, read gay publications and check local organisations (p. 119). **Goa** has 'Gorgeous Goa Gay' on Tuesday and **Alien** (p. 94) goes gay on Saturday. As clubs – and dedicated gay nights – come and go it's wise to check the information first.

Alpheus (3, K4)
It's a fair way from the centre but this is where it happens for gays and lesbians on Friday nights. The 'Muccassassina' DJ crew from the Mario Mieli gang (p. 119) gets things going.
✉ **Via del Commercio 271b ☎ 06 541 39 58**
Ⓜ Piramide
🕘 Fri 10.30pm-4am
$ L18,000/€9.30

Apeiron (5, G1)
Pick the lounge or bar area that appeals to you and hang out, or descend into the basement for erotic videos and dark room activities. Drag queens welcome.
✉ **Via dei Quattro Cantoni 5 ☎ 06 482 88 20 Ⓜ Cavour**
🕘 Mon-Sat 10.30pm-2am (4am on Fri & Sat)
$ L5000/€2.58 annual membership; L6000/€3.10 one-drink min

Buon Pastore Centre (4, H5) It's hardly hip and happening but it's one of the few lesbian spaces in Rome. Gay women meet here weekly for political gatherings of the Coordinamento Lesbiche Italiano (CLI). There's a cafe and a women-only restaurant, Le Sorellastre.
✉ **Via San Francesco di Sales 1a ☎ 06 686 42 01 e cli_network@iol.it**
🚌 23, 280
🕘 10am-9pm $ free

Edoardo II (2, A9)
Named after the infamous English king, this club is decked out like a medieval torture chamber. But it's fairly low-key and tame with a mixed clientele (mostly dressed in black). There's no dancing, it's just a bar and good cruising spot.
✉ **Vicolo Margana 14**
☎ 06 69 94 24 19
🚌 46, 62, 64, 70, 81, 87, 95, 186, 492, 628, H
🕘 Tues-Sat 10pm-2am
$ free

Garbo (2, E4)
About time too! The first gay (and not only) bar catering to couples rather than cruisers. It attracts a mix of Italians and foreigners.
✉ **Vicolo di Santa Margherita 1a**
☎ 06 58 32 07 82
🚌 23, 44, 75, 280, H
🚋 8 🕘 10pm-2am
$ free

Hangar (5, G1)
Rome's oldest gay bar, run by an American, is still one of its most popular. The varied clientele – international and Italian, all ages – includes a significant proportion of gym bunnies. Monday is video night.
✉ **Via in Selci 69**
☎ 06 488 13 97
Ⓜ Cavour 🕘 Wed-Mon 10.30pm-2am $ free

L'Alibi (3, J4)
What was for years Rome's premier gay venue now attracts a mixed crowd and is far from Rome's hippest club. There are two levels, each with bar and dance floor, and a fab roof terrace.
✉ **Via di Monte Testaccio 44 ☎ 06 574 34 48**
Ⓜ Piramide 🕘 Wed-Sun 11pm-4.30am
$ Wed-Thur free, Fri-Sun L20,000/€10.33

Max's Bar (3, G7)
An institution in gay Rome, Max's is an informal place – the ordinary man's bar – with little attitude and great music. It's frequented by young, old and everything in between.
✉ **Via Achille Grandi 3a**
☎ 06 702 01 599 🚌 71, 105, 649 Ⓜ Manzoni
🕘 Tues-Sun 8pm-2am
$ L15,000/€7.75

Clean & Dirty

Scrub up on your gay bath culture. Most have Jacuzzis, Turkish baths or steam rooms, bars and dark rooms. Try these:

- **Apollion** (5, H1) Via Mecenate 59a ☎ 06 482 53 89
- **Europa Multiclub** (4, C15) Via Aureliana 40 ☎ 06 482 36 50
- **Sauna Mediterraneo** (5, J3) Via Villari 3 ☎ 06 772 05 934

SPECTATOR SPORTS

Soccer

Il calcio excites Italian souls more than politics, religion, good food and dressing up all put together. It is one of the great forces in Roman life, and watching a *partita* (match) is one of *the* great cultural experiences for the foreign visitor. Both local teams, AS Roma and Lazio, play in Serie A (the top division). The teams share the **Stadio Olimpico** at Foro Italico, north of the city centre and play all their home matches there. There is great rivalry between the teams and their supporters, and local derbies make for particularly hot clashes.

Basketball

Basketball is the second most popular spectator sport in Rome, but it comes a long way behind soccer. The arrival of several star players from the United States and from the former Yugoslavia has spiced up the Italian league. The season runs over the winter months and matches are played at the **Palazzo dello Sport** in EUR.

Tennis

The Italian Open takes place in May on the clay courts at the Foro Italico. The championships attract the world's best male and female players. Tickets can usually be bought at the Foro Italico each day of the tournament, except for the final days, which are sold out weeks in advance.

Athletics

The Golden Gala athletics meet takes place in June at the Stadio Olimpico. It's organised by the Federazione Italiana di Atletica Leggera.

Equestrian

The annual Piazza di Siena show jumping competition is held in May in Villa Borghese. Phone ☎ 06 322 53 57 for ticket information.

Tickets & Venues

Tickets for sporting events can be purchased through authorised ticketing agencies such as **Orbis** (5, F1) Piazza dell'Esquilino 37, ☎ 06 482 74 03. Tourist information offices and the listings press will also have details. For some events, contact the venues directly:

- **Stadio Olimpico** (3, A2)
  Via dei Gladiatori 2 ☎ 06 323 73 33
- **Foro Italico Tennis Centre** (3, B2)
  Via dei Gladiatori 31 ☎ 06 321 90 64
- **Palazzo dello Sport** (1, C3)
  Viale dell'Umanesimo, EUR
  ☎ 06 592 50 06

places to stay

Rome's hotels run the full gamut from frescoed Renaissance palazzi to *fin-de-siècle* buildings with original features to small *pensioni* or family-run guesthouses. Traditionally the area around the station was where most budget hotels and pensions were located. While this is still true, many have upgraded their facilities and prices. Indeed the term *pensione* is now rarely used – most places call themselves *albergo* (hotel) – and family-run places are being transformed into larger, more commercial affairs.

Hotels in the historic centre charge a premium for their location, and facilities don't always match asking prices. However the convenience of an easily accessible hotel for a post-prandial snooze or to drop off bulky shopping bags is obvious.

Martin Moos

Room Rates

These categories indicate the cost per night of a standard double room.

Deluxe
from L500,000/€258.23

Top End
L321,000-499,000/
€165.89-257.71

Mid-Range
L171,000-320,000/
€88.31-165.27

Budget
under L170,000/
€87.80

Hotels in Rome are quintessentially, well, Roman. Even deluxe category hotels (five-star by international standards) don't offer facilities and comfort levels that are expected elsewhere. Many hotels are in converted *palazzi*, so rooms are often small (albeit luxurious), and gyms and pools are rarely on offer. Deluxe rooms have minibar, air conditioning, television, extremely fine linen, 24-hour room service and private baths with hairdryers and bathrobes. Many top end hotel rooms offer similar facilities. In the mid-range category, facilities are more basic; you won't always find a hairdryer or minibar, there'll be no room service and there mightn't be any air conditioning. Budget hotels often have rooms without private bathrooms.

Martin Moos

Bed & Breakfast

Although a relatively new concept in Rome, B&B has taken off and is a good-value alternative to hotels and pensions. The bonus is that Italian houses are invariably spotlessly clean. The drawback is that keys aren't always provided – night owls find a hotel.

Lists of private B&B operators are available from the APT tourism desk at Termini. An easier option is to use a booking agency. The best of these is **Bed & Breakfast Italia** (Corso Vittorio Emanuele II 282; ☎ 06 687 86 18; fax 06 687 86 19; e md4095@mclink.it; www.bbitalia.it). You can view apartments and book via the Web site.

DELUXE

Hassler Villa Medici (4, C12) This long-standing symbol of Roman hospitality can claim among its guests the royal families of Sweden, Greece and England; President Kennedy and Elizabeth Taylor. The atmosphere is one of discreet glamour, and although the standard rooms aren't huge, features such as the rooftop restaurant (with views to die for) and courtyard bar make up for it.
✉ **Piazza della Trinitá dei Monti 6 ☎ 06 69 93 40; fax 06 678 99 91 e hasslerroma@mclink.it; www.hotelhasslerroma.com 🚌 116, 117, 119 Ⓜ Spagna ✕ Rooftop Restaurant**

Not a hint of poisonous service at Hassler Villa Medici.

Hotel Columbus (4, D4) You can't get much closer to St Peter's than this magnificent 15th century palace. Quiet and surprisingly homely given its history and proportions, it's a Renaissance curiosity with its splendid halls, frescoes by Pinturicchio and heavy wooden furnishings. There's a pretty roof terrace, and a delightful restaurant in the old refectory of the palace, offering Italian and international cuisine.
✉ **Via della Conciliazione 33 ☎ 06 686 54 35; fax 06 686 48 74 e hotel.columbus@alfanet.it 🚌 46, 62, 64, J4, J5 ✕**

Hotel de Russie (4, A10) Rome's newest luxury hotel is also its most beautiful, with decor that's simultaneously opulent, minimal and tasteful. No expense has been spared – from the massive mosaic-tiled bathrooms to the fine linens to the indulgent day spa. But one look at the exquisite terraced gardens out back and you'll realise why it's so special.
✉ **Via del Babuino 9 ☎ 06 32 88 81; fax 06 328 88 888 e hotelderussie@hotelderussie.it; www.rfhotels.com 🚌 117, 119 ✕ restaurant & Stravinsky Bar**

Hotel d'Inghilterra (4, C11) You can smell the history emanating from the wood-panelled corridors of this hotel, originally the guesthouse for the Torlonia family, whose palazzo is opposite. Illustrious guests have included Hemingway, Liszt and Mendelssohn. Decor is a mix of dowdy, tasteful, opulent and over-the-top; rooms on the 5th floor have private balconies.
✉ **Via Bocca di Leone 14 ☎ 06 699 81 204; fax 06 679 86 01 e reservation_hir@charminghotels.it; www.charminghotels.it 🚌 81, 116, 117, 119, 492, 628 Ⓜ Spagna ✕ Roman Garden**

Hotel Eden (4, C12) Originally built in 1889, the Eden was totally revamped in the early '90s and remains one of Rome's most glam hotels. There are all the luxuries you'd expect and a pleasant rooftop restaurant and bar. It's close to Villa Borghese for joggers and power walkers.
✉ **Via Ludovisi 49 ☎ 06 47 81 21; fax 06 482 15 84 e reservations@hotel-eden.it; www.hotel-eden.it 🚌 52, 53, 95, 116, 119 ✕ la Terrazza dell'Eden restaurant & bars**

Hotel Forum (4, H13) Views from this hotel's delightful roof-garden restaurant and the terrace bar above it are breathtaking. Watch Rome come to life over breakfast, have dinner against the impressive backdrop of the Forum and Palatine – or get a room with a view and do it all from bed. The antique-dotted lounge area is a step back in time.
✉ **Via Tor de' Conti 25 ☎ 06 679 24 46; fax 06 678 64 79**

e info@hotelforum.com; www.hotelforum.com 🚌 85, 87, 117, 175, 186, 810, 850 Ⓜ Colosseo, Cavour ✕

Hotel Raphaël (6, B2)
The '70s and '80s were the ivy-clad Raphaël's heyday, when Bettino Craxi and cronies hung out in the penthouse. Today things are less flashy but no less comfortable, and a major refit is planned for 2001. The lobby has magnificent artworks and antiques, including Picasso ceramics.
✉ **Largo Febo 2** ☎ **06 68 28 31; fax 06 687 89 93** e **info@raphaelhotel.com; www.raphaelhotel.com** 🚌 **70, 81, 87, 116, 186, 492, 628** ✕ **Roof Garden**

Minerva (6, D6)
This 17th century palace opposite Bernini's *Elefantino* has had a few touch-ups over the years, most recently by architect Paolo Portoghesi, who added the magnificent Art Deco-style coloured glass lobby ceiling. What hasn't changed is the standard: superior comfort rising to top luxury in the suites. One room is accessible for disabled travellers.
✉ **Piazza della Minerva 69** ☎ **06 69 52 01; fax 06 679 41 65** e **minerva@pronet.it** 🚌 **46, 62, 64, 70, 81, 87, 116, 186, 492, 628, J5** ✕

TOP END

Albergo Teatro di Pompeo (6, F3)
There's plenty of old-world charm in this hotel just off Campo de' Fiori. Parts of the building go back as far as the Roman Republic and guests have breakfast in the remains of Pompey's Theatre (55BC).
✉ **Largo del Pallaro 8** ☎ **06 687 28 12; fax 06 688 05 531** 🚌 **46, 62, 64, 70, 81, 87, 116, 186, 492, 628, J5**

Casa Howard (4, D12)
Someone with *really* good taste and style has created this stunning Campo de' Fiori guesthouse. Each of the five rooms is individually decorated with gorgeous fabrics in a particular colour theme. Two rooms have baths ensuite, the others have a separate but private bathroom (one with a Turkish steam room). Room service breakfast baskets are a nice extra touch.
✉ **Via Capo le Case 18** ☎ **06 699 24 555; fax 06 679 46 44** e **casahowardroma@yahoo.com, www.casahoward.com** 🚌 **52, 53, 62, 71, 95, 116, 117, 119, 492** ✕ **Al 34** **(p. 81)**

Hotel Bramante (4, D4)
This restored 16th century building was designed by the Swiss architect, Domenico Fontana who lived here until he was expelled from Rome by Pope Sixtus V. The superbly decorated guestrooms have marble bathrooms, and there is antique furniture and carpets throughout. One of the most charming in Rome.
✉ **Vicolo delle Palline 24** ☎ **06 688 06 426; fax 06 687 98 81** e **bramante@excalhq.it** 🚌 **23, 64**

Hotel Celio (4, K15)
Celio is a little slice of heaven near the Colosseum. A fortune has been spent on meticulous renovations: stunning mosaic floors decorate corridors and guestrooms, and large-screen TVs feature in most rooms. Art is the theme: each room named after a famous artist and repro oils and frescoes.
✉ **Via dei Santi Quattro 35c** ☎ **06 704 95 333; fax 06 709 63 77** 🚌 **75, 85, 87, 117, 175, 810, 850, J4, J5** Ⓜ **Colosseo** ✕ **Pasqualino** **(p. 83)**

Hotel Locarno (4, A9)
Popular with tourists and business travellers, Hotel Locarno is a friendly alternative to some of the more impersonal top-end hotels. An attractive Art Deco lounge-bar, free use of bicycles and a room equipped for disabled travellers are bonuses.
✉ **Via della Penna 22** ☎ **06 361 08 41; fax 06 321 52 49** e **info@hotellocarno.com; www.hotellocarno.com** 🚌 **81, 117, 119, 628** Ⓜ **Flaminio**

Hotel Nerva (4, G13)
This cosy place takes its name from the Foro Nerva opposite. Rooms aren't huge but what they lack in size is made up for by the friendly management. It's well positioned to explore the nearby archaeological wonders and the epicurial delights of backstreet Monti.
✉ **Via Tor de' Conti 3** ☎ **06 678 18 35;**

fax 06 69 92 22 04 🚌 85, 87, 117, 175, 186, 810, 850 Ⓜ Colosseo, Cavour

Hotel Portoghesi
(4, E9) Located in a quiet street lined with art galleries and jewellers, this is a great place from which to explore Rome on foot. Guestrooms aren't large, but they're nicely furnished and the roof terrace is delightful. It's good value, too, with prices only just above mid-range.
✉ **Via dei Portoghesi 1** ☎ **06 686 42 31; fax 06 687 69 76** e **info@hotelportoghesiroma.com; www.hotelportoghesiroma.com** 🚌 **70, 81, 87, 116, 186, 492, 628**

Hotel Santa Chiara
(6, D5) Get close to the gods at this pleasant but unpretentious hotel right behind the Pantheon. Some of the very comfy rooms have small terraces overlooking the street, although the rooms around the internal courtyard are quieter.
✉ **Via Santa Chiara 21** ☎ **06 687 29 79; fax 06 687 31 44** e **info@albergosantachiara.com; www.albergosantachiara.com** 🚌 **40, 46, 62, 64, 70, 81, 87, 116, 186, 492, 628, J5**

See Rome and ... doze at the Hotel Forum (p. 102).

MID-RANGE

Albergo del Sole
(6, F3) Occupying a crumbling palazzo off Campo de' Fiori, Albergo del Sole is claimed to be the oldest hotel in Rome. It certainly has plenty of character, and some rooms are furnished with antiques. The roof terrace, open to guests until 11pm, is a good place to hang out in hot weather.
✉ **Via del Biscione 76** ☎ **06 687 94 46; fax 06 689 37 87** e **alb.sole@flashnet.it** 🚌 **46, 62, 64, 116, J5** ✕ **Insalata Ricca (p. 78)**

Aventino Sant'Anselmo Hotels
(3, H4) The perfect place if you prefer quieter surroundings, these five separate Art Nouveau villas, each with gardens and courtyards, are situated on the largely residential Aventine hill, but still close to the historic centre and Testaccio's restaurants and nightlife.
✉ **Piazza di Sant' Anselmo 2** ☎ **06 574 51 74; fax 06 578 36 04** e **frpiroli@tin.it; www.aventinohotels.com** 🚌 **81, 160, 175, 715** Ⓜ **Circo Massimo**

Hotel Amalia (4, B3)
Located in a residential palazzo a stone's throw from the Vatican, the Amalia is one of the best-value hotels here. Simple but comfortable rooms are bright, spacious and spotlessly clean, although the lack of air-con means they get a bit hot in summer.
✉ **Via Germanico 66** ☎ **06 39 72 33 54; fax 06 39 72 33 65** e **hotelamalia@iol.it; www.hotelamalia.com** 🚌 **23, 49, 70, 81, 492** Ⓜ **Ottaviano**

Hotel Campo de' Fiori
(6, F3) Guest rooms of this quirky hotel are a decorator's nightmare – garish blue carpet and clashing floral wallpaper – not recommended to wake up in with a hangover. Some

Apartment Rentals

For longer stays, consider renting an apartment. Expect to pay a minimum of L1,500,000/€775 a month (plus bills and a hefty deposit) for a studio apartment or a small one-bedroom place. The fortnightly listing magazine *Wanted in Rome* (from newsstands; e www.wantedinrome.com). has classified short-term rental ads and lists English-speaking estate agencies.

'bathrooms' are just shower stalls plonked unceremoniously in the room, so check first. Six floors are walk-up, but the roof terrace is worth the climb.
✉ **Via del Biscione 6**
☎ **06 688 06 865; fax 06 687 60 03**
🚌 **46, 62, 64, 116**

Hotel Columbia (5, E1)
The tasteful, tranquil Columbia is an anomaly in a part of town renowned for characterless hotels and insalubrious surroundings. Good for business or leisure travellers, rooms are large and bright and all have data plugs. There's a nice breakfast terrace. Like its sister hotel the Venezia (this page) it's a bargain.
✉ **Via del Viminale 15**
☎ **06 474 42; 89 fax 06 474 02 09** e **info@hotelcolumbia.com; www.hotelcolumbia.com**
🚌 **16, 64, 70, 71, 75, 170, H, J2**
Ⓜ **Repubblica, Termini**

Hotel d'Este (5, G3)
Mosaic lovers would find this hotel convenient for its proximity to Santa Maria Maggiore and nearby churches. Prices are at the upper end of mid-range, but the beautifully furnished rooms and a pleasant roof garden are worth it. Selling points include a bar, restaurant and laundry/dry cleaning service.
✉ **Via Carlo Alberto 4b**
☎ **06 446 56 07; fax 06 446 56 01** e **d.este@italyhotel.com; www.hotel-deste.com** 🚌 **16, 71, 590** Ⓜ **Vittorio** ✗

Hotel Dolomiti (5, C4)
What was once a run-down pensione has been renovated into an elegant and airy hotel. Rooms have all mod-cons and breakfast taken in the lovely marble-panelled bar area makes for a good start to the day. Well positioned for access to trains.
✉ **Via San Martino della Battaglia 11** ☎ **06 495 72 56; fax 06 445 46 65** e **dolomiti@hotel-dolomiti.it; www.hotel-dolomiti.it**
🚌 **16, 38, 75, 492** Ⓜ **Castro Pretorio, Termini**

Hotel Margutta
(4, B10) The shoppers' paradise around Via Condotti is dangerously close here. Rooms are rather dark, although two of them share a terrace and one has a terrace of its own – book ahead for these. Some ground floor rooms have wheelchair access.
✉ **Via Laurina 34**
☎ **06 322 36 74; fax 06 320 03 95**
🚌 **81, 117, 119, 628**
Ⓜ **Spagna, Flaminio**

Hotel Positano (5, C4)
This family-run hotel is a particularly good choice for families, as kids under six stay free. Guestrooms are simply furnished with bathrooms and all the trimmings (air-con, TV, phone, safe, minibar and hairdryer). The central position has easy access to transport.
✉ **Via Palestro 49**
☎ **06 49 03 60; fax 06 446 91 01** e **hotposit@tin.it** 🚌 **16, 38, 75, 492**
Ⓜ **Castro Pretorio, Termini**

Hotel Primavera
(6, D2) Well located in a pretty palazzo near Piazza Navona, Primavera is clean and comfy. Rooms have air-con and double glazing to combat the heat and traffic noise. Bathrooms, added as an afterthought, are a bit cramped. No credit cards.
✉ **Piazza di San Pantaleo 3** ☎ **06 68 80 31 09; fax 06 686 92 65**
🚌 **46, 62, 64, 116, J5**

Hotel Venezia (5, D4)
If this hotel were in a slightly more upmarket locale, the rates would double. As it is they're good value, and this is the nicest hotel – a haven of tranquillity in the Termini area. Antiques and beautifully upholstered furniture feature throughout, and multilingual staff are ready to satisfy your every whim. A bargain!
✉ **Via Varese 18**
☎ **06 445 71 01; fax 06 495 76 87** e **www.hotelvenezia.com**
🚌 **16, 38, 75, 492**
Ⓜ **Termini**

Credit Cards
Don't get caught short! Many mid-range and budget hotels in Rome don't accept cards, so check payment terms when you book.

Suore di Santa Brigida (6, F1)
The rooms are simple and you *are* dossing down with nuns, but as far as location is concerned you really can't do much better than Piazza Farnese. The 11pm curfew might bother some people, the church bells may bug others.
✉ **Piazza Farnese 96 (entrance in Via del Monserrato)** ☎ **06 688 92 596; fax 06 682 19 126** e **brigida@mclink.it**
🚌 **116** ✗ **Ristorante Moserrato** **(p. 78)**

BUDGET

Albergo Abruzzi
(6, B6) Smack opposite the Pantheon, the Abruzzi is *centralissimo*, although the rooms can be very noisy till late at night when the piazza finally clears. There's nothing fancy about the rooms and shared baths, but the chatty management make it a perennial budget fave. Bring cash – credit cards not accepted.
✉ **Piazza della Rotonda 69** ☎ **06 679 20 21** 🚌 **46, 62, 64, 70, 81, 87, 116, 186, 492, 628, J5**

Albergo della Lunetta
(6, F3) This old-fashioned pensione, run by three rather cantankerous but somewhat charming *signore*, is popular with young foreign students who stay for months at a time. It's much bigger than it looks, with labyrinthine corridors and staircases leading to small but spotless rooms.
✉ **Piazza Paradiso 68** ☎ **06 686 10 80; fax 06 689 20 28** 🚌 **46, 62, 64, 70, 81, 87, 116, 186, 492, 628, J5**

Albergo Sandra (5, C4)
A house-proud Italian *mamma* and her English-speaking son run this medium-sized pensione north of the Termini. Rooms are clean and pleasant and bathrooms are shared. Good for a quick escape by train.
✉ **Via Villafranca 10** ☎ **06 445 26 12; fax 06 446 08 46** 🚌 **16, 38, 75, 492** Ⓜ **Castro Pretorio**

Hotel Carmel (3, H3)
The shady roof terrace is one of Carmel's attractions, as is its proximity to the bars and restaurants of Trastevere. Clean, simple rooms come with private bathrooms; two have private terraces. Book ahead.
✉ **Via Mameli 11** ☎ **06 580 99 21; fax 06 581 88 53** 🚌 **44, 75** 🚋 **8**

Casa Kolbe (4, J12)
Tour groups tend to take over this former Franciscan monastery, opposite the Palatine, but it's a comfortable place with a large sheltered garden in a quiet but central area of the city. The name comes from a Polish monk who lived there before his death during WWII in Auschwitz.
✉ **Via di San Teodoro 44** ☎ **06 679 49 74; fax 06 69 94 15 50** 🚌 **81, 160, 628**

Martin Moos

Basil!

Fawlty Towers (5, E3)
The hostel-style accommodation on offer in this converted apartment near Termini is Rome's best, and it's a popular travellers' meeting spot. Book in advance for the private rooms; you have to reserve a dorm place the night before. The sunny terrace is a bonus.
✉ **Via Magenta 39** ☎**/fax 06 445 03 74** **e hotelfawltytowers@hotmail.com** 🚌 **62, 64, 75, 90, 492, J2, J3** Ⓜ **Termini**

Hotel Lady (4, B5)
There's a sense of eccentric elegance about this little hotel in a leafy residential street. Furnished with rustic antiques, the pleasant rooms (two of which still have original beamed ceiling) have stunning wooden doors and the bathrooms (mostly shared) are new, tasteful and very clean.
✉ **Via Germanico 198** ☎ **06 324 21 12; fax 06 324 34 46** 🚌 **70, 186, 280, 913** Ⓜ **Lepanto**

Hotel Trastevere
(2, E3) What used to be a well-located dive has been transformed into one of the city's best deals, with three-star quality at excellent prices. Most rooms look out over the bustling market square of Piazza San Cosimato; all are spotlessly clean with all mod-cons. Independent apartments are also available.
✉ **Via Luciano Manara 24a-25** ☎ **06 581 47 13; fax 06 588 10 16** 🚌 **44, 75, H** 🚋 **8** ✕ **Pizzeria Ivo (p. 85)**

Pensione Restivo
(5, D4) If the proud display of letters and gifts sent by former guests is any indication, this small pensione run by a former *carabiniere* officer and his elderly mother is a big hit. This quaint place is immaculately clean, but the midnight curfew might be a drawback for some.
✉ **Via Palestro 55** ☎ **06 446 21 72** 🚌 **62, 64, 75, 90, 492, J2, J3** Ⓜ **Termini**

facts for the visitor

Martin Moos

ARRIVAL & DEPARTURE

Rome can be reached by air from most places in the world. Direct flights are available from most European capitals, and from Australia, Asia, Africa and the USA, although some carriers use Milan as their Italian gateway. The city is also linked by good train services to neighbouring countries.

Air

Rome's main airport is Leonardo da Vinci, commonly referred to as Fiumicino (1, C2), 30km south-west of the city. The arrivals area is on the ground floor, departures on the first floor. Facilities include banks, exchange booths, post offices and shops; the new satellite terminal for long-haul flights has especially good shops and boutiques.

A growing number of discount airlines and charter flights operate out of the much smaller Ciampino airport (1, C4), 15km south-east of the centre.

Left Luggage

Luggage can be left at the arrivals area of Fiumicino (L4100, €2.07/ day).

Information

General Inquiries
Fiumicino ☎ 06 659 53 640, 06 659 54 455
Ciampino ☎ 06 79 49 41

Airport information online
e www.adr.it

Airport Access

Train Two trains connect Fiumicino to the city. The Leonardo Express runs hourly (sometimes half-hourly) to Termini. The trip takes 30mins and costs L16,000/€8.26 one way. The other train (a local service) is more frequent, stopping at Trastevere (25mins), Ostiense (30 mins) and Tiburtina (40mins) stations but not at Termini. From the airport, trains run about every 20mins (L9000/€4.65 one way). Tickets for both trains can be bought from vending machines in the main airport arrivals hall (have some small change/notes handy).

Bus A night bus operates from Fiumicino to Termini and Tiburtina (around 1hr) stations from midnight to 5am (L9000/€4.65 one way). From Ciampino, take the LiLa/COTRAL bus to Anagnina (L1200/€0.62; every 60-90mins), then Metro to the centre (L1500/€0.77). Combined trip takes 1-2½ hrs depending on connections.

Taxi From Fiumicino, taxis to the centre take about 45mins (longer in rush hour) and cost around L75,000/ €38.73 (including airport supplement L15,000/€7.75). From Ciampino (40-60mins) fares are about L70,000/ €36.15 (with airport supplement).

Train

Rail travel is generally efficient and comfortable (but not always fast) within Italy. The Ferrovie dello Stato (FS; State Railway) has regular services connecting Rome to most Italian destinations. Intercity (IC) and Eurostar (ES) trains are express services to major cities and towns; they cost significantly more than the slow Regionale (R) and InterRegionale (IR) services which cover small towns and link regions.

EuroCity trains operate between Rome and major destinations throughout Europe – including Paris, Geneva, Zürich, Frankfurt and Vienna. Both 1st and 2nd class are available and on overnight hauls you can book a *cuccetta* or sleeping berth for most international trains. It's wise to reserve a seat for international journeys. Tickets must be validated at the yellow boxes on platforms.

Almost all trains depart from/ arrive at Stazione Termini (5, F3), although a few go to Tiburtina (3, E9). Tickets can be purchased at any train station, most travel agents and at e www.fs-on-line.com. For information go to the busy bureau at Termini (7am-9.45pm) or ring ☎ 1478 880 88 (7am-9pm; Italian only). Left luggage deposit is under platform 24 (L6000, €3.10/5hrs, then L1000, €0.52/hr).

Bus

Linee Laziali (LiLa, formerly known as COTRAL; ☎ 800 431 784; e www.atac.roma.it.) buses service the Lazio region and depart from numerous points throughout the city (usually at Metro stations), depending on their destinations.

Eurolines (Circonvallazione Nomentana 574; ☎ 06 440 40 09; e www.eurolines.com) is the main carrier for European destinations, and is connected with coach operators throughout Europe. Buses leave from Stazione Tiburtina.

Travel Documents

Passport

If you need a visa for entry to Italy, your passport will have to be valid for several months after the date of entry.

Visa

EU citizens only need to pack a passport or ID card. Nationals of Australia, Canada, Japan, New Zealand and the USA do not need a visa if entering as tourists for up to three months. Other nationals and those who wish to stay for lengthy periods or for work or study purposes should check with their local Italian embassy.

Customs

There is no limit on the amount of lire brought into the country. Goods brought in and exported within the EU incur no additional taxes, provided duty has been paid somewhere within the EU and the goods are for personal consumption.

Duty Free

Duty-free sales within the EU no longer exist. Travellers coming into non-EU countries can import, duty free, 200 cigarettes, 1L of spirits, 2L wine, 60mL perfume, 250mL eau de toilette and other goods up to a total of L340,000/€175.60; anything over this limit must be declared on arrival and the appropriate duty paid.

Departure Tax

Airport taxes are always prepaid with your air ticket into or out of Italy.

GETTING AROUND

Rome's buses, trams, subway (Metropolitana) and suburban railways are part of an integrated system run by ATAC. Regional bus services covering the Lazio region are operated by Linee Laziali (LiLa, formerly COTRAL). For information on fares and routes call ☎ 800 431 784 or see e www.atac.roma.it. Tickets must be bought in advance and validated as you get onto the bus/tram or enter the station.

In addition to the ATAC system, Rome also has private network of

J buses (☎ 800 076 287, ⓔ www.linee-j.com) which cover a limited number of routes.

Travel Passes

ATAC's **Metrebus tickets** *(biglietti integrati)* are valid for all modes of transport within the metropolitan area: 75mins L1500/€0.77, daily L6000/€3.10, weekly L24,000/€12.39, monthly L50,000/€25.82. Children up to 1m tall travel free. J buses cost L1900/€0.98 for 75mins. Buy tickets for both from tobacconists, newspaper stands and from vending machines at main bus stops.

Separate tickets are required for LiLa bus travel outside the metropolitan area. Daily regional tickets, known as BIRG, are useful for travel on both the ATAC metropolitan network, FS trains and the Linee Laziali buses; they are generally available only from bus termini/Metro stations.

Bus & Tram

Many of the main ATAC bus routes terminate in Piazza dei Cinquecento at Stazione Termini. Other useful bus hubs are Piazza Venezia, Largo Argentina and Piazza San Silvestro. Night buses run from 12.30am-5.30am from Piazza dei Cinquecento and the other main bus termini. Tourist booths, and the information booth at Piazza dei Cinquecento (stand C), can provide bus & tram maps.

J buses operate every 10mins 7am-11pm. The nine routes include: J3 Termini-San Giovanni, Catacombs; J4 San Paolo fuori—le-Mura, Colosseum, Ponte Sisto, Vatican; J5 St Peter's, Largo Argentina, Colosseum, Stazione Tiburtina.

Metropolitana

The Metro operates 5.30am-11.30pm (12.30am Sat) and trains run about every 5-10mins. Both lines, A and B, pass through Stazione Termini.

Train

Suburban trains *(ferrovia metropolitana)* are operated by FS. ATAC Metrebus tickets are valid for journeys within the metropolitan area.

Taxi

Rome's taxis are expensive. Flagfall is L4500/€2.07 (for the first 3km), then L1200/€0.62 per km; supplements for luggage (L2000/€1.03), night travel (L5000/€2.58) and to/from the airports. Pick one up from a taxi rank as, strictly speaking, they aren't allowed to be hailed in the street. To call a taxi dial ☎ 06 55 51, ☎ 06 4994 or ☎ 06 35 70.

Car & Motorcycle

Do you *really* want to take 10 years off your life? Driving in Rome is a complete nightmare. Only residents with permits can enter the historic centre (although tourists are sometimes permitted to drive to their hotels), streets are badly signposted with a complicated one-way system, parking is difficult and/or expensive and Roman drivers are completely mad. *Motorini* (scooters) can enter the historic centre and are a fast way to get around.

Road Rules

Italians drive on the right. Seatbelts are compulsory but no one in Rome seems to follow the law. In built-up areas, the speed limit is 50km/h, 90 km/h on country roads, 110km/h on main roads/highways and 130 km/h on motorways. The blood-alcohol limit when driving is 0.08%.

Rental

At most you'll need a car for excursions out of Rome. Rental cars cost from L120,000/€61.97 a day; good 3-day weekend deals are available. Main companies include Avis (☎ 199 100 133), Europcar (☎ 06 52 08 11) and Maggiore National (☎ 1478 670 67), all of which have outlets at Fiumicino and Termini.

Driving Licence & Permit

Bring either an EU driving licence or an International Driving Permit plus your home-country licence.

Motoring Organisations

Automobile Club Italiano (ACI), Via Marsala 8 (☎ 06 4 99 81) offers free emergency roadside assistance (to deliver you and your vehicle to the nearest garage) to members of allforeign automobile associations. The cost for non-members is L116,000/€59.91. For roadside assistance call ☎ 116.

PRACTICAL INFORMATION

Climate & When to Go

Rome is a city for all seasons. Apr-May and Sept-Oct are the high seasons for tourists, and accommodation can be hard to come by. From late June to Aug it gets hot and humid, sometimes unbearably so, but this is when Rome is at its most vibrant, with life spilling onto the streets and open-air festivals in abundance. It can be cold from Dec to Feb, but it's rarely grey and gloomy.

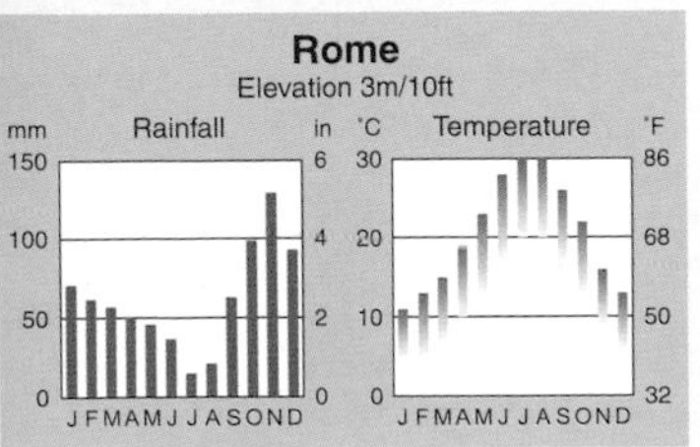

Tourist Information

Tourist Information Abroad

Information on Rome and Italy is available from the Ente Nazionale Italiana di Turismo (ENIT; ⓔ www.enit.it), known internationally as the Italian State Tourist Office. ENIT offices include:

Australia
Level 26, 44 Market Street, Sydney 2000 (☎ 02-9262 1666)

Canada
Suite 907, South Tower, 17 Bloor Street East, Toronto, Ontario M4W3R8 (☎ 416-925 4882)

UK
1 Princess St, London W1R 9AY (☎ 020-7355 1557)

USA
630 Fifth Avenue, Suite 1565, New York, NY 10111 (☎ 212-245 4822)

Local Tourist Information

There are two information offices run by the Comune di Roma at Stazione Termini, at the end of Platform 4 (8am-9pm), and in the Ala Mazzoniana next to Platform 24 (8am-8pm). Free city maps, transport guides and brochures on museums, festivals and events are available. Comune tourism infoline on ☎ 06 360 04 399 operates 9am-7pm.

There are also 10 comune tourist information kiosks dotted around the city, open 9am-6pm daily: Piazza dei Cinquecento (5, D2); Via dei Fori Imperiali (4, H13); Via Nazionale (4, E14); Via del Corso, at Via Minghetti (6, B8); Via del Corso, at Largo Goldoni (4, C10); Castel Sant'Angelo (4, D5); Trastevere (2, D5); Santa Maria Maggiore (5, G1); Piazza Navona (6, B3); Piazza San Giovanni in Laterano (3, G7).

The Azienda di Promozione Turistica (4, D15; APT; ☎ 06 488 99 253) Via Parigi 5 is open Mon-Fri 8.15am-7.15pm, Sat 7.15am-1.45pm. The APT is operated by the regional authorities and has information on destinations outside the city centre. Other offices are at Fiumicino in the arrivals hall and at Stazione Termini in the Ala Mazzoniana next to platform 24.

Embassies & Consulates

Australia
Via Alessandria 215 (3, D7; ☎ 06 85 27 21)

Canada
Via Zara 30 (3, D7; ☎ 06 44 59 81)

New Zealand
Via Zara 28 (3, D7; ☎ 06 441 71 71)

South Africa
Via Tanaro 14 (3, D7; ☎ 06 841 97 94)

UK
Via XX Settembre 80a (5, B3; ☎ 06 482 54 41)

USA
Via Vittorio Veneto 119a-121 (4, C14; ☎ 06 4 67 41)

Money

Currency

From 1 Jan 2002, Italy will be one of 11 countries to use the new European single currency, the euro (€). Notes and coins will be introduced over the few months of 2002 and existing currencies phased out.

Until the 28th Feb 2002 cut-off date, Italy's currency remains the *lira* (plural: *lire)*. Lire note denominations are L1000, L2000, L5000, L10,000, L50,000, L100,000 and L500,000. Coins come in L50, L100, L200, L500 and L1000 units. Euros will be available in €1 and €2 coins and €5, €10, €20, €50, €100, €200 and €500 notes. Euro coins (cents) be will issued in €0.01, €0.02, €0.05, €0.10, €0.20 and €0.50 units.

Banks will continue to exchange lire after the cut-off date. For further information visit the European Union's Web site at e www.europa.eu.int/euro/html/entry.html.

Lire are converted at a rate of L1936.27 to €1. Euro prices listed in this book are direct conversions based on the official rate. There may be some price variations as it is difficult to predict individual price movements prior to the change.

Lire – Euro Conversion

L	€	L	€
500	0.26	30,000	15.49
1000	0.52	40,000	20.66
2000	1.03	50,000	25.82
3000	1.55	60,000	30.99
4000	2.07	70,000	36.15
5000	2.58	80,000	41.32
6000	3.10	90,000	46.48
7000	3.62	100,000	51.65
8000	4.13	200,000	103.29
9000	4.65	300,000	154.94
10,000	5.16	400,000	206.58
15,000	7.75	500,000	258.23
20,000	10.33	1,000,000	516.46

Travellers Cheques

Travellers cheques can be cashed at any bank or exchange office. American Express (4, C11; ☎ 06 6 76 41) Piazza di Spagna 38 is open Mon-Fri 9am-5.30pm, Sat 9am-12.30pm. Call toll-free ☎ 800 872 000 for lost cheques.

Credit Cards

Major credit cards, such as AmEx, Visa, MasterCard, Eurocard, Cirrus and Euro Cheques, are accepted in Rome and throughout Italy although smaller hotels and restaurants may not accept them. Diners Club and JCB are accepted less frequently. Credit cards can also be used in ATMs displaying the appropriate sign. For 24hr card cancellations or assistance, call:

American Express	☎ 06 7 22 82
MasterCard	☎ 800 870 866
Visa	☎ 800 877 232

ATMs
Automatic Teller Machines can be found outside most banks, in the airport halls and at Stazione Termini. Visa and Mastercard/ Eurocard are widely accepted, as well as cash cards that access the Cirrus/Maestro network.

Changing Money
Banks generally offer better rates than *cambi* (bureaux de change) although commissions can vary – anything from flat fee of L3000/ €1.55 to a hefty percentage of the amount exchanged. Exchange bureaux are open longer hours than banks – so you're paying for convenience.

Tipping

In restaurants where service is not included it's customary to leave a 10% tip; if service is included, you can (but are not obliged to) leave a small amount (L2000-5000/€1.03-2.58). In bars, Italians often leave small change as a tip. Tipping taxi drivers is not common practice, but you should tip the porter at upmarket hotels (about L1000/€0.52 a bag).

Discounts

Children under 18 and seniors over 65 get free entry to all state and city museums, and discounted admission to private museums and sights. Those aged 18-25 and card-carrying students and teachers get reduced admission *(prezzo ridotto)* to most museums and sights. A 5-day museum pass (see p. 14) is available for entry to the Colosseum, Palatine, and the various departments of the Museo Nazionale Romano.

Student & Youth Cards
The International Student Identity Card (ISIC) is the most widely accepted form of student identification.

Seniors' Cards
Senior travellers are entitled to discounts on FS rail travel but they have to purchase the Carta Argento (L40,000/€20.66) first, so it's only worth it if a lot of train travel is being undertaken. There are no discounts for metropolitan public transport.

Travel Insurance

A policy covering theft, loss, medical expenses and compensation for cancellation or delays in your travel arrangements is highly recommended. If items are lost or stolen, make sure you get a police report straight away – otherwise your insurer might not pay up.

Opening Hours

Banks
: Mon-Fri 8.30am-1.30pm, 2.45-4.30pm; some central banks also Sat 9am-12.30pm

Shops
: Mon-Sat 9am-1pm, 3.30-7.30pm; some stay open all day, close Thurs pm and/or open Sun

Offices
: Mon-Fri 9am-1.30pm, 4-7.30pm; some also Sat 9am-1.30pm

Public Holidays

Jan 1	New Year's Day
Jan 6	Epiphany
Mar/Apr	Easter Monday
Apr 25	Liberation Day
May 1	Labour Day
June 29	Feast of SS Peter & Paul
Aug 15	Ferragosto (Feast of the Assumption)
Nov 1	All Saints' Day
Dec 25	Christmas Day
Dec 26	Santo Stefan (Boxing Day)

Time

Rome Standard Time is 1hr ahead of GMT. Daylight savings time is practised from the last Sunday in Mar to the last Sunday in Oct. At noon in Rome it's:

6am in New York
3am in Los Angeles
11am in London
1pm in Johannesburg
9pm in Sydney
11pm in Auckland

Electricity

The electric current in Italy is 220V, 50Hz, but make a point of checking with your hotel because some older buildings may still use 125V. Plugs have either two or three round pins and power points have two or three holes. Bring international plug adaptors for your appliances. Travellers from North America need a voltage converter (although many of the more expensive hotels have provision for 110V appliances such as electric razors).

Weights & Measures

The metric system is standard. Like other Continental Europeans, Italians use commas in decimals, and points to indicate thousands. See the conversion table (p. 121).

Post

Italy's postal system is notoriously unreliable, although things look better today than a decade ago with the more efficient *posta prioritaria* service used for domestic and international mail. Stamps are sold at post office counters and most tobacconists. The Vatican Post (available only in the Vatican City) has a reputation for being more reliable for international mail.

Postal Rates

Postcards and letters (up to 20g) sent *posta prioritaria* cost L1200/€0.62 within Europe, L1500/€0.77 to the Americas, Africa, Asia, Australia and New Zealand. Letters weighing 21-100g cost L2400/€1.24 within Europe, L3000/€1.55 to Africa, Asia and the Americas and L3500/€1.81 to Australia and New Zealand.

Opening Hours

Rome's main post office is at Piazza di San Silvestro 18-20 (4, D11). It is open Mon-Fri 8.30am-6pm, Sat 8.30am-2pm and Sun 9am-2pm. Local post offices are open Mon-Fri 8.30am-1.50pm and Sat 8.30-11.50am.

Telephone

A local call *(comunicazione urbana)* from a public phone will cost around L200/€0.10 for 3-6mins, depending on the time of day you call. Phone booths are operated by Telecom Italia, Infostrada and Albacom; each needs its own dedicated phonecard, available from tobacconists and some newsstands. Most phone booths also take coins.

Phonecards

Telecom Italia, Infostrada and Albacom phonecards are available in L5000-50,000/€2.58-28.41 denominations; buy them from post offices, tobacconists and some newsstands. They can be used for both local and long-distance/international calls. Lonely Planet's eKno Communication Card, specifically aimed at travellers, provides competitive international calls (avoid using it for local calls), messaging services and free email. Visit e www.ekno.lonelyplanet.com for information on joining and accessing the service.

Mobile Phones

Italy uses the GSM cellular phone system, compatible with phones sold in the UK, Australia and most of Asia, but not those from North American or Japan. Check with your service provider before you leave home that they have a roaming agreement with a local counterpart.

Country & City Codes

Italy	☎ 39
Rome	☎ 06

For local calls, the 0 at the start of the phone number is an integral part of the phone number. From outside Italy the 0 in the area code (eg, ☎ 06 66 66 66) must be retained after the country code (eg, ☎ +39 06 66 66 66). However for calls to mobile phones in Italy (eg, ☎ 0330 66 66 66) the 0 is dropped after the country code (☎ +39 330 66 66 66).

Useful Numbers

Local Directory Inquiries	☎ 2
International Directory Inquiries	☎ 176
International Operator	☎ 170
Reverse-Charge (collect)	☎ 170

International Codes

Australia	☎ 0061
Canada	☎ 001
Japan	☎ 0081
New Zealand	☎ 0064
South Africa	☎ 0027
UK	☎ 0044
USA	☎ 001

Email/www

After a slow start, Italy has taken to the internet with gusto. If you packed your laptop, note that Italy uses a three-pin phone plug that accommodates a US, French or Australian-style jack. Newer plugs (including modern plugs in many hotels) take the jack directly into the wall.

Internet Service Providers

Most major global ISPs have dial-in nodes in Italy; it's best to download a list of the dial-in numbers before you leave home. If you access your Internet through a smaller ISP, your best option is either to open an account with a global ISP or to rely on cybercafes.

Internet Cafes

If you can't access the Internet from where you're staying, head to a cybercafe:

Netgate
Piazza Firenze 25 (4, E9; ☎ 06 689 34 45; e roma.pantheon@thenetgate.it; L10,000, €5.16/hr)

Rimaweb Internet Point
Via del Portico d'Ottavia 2a (2, B6; ☎ 06 688 91 356; e www.rimaweb.com; L3000, €1.55/15mins or L50,000, €25.82/5hrs)

Bibli
Via dei Fienaroli 28 (2, E4; ☎ 06 588 40 97; L50,000, €25.82/10hrs)

Splashnet
Via Varese 33 (5, D4; ☎ 06 493 82 073; e www.splashnet.it; L6000, €3.10/hr)

Useful Sites

The Lonely Planet web site (e www.lonelyplanet.com) offers a speedy link to many of Rome's Web sites. Others to try include:

Comune di Roma database
e www.informaroma.it

Enjoy Rome tourist office & travel agent
e www.enjoyrome.com

Vatican Web site
e www.vatican.va

Wanted in Rome
e www.wantedinrome.com

Museums in Italy
e www.museionline.it

Doing Business

The trade office at the Italian embassy in your home country can provide initial information and help to establish contacts, as can your embassy's trade office in Rome. The Istituto Nazionale per il Commercio Estero, Via Liszt 21 (☎ 06 5 99 21; e ice@ice.it, www.ice.it 92 68 99), is the main Italian foreign trade commission. The British Chamber of Commerce in Italy (e www.britchamitaly.com) is based in Milan but has a Rome agent (☎ 06 862 06 459).

Executive Services Business Centres, Via Savoia 78 (☎ 06 852 37 250, e www.executivenetwork.it), provides secretarial services, meeting rooms with video conferencing, company addresses, voice mailboxes, translators and interpreters and other services. World Translation Centre, Via Merulana 259 (☎ 06 488 10 39, e wtc@iol.it), does sworn translations for legal and corporate needs.

Newspapers & Magazines

Rome's main daily newspapers are *Il Messaggero, La Repubblica* and *Corriere della Sera.* The conservative daily *L'Osservatore Romano,* the official voice of the Vatican, has weekly editions in English and other foreign languages.

The *International Herald Tribune* (Mon-Sat) has a supplement on Italian news, *Italy Daily*. Major British and US daily papers and weekly news magazines are available same (or next) day from larger newsstands.

Radio

There are three state-owned stations: RAI-1 (1332AM or 89.7FM), RAI-2 (846AM or 91.7FM) and RAI-3 (93.7FM). They combine classical and light music with news broadcasts and discussion programs.

Commercial radio stations are a better bet if you're after contemporary music. Try Radio Centro Suono (101.3FM) or Radio Città Futura (97.7FM) which broadcasts a listing of the day's events in Rome at 10am.

You can pick up the BBC World Service on medium wave at 648kHz, short wave at 6195kHz, 9410kHz, 12095kHz, 15575kHz, and on long wave at 198kHz, depending on where you are and the time of day.

TV

Italian television is so bad that it is compelling, with an inordinate number of quiz shows and variety programs featuring troupes of scantily-clad women prancing across the screen. Watch at your peril.

The state-run channels are RAI 1, RAI 2 and RAI 3. The main commercial stations are Canale 5, Italia 1, Rete 4 and Telemontecarlo (TMC). Most of Rome's mid- to top- range hotels, as well as many bars and restaurants, have satellite TV and can receive BBC World, Sky Channel, CNN and NBC Superchannel.

Photography & Video

Print and slide film are readily available from all photo shops and some supermarkets. There are plenty of photo shops that sell camera gear and do repairs. Developing slide film can be very cheap – as low as L7000/€3.62 a roll.

Italy uses the PAL video system (the same as in Australia and most of Europe). This system is not compatible with NTSC (used in North America, Japan and Latin America) or Secam (used in France, other Francophone countries and Germany) unless the machine is multi-system.

Health

Immunisations

There are no vaccination requirements for entry to Italy.

Precautions

Rome's tap water is safe to drink (although it contains a lot of calcium and many people prefer the bottled stuff), and food preparation is fairly hygienic. It's advisable to wash fruit bought from markets. Heat and humidity are the only things liable to get you down; wear a hat and loose comfortable clothing and drink plenty of fluids.

Like anywhere else, practice the usual precautions when it comes to sex; condoms are available in pharmacies and supermarkets.

Insurance & Medical Treatment

Travel insurance is advisable to cover any medical treatment you may need while in Rome. All foreigners have the same right as locals to emergency or essential medical treatment, including ongoing treatment, in a public hospital or clinic.

In addition, various countries (including Australia) have longstanding reciprocal agreements with Italy, which won't effect the treatment you receive in a public hospital, but might make the paperwork easier. Citizens of EU countries should have an E111 form.

The quality of medical treatment in public hospitals in Rome is well below the standards of many other major Western European cities, not because of a lack in professional expertise – Italy's doctors are highly regarded on an international level – but because hospital facilities and equipment are outdated, the services are oversubscribed and the standard of nursing care is low.

Medical Services

Hospitals with 24hr accident and emergency departments include:

Ospedale Bambino Gesù (children)
Pza Sant'Onofrio (4, F4; ☎ 06 685 9 23 51)

Ospedale Fatebenefratelli
Pza Fatebenefratelli (2, C6; ☎ 06 6 83 71)

Ospedale San Giacomo
Via Canova 29 (4, B9; ☎ 06 3 62 61)

Policlinico Umberto I
Via del Policlinico 155 (5, B5; ☎ 06 4 99 71)

Dental Services

If you chip a tooth or require emergency treatment, head to Ospedale di Odontoiatria, Viale Regine Elena 287b (3, E8; ☎ 06 844 83 232).

Pharmacies

Pharmacies or chemists *(farmacie)* are usually open Mon-Sat 9am-1pm and 4-7.30pm. They open after hours on a rotation basis. Night pharmacies are listed in the daily newspapers. When closed, pharmacies display a list of others open nearby. There's a 24-hr pharmacy at Piazza dei Cinquecento 51 (5, E2; ☎ 06 488 00 19) and one inside Stazione Termini (on the lower ground floor) that opens 7.30am-10pm.

Toilets

It is estimated that there are less than 40 public toilets in Rome. Residents and tourists alike are waiting with crossed legs to see whether all the semi-permanent 'portaloos' brought in for the Jubilee year will remain. Most people use the toilets in bars and cafes – although you might need to buy a coffee first.

Stazione Termini's public toilets are on the lower ground level (L1000/€0.52). Toilets on the Via Giolitti side also have showers (L15,000/€7.75).

Safety Concerns

Rome is a very safe city and violent crime against tourists is rare. It's generally safe to walk anywhere in the historic centre at night. However, theft is common, especially at major tourist sights like the Colosseum, Trevi Fountain and Spanish Steps. Watch out for nimble-fingered gypsies working in groups – before you know it they'll be off with your wallet. It's wise to keep your valuables in a safe place on your person (or in your hotel safe) and wear your handbag across your chest rather than slung over a shoulder.

Lost Property

For items lost on a bus call ☎ 06 581 60 40, on the metro call ☎ 06 487 43 09, and on a train ☎ 06 473 06 682.

Keeping Copies

Make photocopies of all your important documents, keep some with you, separate from the originals, and leave a copy at home. You can also store details of documents in Lonely Planet's free online Travel Vault (e www.ekno.lonelyplanet.com) is password-protected and accessible worldwide.

Emergency Numbers

Police, ambulance, fire ☎ 113

Women Travellers

Rome is not a dangerous city for women, but women travelling alone will often find themselves plagued by unwanted attention from men. Most of the attention falls into the nuisance/harassment category. However, women on their own should use their common sense. Avoid walking alone in deserted and dark streets, and look for hotels which are centrally located and within easy walking distance of places where you can eat at night.

Beware of men with wandering hands on crowded buses (especially the No 64). A loud *che schifo!* (how disgusting!) will usually do the trick.

Tampons (and more commonly, sanitary towels) are available in pharmacies and supermarkets. Prescriptions are needed for the contraceptive pill.

Gay & Lesbian Travellers

Homosexuality is legal in Italy and well tolerated in Rome if you ignore the Vatican's periodic anti-gay diatribe such as Pope John Paul II referring to homosexual men and women as 'morally corrupt'. The legal age of consent is 16. Previously a subculture that operated behind closed doors, Rome's gay scene is now a lot more open and there are numerous bars and clubs, with new venues opening all the time. World Pride held in July 2000 was a watershed for gay Rome, notwithstanding the protests about it from conservative and religious groups.

There is no centre for gay life, although there are a number of bars and saunas in the Monti/Esquiline Hill.

Information & Organisations

The hub of gay and lesbian activity in Rome is the Circolo Mario Mieli di Cultura Omosessuale, Via Efeso 2a (☎ 06 541 39 85; e info@mariomieli.it, www.mariomieli.it). The Co-ordinamento Lesbiche Italiano

(Via San Francesco di Sales 1; ☎ 06 686 42 01; e cli_network@iol.it), also known as Buon Pastore Centre, has regular political gatherings and social events for lesbians.

Senior Travellers

Senior travellers are well catered for in Rome, but it's important to realise that wherever you stay or whatever you do, it will involve at least some walking – often on uneven cobblestones – and invariably some hills and stairs. Not all hotels have lifts – if stairs are a problem, find out before you arrive.

Disabled Travellers

Rome is not an easy city for disabled travellers and getting around can be a problem for the mobility impaired. Wheelchair-accessible buses have been introduced on several busy ATAC bus routes and J buses are also accessible. Rome's newer trams are generally accessible. On the Metro, only the newer stations at the end of the lines have lifts. Bus No 590 follows the route of Metro Linea A and is specially equipped for disabled passengers and wheelchairs.

Although many buildings have lifts, they are not always wide enough to accommodate a wheelchair. Some taxis are equipped to carry passengers in wheelchairs; it is advisable to book these by phone, and ask for one suitable for a *sedia a rotelle*. Many of the city's main museums have been overhauled in recent years so things are looking better now for disabled travellers than ever before.

Braille labels are being introduced in several museums, as are audioguides for the hearing impaired, but there's a long way to go.

Information & Organisations

COIN (☎ 06 712 90 11, e www.coinsociale.it) is a proactive organisation which assists disabled tourists; its free publication *Roma Accessible* is available by phone order or online.

Language

Italian is a Romance language related to French, Spanish, Portuguese and Romanian. As English and Italian share common roots in Latin, you'll recognise many Italian words.

The Roman accent is melodic and lilting. The Romans have their own Italian dialect and slang, which is virtually indecipherable to a non-Roman (let alone a foreigner).

Many Italians speak some English because they study it at school. Staff at most hotels and restaurants usually speak a little English, but you will be better received if you at least attempt to communicate in Italian. Here's some useful phrases that will get you started. Grab a copy of Lonely Planet's *Italian phrasebook* if you'd like to know more.

Basics

Hello	*Buongiorno* (polite) *Ciao* (informal)
Goodbye	*Arrivederci* (polite) *Ciao* (informal)
Yes	*Sì*
No	*No*
Please	*Per favore/ Per piacere*
Thank you	*Grazie*
That's fine/ You're welcome	*Prego*
Excuse me	*Mi scusi*
Sorry (forgive me)	*Mi perdoni*
Do you speak English?	*Parla inglese?*
How much is it?	*Quanto costa?*

Getting Around

When does the … leave/arrive	*A che ora parte/arriva...?*
bus	*l'autobus*
train	*il treno*
left luggage	*deposito bagagli*
I'd like a ticket …	*Vorrei un biglietto di …*
one-way	*solo andata*
return	*andata e ritorno*
Where is...?	*Dov'è...?*
Go straight ahead	*Si va sempre diritto*
Turn left/right	*Giri a sinistra/destra*

Around Town

a bank	*una banca*
chemist/pharmacy	*la farmacia*
the tourist office	*l'ufficio di turismo*
What time does it open/close?	*A che ora (si) apre/chiude?*

Accommodation

hotel	*albergo*
Do you have any rooms available?	*Avete delle camere libere?*
How much is it …?	*Quanto costa …?*
per night	*per la notte*
per person	*per ciascuno?*
a … room	*una camera …*
single	*singola*
twin	*doppia*
double	*matrimonia*

Eating

The bill, please	*il conto, per favore*
I'm a vegetarian	*Sono vegetariana/o*

Time, Days & Numbers

What time is it?	*Che ora è?*
today	*oggi*
tomorrow	*domani*
yesterday	*ieri*
morning	*mattina*
afternoon	*pomeriggio*
day	*giorno*
hour	*ora*

Monday	*lunedì*
Tuesday	*martedì*
Wednesday	*mercoledì*
Thursday	*giovedì*
Friday	*venerdì*
Saturday	*sabato*
Sunday	*domenica*

1	*uno*	7	*sette*
2	*due*	8	*otto*
3	*tre*	9	*nove*
4	*quattro*	10	*dieci*
5	*cinque*	100	*cento*
6	*sei*	1000	*mille*

Conversion Table

Clothing Sizes

Measurements approximate only; try before you buy.

Women's Clothing

Aust/NZ	8	10	12	14	16	18
Europe	36	38	40	42	44	46
Japan	5	7	9	11	13	15
UK	8	10	12	14	16	18
USA	6	8	10	12	14	16

Women's Shoes

Aust/NZ	5	6	7	8	9	10
Europe	35	36	37	38	39	40
France only	35	36	38	39	40	42
Japan	22	23	24	25	26	27
UK	3½	4½	5½	6½	7½	8½
USA	5	6	7	8	9	10

Men's Clothing

Aust/NZ	92	96	100	104	108	112
Europe	46	48	50	52	54	56
Japan	S		M	M		L
UK	35	36	37	38	39	40
USA	35	36	37	38	39	40

Men's Shirts (Collar Sizes)

Aust/NZ	38	39	40	41	42	43
Europe	38	39	40	41	42	43
Japan	38	39	40	41	42	43
UK	15	15½	16	16½	17	17½
USA	15	15½	16	16½	17	17½

Men's Shoes

Aust/NZ	7	8	9	10	11	12
Europe	41	42	43	44½	46	47
Japan	26	27	27.5	28	29	30
UK	7	8	9	10	11	12
USA	7½	8½	9½	10½	11½	12½

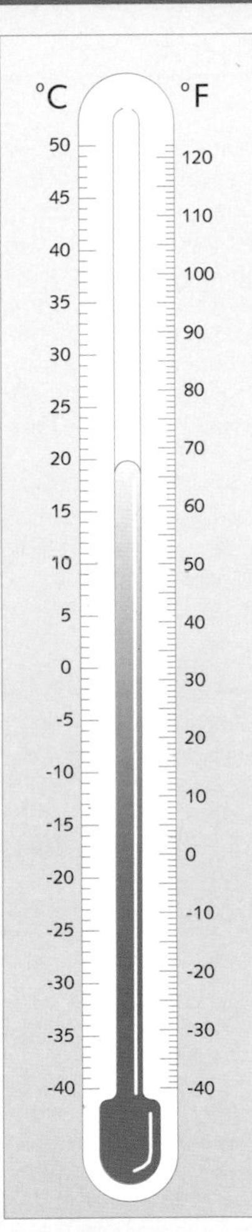

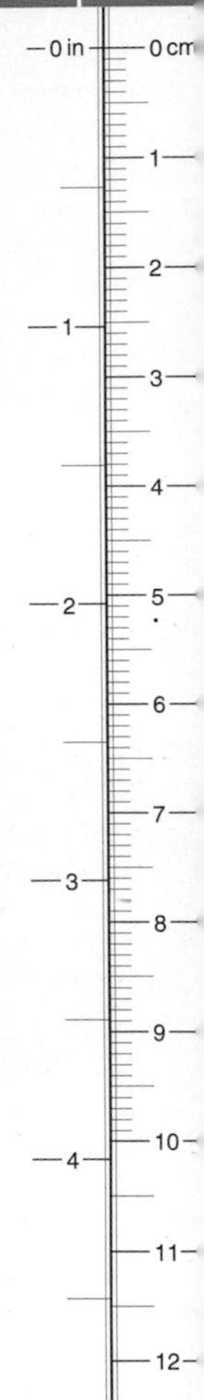

Weights & Measures

Length & Distance

1 inch = 2.54cm
1cm = 0.39 inches
1m = 3.3ft = 1.1yds
1ft = 0.3m
1km = 0.62 miles
1 mile = 1.6km

Weight

1kg = 2.2lb
1lb = 0.45kg
1g = 0.04oz
1oz = 28g

Volume

1 litre = 0.26 US gallons
1 US gallon = 3.8 litres
1 litre = 0.22 imperial gallons
1 imperial gallon = 4.55 litres

THE AUTHOR

Sally Webb

Sally's addiction to Rome started when she moved there to research the myth of the Latin lover. Four years, several Latins, five leather jackets and 30 pairs of shoes later, she severed the umbilical and returned to her native Australia. When she's not in therapy in Sydney dealing with the absence in her life of real mozzarella di bufala and properly cooked pasta, she writes for publications including *The Independent on Sunday* and *Vogue Entertaining & Travel.*

Thanks to friends, Romans and countrymen and women, especially Rob Allyn and Rosario Gorgone, Nick Rigillo and Lisbeth Davidsen, Michele Pozzi, Rory Carroll, James Walston, Sari and Alessandro Taddei, Orla Guerin, Lisa Triulzi, Laura Clarke and everyone at Wanted in Rome.

ABOUT THIS BOOK

• Design by James Hardy • Maps by Charles Rawlings-Way • Edited by Gabrielle Green and Janine Eberle • Cover by Daniel New and Maria Vallianos • Publishing Manager Diana Saad • Thanks to Annie Horner, Bibiana Jaramillo, Gerard Walker, Jane Hart, Kerrie Williams, Mary Neighbour, Natasha Velleley, Paul Piaia and Quentin Frayne.

OTHER CONDENSED GUIDES

Other Lonely Planet Condensed guides include: *Amsterdam, Boston, California, Chicago (due September 2001), Crete, Frankfurt, Hong Kong, London, New York City, Paris* and *Sydney*.

ABOUT LONELY PLANET

The story begins with a classic travel adventure: Tony and Maureen Wheeler's 1972 journey across Europe and Asia to Australia. Useful information about the overland trail did not exist at that time, so Tony and Maureen published the first Lonely Planet guidebook to meet a growing need.

From a kitchen table, then from a tiny office in Melbourne, Australia, Lonely Planet has become the largest independent travel publisher in the world, an international company with offices in Melbourne, Oakland, London and Paris.

Today there are over 400 titles, including travel guides, city maps, cycling guides, first time travel guides, healthy travel guides, travel atlases, diving guides, pictorial books, phrasebooks, restaurant guides, travel literature, walking guides, watching wildlife and world food guides.

At Lonely Planet we believe that travellers can make a positive contribution to the countries they visit – if they respect their host communities and spend their money wisely. Since 1986 a percentage of the income from books has been donated to aid and human rights projects.

LONELY PLANET ONLINE

www.lonelyplanet.com or AOL keyword: lp
Lonely Planet's award-winning Web site has insider info on hundreds of destinations from Amsterdam to Zimbabwe, complete with interactive maps and colour photographs. You'll also find the latest travel news, recent reports from travellers on the road, guidebook upgrades and a lively bulletin board where you can meet fellow travellers, swap recommendations and seek advice.

PLANET TALK

Our FREE quarterly printed newsletter is full of tips from travellers and anecdotes from Lonely Planet authors. Every issue is packed with up-to-date travel news and advice, and includes a postcard from Lonely Planet co-founder Tony Wheeler, mail from travellers, a look at life on the road through the eyes of a Lonely Planet author, topical health advice, prizes for the best travel yarn, news about forthcoming Lonely Planet events and a complete list of Lonely Planet books and products.

To join our mailing list, email us at: go@lonelyplanet.co.uk (UK, Europe and Africa residents); info@lonelyplanet.com (North and South America residents); talk2us@lonelyplanet.com.au (the rest of the world); or contact any Lonely Planet office.

COMET

Our FREE monthly email newsletter brings you all the latest travel news, features, interviews, competitions, destination ideas, travellers' tips & tales, Q&As, raging debates and related links. Find out what's new on the Lonely Planet Web site and which books are about to hit the shelves.

Subscribe from your desktop: www.lonelyplanet.com/comet

LONELY PLANET OFFICES

Australia
90 Maribyrnong St, Footscray, Vic 3011
☎ 613 8379 8000 fax 613 8379 8111
email: talk2us@lonelyplanet.com.au

USA
150 Linden St, Oakland, CA 94607
☎ 510 893 8555 TOLL FREE: 800 275 8555
fax 510 893 8572
email: info@lonelyplanet.com

UK
10a Spring Place, London NW5 3BH
☎ 020 7428 4800 fax 020 7428 4828
email: go@lonelyplanet.co.uk

France
1 rue du Dahomey, 75011 Paris
☎ 01 55 25 33 00 fax 01 55 25 33 01
email: bip@lonelyplanet.fr
minitel: 3615 lonelyplanet

World Wide Web: www.lonelyplanet.com or AOL keyword: lp
Lonely Planet Images: lpi@lonelyplanet.com.au

index

See also separate indexes for Places to Eat (p. 126), Places to Stay (p. 127), Shops (p. 127) and Sights with map references (p. 128).

A

B

C

D

E

F

G

PLACES TO EAT

PLACES TO STAY

SHOPS

sights – quick index